School-Based Curriculum Development

School Based Curriculum Development

School-Based Curriculum Development

Malcolm Skilbeck

Harper & Row, Publishers
London

Cambridge
Hagerstown
Philadelphia
New York

San Francisco
Mexico City
São Paulo
Sydney

First published 1984

Harper & Row Ltd
28 Tavistock Street
London WC2E 7PN

British Library Cataloguing in Publication Data

Skilbeck, Malcolm
    School based curriculum development.
    1. Curriculum planning—Great Britain
    I. Title
    375'.001'0941   LB1564.G7

    ISBN 0–06–318266–1

Typeset by Inforum Ltd, Portsmouth
Printed and bound by Butler & Tanner Ltd, Frome and London

CONTENTS

ACKNOWLEDGEMENTS

The ideas and experiences discussed in this book have been gathered over several years, in different parts of the world and with the advice and assistance of many hands. I am grateful to a wide circle of colleagues, friends, students and professional associates, upon whose knowledge and understanding I have drawn, and to the many teachers in primary and secondary schools who, often unknowingly, have helped me to appreciate the distinctive challenges of curriculum development in the school setting. Thanks are due to colleagues and friends in the Universities of London, Bristol and Ulster, the Australian Curriculum Development Centre, Unesco (Bangkok) and OECD (Paris) and to members of project teams and curriculum groups, with whom I have been associated in curriculum research and development.

I owe a particular debt to my former research assistants, Wendy Edgar and Claire Runciman and to Lynn Cairns who admirably sorted out and typed the manuscript.

PREFACE

As in other countries, education in England and Wales has witnessed far-reaching structural and organizational changes in recent decades. These result not only from policy changes with a strong ideological or pedagogical flavour, such as the establishment of the basic, common, or comprehensive school and the abandonment of external examining for selection for secondary education, but also from demographic, economic and other pressures in society. National as well as international studies and experience have shown that there have not been changes of a comparable order in the curriculum of schools, despite the energetic attempts to revitalize subject content, as in the large-scale curriculum development projects of the Schools Council and other agencies in the 1960s and 70s. We are becoming increasingly aware of grave weaknesses of scope, quality and priorities in the curriculum for all students, of such a kind as to require a more comprehensive critique and reconstruction than has yet been attempted, except in isolated instances.

One kind of challenge comes from groups and agencies which sometimes seem to regard the schools as having failed or as being incapable of reform from within. This is illustrated by the insertion of new programmes of vocational and practical skills, usually heavily supported with earmarked funds and with high political and bureaucratic salience. However, it is recognized now that the success of these programmes depends on the closest possible collaboration with schools. What, at first, appeared to some educationists like an external and independent initiative for curriculum change will provide, at the very least, an opportunity for schools to review and modify their curricula, taking in new perspectives and possibilities.

I do not believe that any substantial reform movement for the school curriculum can proceed unless questions of curriculum review, planning, design, development, implementation and innovation are placed quite centrally *in* the context of school life. Thus I do not see the school as merely 'recipient' or 'vehicle' or 'adopter' but as a partner, collaborator and, often, initiator in the change process. This position does not lead me to think of the school as a self-sufficient institution, or to regard indifference or resistance to the attempt, in contemporary Britain, to establish a national curriculum framework as a healthy form of local autonomy. On the contrary, the task is to redefine the school's role in curriculum development by determining certain principles of action and seeing how they might work out in the shifting relationships between schools, local education authorities, central government, professional bodies, local communities and others.

A fresh perspective on school-based curriculum development can provide us with the means of addressing these larger shifts and changes in education and other sectors of our society. My central argument is that a new, common core of studies for all students is needed and that the school has a major role in helping to define, as well as teach, this core. The purpose of this book and its companion volume of readings, accordingly, is to contribute towards a better and wider understanding of school-based curriculum development, what it is and how it may be undertaken in circumstances very different from only a decade ago.

Despite a welcome increase in curriculum writing, in research, experiential inquiry and theoretical analysis, the role of the school in curriculum development is still too little appreciated. Partly this is due to a lingering tendency to treat the school as a recipient of policy and other kinds of wisdom generated in the loftier parts of our society. It must be admitted that the problem is not only one of insensitive criticisms of schools for failing to solve this or that problem in society at large, or of the disquieting expansion of the political and bureaucratic domains, but is also in part that of the school's own making. Curriculum, there, is too often treated superficially, as a list of subjects, a set of topics, and periods on timetables. These, in turn, are conceived as the province of professionals and specialists, instead of being seen as a common set of concerns for the whole school – staff, students, parents, community groups and others. There are, of course, many exceptions and some of them are discussed in the companion *Readings*. Nevertheless, there is ample evidence that many schools have been unable, or unwilling, to take seriously the legitimate social challenge to rethink their curricula, fundamentally and globally, to adapt their policies to the great changes of contemporary life and to devise learning programmes that will meet the needs of all students.

Curriculum development certainly includes changes in items of subject matter and the planning of the timetable: much work is done and is needed to maintain the vitality of day-to-day classroom practice in order to meet the needs of particular groups. The focus in this volume, and its companion, however, is the whole curriculum for all students – its conceptualization, planning, design and development, set firmly against national – and international – movements in education. There is, I believe, a very profound need to evaluate and find ways of improving curriculum in this wider sense, treating it not as a collection of separate subjects and topics (not a few of them outmoded and largely useless for learning purposes) but as a powerful framework for the enhancement and organiz- ation of the varied and numerous experiences of students in the school setting and beyond the school.

The key to all of this, in curriculum terms, is the process of *design*, within the school itself but with constant reference to relevant contexts beyond the school. Thus, emphasis needs to be given by school leaders and managers to ways of thinking through and planning the whole curriculum. The school will be burying its head in the sand if it ignores the new forces in our national education system which are changing conditions of teaching and learning even when those affected do not realize the full import of what is happening. Hence the emphasis I have given throughout to development strategies and such matters as national aims and core curriculum.

In this book, in the main I consider general questions of curriculum policy, planning, design and development in so far as they seem to me to indicate possibilities for action and roles for schools. The companion *Readings* provide more concrete illustrations and examples of curriculum developers at work in schools and in supporting institutions. The two books have been written together to serve complementary purposes. A substantial bibliography has been included since one of my aims is to facilitate the study of school curriculum development in a wider context of curriculum theory, research and scholarship than has been usual in earlier (including my own) treatments of the subject.

It is worth mentioning that I have preferred the term 'student' to the more commonly used 'pupil'. The reasons for this are perhaps most apparent in Chapter 9, where I argue that one of our most pressing needs in education is to relate the curriculum quite centrally to student needs, and to bring the students themselves into a renewed partnership in curriculum decision making.

Malcolm Skilbeck 1984

CHAPTER 1

THE SCHOOL
AND CURRICULUM DECISIONS

'Whenever we have in mind the discussion of a new movement in education, it is especially necessary to take the broader, or social, view.'
(John Dewey, *The School and Society*)

School-based curriculum development may be thought of as a set of inter-related ideas about, or proposals for, how whole curricula are to be designed and how the related teaching and learning are to be planned and organized. It includes the roles and relations of the various parties and interests who are or might be involved in curriculum decisions. This is to approach the matter reflectively and critically, as a way of thinking about and organizing action to be taken. On the other hand, we may conceive of school-based curriculum development as a very loosely applied, descriptive label for a varied and perhaps miscellaneous collection of activities in schools. Whatever schools do that is in some measure related to the curriculum, whether in whole or part, and their ways of deliberately changing the curriculum, would fall under this definition, as would the shifting balance of control over the curriculum, as between schools and other agencies. Studying school-based curriculum development, trying to understand it in order, perhaps, to improve or perfect our actions, requires us to adopt both of these approaches. On the one hand, we need clear and strong organizing ideas: robust concepts that help us in the tasks of observation, analysis, appraisal and generalization that are essential in planning and in theory building. But, on the other hand, we need to be open to the diversity, variety and the ordinariness of a great deal of practice that arises through the actions and interactions of people in specific situations. It is indeed one of the characteristic features of curriculum theory that it serves as a bridge between the concreteness and variability of practical activities in teaching and learning, and the systematically analysed research data and constructs of the several branches of educational knowledge.

A question of definition

A book on school-based curriculum development may lean more towards the theoretical issues and problems and towards planning and design, as this one does, or towards the achievements, problems, puzzles and issues in practice, as does the companion volume *Readings in School-Based Curriculum Development* (Skilbeck 1984a).* Each, however, will have to call in some degree on the other, with the proviso that in talking about curriculum development in any form we must give our main attention to plans, designs and ideas for action: our theory is a theory of action and its tests must go beyond the canons of discourse, evidence and logical argument to the arenas of teaching and learning and the test of experience in classrooms, workshops, field centres, libraries, laboratories and so forth. This require-ment is all the greater in a study of school-based curriculum development, as is immediately apparent if we consider in a preliminary way a definition of that term: 'the planning, design, implementation and evaluation of a programme of students' learnings by the educational institution of which those students are members'. To extend this definition a little further, the educational institution may be a school, a study circle, a college or uni-versity, and so on, but what we have in mind is that the institution should be a living educational environment, defined and defining itself as a distinct entity and characterized by a definite pattern of relationships, aims, values, norms, procedures and roles. The curriculum in school-based curriculum development is internal and organic to the institution, not an extrinsic imposition. The institution also has a network of relationships with other institutions, groups and bodies, as for example a school is part of a local education authority and a national educational system and it relates to community bodies. The curriculum should not be parochially conceived. A further point to note is that it is not only the teachers that we have in mind when referring to what the institution determines and decides. It is a recurring theme of this book that school-based curriculum development ought not and indeed cannot be reduced by professional sleight of hand to teacher-based curriculum development, important as teachers' roles are

---

* This companion volume will be referred to as the *Readings* throughout the book.

at every stage. Decision making in the curriculum should be shared, participatory, with students involved in determining the pattern of experiences they are to undergo.

A final observation to make on this preliminary definition of school-based curriculum development is that it will not prove very serviceable if we think of it as conferring upon individual institutions powers and prerogatives – and resources – that they do not and arguably ought not to command. As we shall see a little later in this chapter and in greater detail in subsequent chapters, the school must apprehend its role in curriculum development as a close yet ever-changing partnership with other institutions and agencies in society. It no longer makes sense, if ever it did, to treat the school as the sole and exclusive determiner of the curriculum. That is not how our educational and social systems work, so we need to be especially sensitive to the relationship issue. In defining the school's role, however, we must also be prepared to define, or redefine, related roles: the school is not merely a reflexive agent of other institutions or forces in society. By drawing attention to the school's role we are bringing to its notice the problematic nature of its social relations. If, as some sociologists have claimed, the school unconsciously (or perhaps at times deliberately) reproduces existing relationships of power and control (Apple 1982a) it needs to learn ways of constructive social criticism in order to perform its educative role of social reconstruction (Skilbeck 1975, 1982b).

Turning for a moment to the aims and processes of curriculum development, to give to the school a central role is to raise challenging questions about the source and authority of the aims and values it adopts, the manner in which it selects and arranges curriculum content and its capability as an organization to handle the time-consuming and often difficult tasks of planning, designing, implementing and evaluating curricula. Changes in school management, organization and climate are required if schools are to be effective in their curriculum roles. We cannot, perhaps on ideological grounds or as a matter of administrative convenience, simply confer roles. Consequent changes in the life of the institution and its need for resources and support must be addressed.

A context for school-based curriculum development

The central ideas in school-based curriculum development may seem quite straightforward, but in order to see them clearly, to understand their implications and to know how to act upon them we have to study and think about a wide assortment of issues and developments in modern education. Like all simple yet profound ideas that get caught up in institutional life, they have become surrounded by a complex array of beliefs, values, theories, practical arrangements – and ambiguities and misunderstandings. Because the role of the school and the task of the teacher in curriculum development cannot be understood in isolation, we need to be prepared to take a broad overview of other agencies and forces at work in curriculum. School-level decisions inevitably affect and are affected by other kinds of curriculum decisions outside the school. Not to try to relate the one to the other is to risk parochialism and indeed a failure of effort.

Paradoxical as it may seem, approaching school-based curriculum development as a practical and potentially effective approach to educational change requires that we give particular attention to structures and processes which lie at the heart of the national educational system. There are several reasons for this. First, in most educational systems around the world, policy is centrally determined and funds centrally allocated even where they are regionally and locally administered. By central, we do not necessarily mean the political and bureaucratic apparatus of the nation state. Within federal systems, for example, policy may be – and usually is – centralized at the state or provincial level and control may be divided. However, whether the concentration of power and decision making is state, provincial or national, for school-based curriculum development to work or to be seen to have a role to play, its relationship with that central apparatus of policy and resource allocation needs to be explored.

A second consideration is that, significant among the factors affecting local decisions about the curriculum are the general outlines, guides or frameworks, voluntary or mandatory, which are an increasingly common feature of central educational administrations. Even among countries traditionally identified as decentralized or having strong and seemingly durable local decision-making structures, such as Britain and the United States, there have for long been influential curriculum proposals emanating from central bodies.

Thirdly, in most parts of the world since the Second World War considerable sums of central government money for education have come to be directed towards the achievement of curriculum values and objectives identified at the national level, whether these be in the form of government-sponsored curriculum development projects and agencies, or government funding of local initiatives within the broad framework of these values and objectives. A good example is to be found in the emergence in Australia, since the late 1960s, of a powerful set of federal government educational funding and development agencies including a national Schools Commission, in a system where, until then, the federal role in education was minimal – as it still is, for example, in Canada (Schools Commission 1981; Harman and Smart 1982).

A fourth reason for approaching the subject of school-based curriculum development through its relationships with the structures, policies and programmes for curriculum that are external to the school is that it is now accepted that neither the independent initiatives of the school nor those larger external forces in the curriculum are by themselves sufficient for achieving the systemwide kinds of changes that are needed. Imposed change from without does not work, because it is not adequately thought out, or it is not understood, or resources are not available to carry it through, or because it is actively resisted. Within-institution change is, by its nature, situation specific, often piecemeal, incomplete, of mediocre quality and so on. Each process requires the other, in a well worked out philosophy and programme of development.

It is the interrelationship, including the quest for better communication, a more concrete kind of partnership and shared decision making, between the school and the larger educational environment that has to be the focus of our efforts in future. This is shown both in the experience of those all too numerous curriculum development projects that have failed to engage significant proportions of teachers and in those many school projects that have remained partial, parochial and inconclusive. The theory of curriculum has had to be revised in an effort to comprehend these problems, provide explanations for them and suggest better and more effective designs, structures, models and processes for the future. By way of illustration, one of the best known of the curriculum development design models is the so-called 'Tyler rationale'. Formulated in the late 1940s, by Herrick and Tyler, the rationale was intended to show that there are four fundamental elements of a curriculum design: decisions about the educational purposes the school seeks to attain; experiences provided to attain these purposes; organization of these experiences; and assessment and evaluation to determine whether the purposes have been attained (Herrick and Tyler 1950; Tyler 1949). The design is, in fact, more elaborate and sophisticated than this, for example in its incorporation of data about society, subject matter and student learning needs, but these four stages, related as a linear sequence, are how the Tyler rationale has come into curriculum discourse, as a design model.

In a discussion with one of his critics, John Goodlad, Ralph Tyler some years later conceded that his rationale needed to be changed in significant ways, to give a definite role to teachers in curriculum design, to avoid an oversimplified linearity whereby all designs were supposed to commence with a statement of purposes to be attained, and to give a more definite place to local and personal assessment of student needs than the rationale allowed (Klein 1976). We discuss this general view of curriculum development in greater detail in Chapters 2 and 8. For the present, let us notice that the 'concessions' Tyler had in mind all take us towards a more open, school-focused modification of the rationale. Here is an example of one of the most influential of modern curriculum theorists acknowledging the need for a revision of theory in the light of the results and experience of large-scale sponsored curriculum research and development which frequently by-passed schools except for purposes of 'trialling' materials and 'implementing' change.

Conversely, in Britain since the late 1960s, school-based or school-focused discussions of the curriculum have had increasingly to come to terms with a new national dynamic, itself embodying social and economic forces of far-reaching effect. Throughout this book I refer to this emerging policy response as the *national framework*, or *national curriculum framework*. This is a complex of general aims, proposals for curriculum content – whether subjects or areas of knowledge or experience – and changing patterns of student assessment. However inadequately as yet, the national framework is helping schools and educationists to relate their activities to changes in our society and its culture which pose a dramatic challenge to the older notions of schooling. This framework, together with the theory of core curriculum and attempts in some countries such as Australia and England to set in motion a national dialogue on core curriculum, form a considerable part of this book.

The reasons for setting school-based curriculum development in this context of national initiatives and core curriculum are discussed, together with the details of these initiatives, in Chapters 4 to 7. What I argue there is the need for reconceptualizing school-based curriculum development, not by abandoning the by now established rationales and design models, but by locating it in a wider context. What is intended to emerge from all this is a redefined theory of curriculum action for schools and educational systems. It is evident that a quite fundamental change in the balance of educational forces is taking place, not only in Britain but in many other countries and, looking forward rather than to the past, we must now take the discussion of school-based curriculum development out of the localist context in which it emerged as a distinct philosophy of curriculum in the 1960s and earlier, and try to relate it to the changing circumstances and needs of schools, the newer perspectives in curriculum theory and the changes in national curriculum policies, structures and practices.

Schooling has lost much of its isolation or distance from the larger society, and the development of the curriculum is now rightly regarded as a matter of public policy not an exclusive professional preserve. Although we cannot, in a book of this scope and length, hope to treat the social and cultural phenomena of curriculum development in any kind of detail, some effort has to be made to bring the analysis of curriculum issues into the arena of changing social and cultural realities. It is these as much as our improved understanding of curriculum dynamics that oblige us to rethink school-based curriculum development. There is discussion of this kind in several chapters that follow, and suggestions are made as to how schools, in their activities of curriculum review, evaluation and development, might give much more attention in whole curriculum planning to social and cultural change than they have been accustomed to giving. My colleague, Denis Lawton, has pointed the way in his *Curriculum Studies and Educational Planning* (1983), a practical guide to planning the curriculum according to a concept of cultural analysis which he and I largely share.

The central strategy, then, that I have adopted conceives the school in an organic, historical relationship with defined educational system changes and seeks to elucidate its practice with the aid of theories about change, development, planning and design. The attempt that is made is to invest the school with a capability and a role that it can legitimately perform. It is therefore in the latter part of this book, in Chapter 8, that a design model for school-based curriculum development is proposed as a way whereby schools may and, I shall argue, ought to respond creatively and constructively to the ideas and changes discussed throughout the book.

Following that chapter on a design model for school-based curriculum development is a student-focused discussion of participation in the processes of reviewing, evaluating and developing curricula. The elevation of the student is not accidental or arbitrary but deliberate: in all of the recent debate on the curriculum far too little attention has been given to the students as partners in the educational enterprise. It seemed necessary to try to redress the balance even at the expense of forgoing the detailed consideration of the roles of all of the partners, parents included – a topic which in itself justifies a book.

The case for school-based curriculum development

We have been proceeding in this chapter on an assumption which now needs to be examined: the assumption that the school is properly to be regarded as an agency – a principal agency – of curriculum *development*. Because school-based curriculum development as a philosophical stance in education expresses some profound truths, it is not for that reason self-justifying. It is now more than ever necessary that practitioners in education, whether in or out of the classroom, should be able to explain and justify their curriculum ideas and decisions to a wider public. Just why the school ought to be singled out as the arena for special attention in curriculum making is a question that is not answerable by comfortable assumptions and traditionalist assertions of school and teacher autonomy. Those assumptions are under challenge and the assertions can very easily sound defensive. Nor can we accept the pinchpenny argument that curriculum development as a whole can simply be left to schools, as a means of economizing, with no recognition or provision of the essential resources. We need, in short, a rationale for the school's role in curriculum development, an understanding of the school's place in the wider field of curriculum, a sure grasp of the principles and procedures of curriculum review, evaluation and development, and well-reasoned arguments for essential resources – notably, adequate staffing and professional expertise. If we lack these, our moves to promote and seek support for school-based curriculum development will seem like special pleading by interested parties – the teachers.

It is frequently assumed that schools have a fundamental right to deter-mine their own curricula and there have been many declarations of teachers' professional responsibility for curriculum decisions. In England, par-ticularly, school control of the curriculum has had the status of an article of faith which has been rephrased and reiterated over the generations not only by individual teachers and schools but by philosophers, committees, civil servants, development agencies, teachers' unions and local and central government (Board of Education 1943; Morrell 1963; National Union of Teachers 1981; Whitehead 1932).

Like other articles of faith, school and especially teacher control of the curriculum is coming under question. That control never has been un-conditional and changing circumstances in school and society require its reappraisal. While there are rights for teachers which need to be affirmed and worked out in practice, it is not clear that they extend into all aspects of the curriculum. Nor are teachers the only people in or related to the school with curriculum rights. For example, would we concede that the decisions of the school teacher as to what the student should be taught ought to be made in all cases independently of parents' views and the preferences of students themselves? Would we accept that the teacher's role in curriculum decision making is in any way constrained or needs to be moderated by such wider social requirements as the needs of the employment market for trained personnel, the State's interest in responsible citizenship, or the views of people in higher and further education about appropriate areas of knowledge for young people to study and standards for them to attain? It is because teachers are but one of the groups and schools but one of the agencies with a stake in the school curriculum that the issues of how far and in what manner schools can or should seek to determine the curriculum have become so much a matter of public, political and professional concern in recent years (Becher 1984; Department of Education and Science (DES) 1981a; Weinstock 1976).

The question, 'Who should control the curriculum?', inevitably raises philosophical and political issues about rights and participation. These can be endlessly debated; in addressing them we need to keep a sense of balance about the school's legitimate rights over the curriculum as they exist and have evolved. If we look at the matter historically and go far enough back in time, schools were set up as places where, among other things, decisions would be taken corporately about what to teach and how to teach it. There were no other agencies for this purpose. The school was formally established, as an institution, just because there was felt to be a need for these decisions to be taken in respect of moral, aesthetic and physical as well as intellectual training or because individuals and groups, such as the teachers of Athens in the classical period, believed they had something to teach – a curriculum – for which there would be a ready demand (Butts 1955, pp. 9ff.; Freeman 1907; Marrou 1956, pp. 39–45 et seq.).

The overlaying in modern times of this concept of the school as itself the place where the curriculum would be decided, by the massive apparatus of local and national educational bureaucracies, examining and accrediting bodies, the publishing industry, teacher education institutions, professional associations and so forth, although now so well established is, historically speaking, of relatively recent origins. We need to appraise it in the course of reviewing school roles. Yet it would be a mistake to suppose that schools ever were or are, except in a very small minority of cases, just places where a group of teachers get together to organize learning for others. A closer analysis shows that school policies, including curriculum policies, embody and express the preferences and decisions of community groups, and of governments both local and national: the school never has been entirely shut off from the larger society as a specialized 'teaching shop'. We shall be returning to this question of the relationships between 'school' as an institution and the teaching staff in later chapters. For the present, and allowing for these relations between school–community–society, we can say that the very establishment of the school casts the teaching staff into the role of curriculum makers in some quite basic but not unrestricted ways.

It is all too easy to lose sight of the intimate interplay of school–community–society relations in everyday school life when so much of the contemporary discussion of curricula is dominated by the larger issues of government policies, the state of the economy, society's changing needs, the future prospects for young people and other macro concerns. To an extent this is inevitable, reflecting as it does the scale of public schooling. We are reaping the fruits of the setting up of State-supported or controlled systems of elementary education, mainly in the eighteenth and nineteenth centuries in the nations of Europe and the USA, and in the twentieth century in the developing countries and in revolutionary societies. Throughout the world, these movements have resulted in State dominance of schooling, with a great deal of curriculum decision making centralized in bureaucratic structures and reflecting broad social policies or contributing to the implementation of State plans (Connell 1980, part 3).

It is only exceptionally, in countries such as England and Wales (but not Scotland), that there has persisted, as if in an unbroken chain, a belief that the curriculum in some quite fundamental respects is the school's responsibility, independent of central government. The historical authenticity of this view has been debated (Gordon and Lawton 1978; White 1975) and it is true that the English Elementary Code during the nineteenth century imposed quite specific constraints on teachers' freedom of action, but the tradition – or myth – has persisted in spite of that and it is certainly the case in the twentieth century that the teacher in the school has been widely accepted – and proclaimed – as a kind of prince regent in curriculum making (Central Advisory Council 1967; Morrell 1963).

There is another sense – additional that is to this historical train of events, or myth if you like – in which it is scarcely disputable that the teacher's role in curriculum making is crucial, regardless of whether the educational system is centralized or decentralized. This point is well expressed by the American educator, J.J. Schwab, one of the sharpest critics of those mid-twentieth-century curriculum development projects and programmes which, in the USA, bypassed teachers and led to unenlightening squabbles amongst curriculum theorists. Schwab wrote:

> There are a thousand ingenious ways in which commands on what and how to teach can, will, and must be modified or circumvented in the actual moments of teaching. Teachers practise an art. Moments of choice of what to do, how to do it, with whom and at what pace, arise hundreds of times a school day, and arise differently every day and with every group of students. No command or instruction can be so formulated as to control that kind of artistic judgement and behaviour . . .
>
> . . . teachers *must* be involved in debate, deliberations, and decision about what and how to teach. (1983, p. 245)

This sense of the indivisibility of the teacher's classroom decisions was often submerged in the great surge of curriculum development through national projects that occurred in many English-speaking countries starting in the USA in the 1950s and then spreading to the UK, Canada, Australia and others. Hence there arose the notion of the 'teacher proof' curriculum – a course of studies so well structured, so tightly integrated, so well sustained by rich and stimulating materials that teachers either would not wish to or could not stand in the way of a direct transaction between the learner – the student – and the learning resources – the curriculum package.

Easy as it is to dismiss this as an aberration of the technological imagination, or as academic imperialism, not all teachers are inspirational, creative, effective. The projects in some cases went too far but their mission was to support teachers. Moreover, these exuberant curriculum designers and developers were quite reasonably concerned primarily with children's learning – not with the teacher's sense of propriety or views about curriculum ownership. Nevertheless, the aspiration sometimes had unfortunate consequences in practice for the reasons Schwab and many other critics of the 'teacher proof' curriculum advanced.

Some of the large-scale curriculum development projects involved considerable numbers of teachers in school trials of new materials and methods of teaching; others stimulated school developments which continued beyond the project; others again more nearly constituted loose networks of collaborating schools and teachers than tightly controlled national development schemes (OECD/CERI 1979; Stenhouse 1980). But they were still regarded by some educationists as an alternative to either school-based curriculum development on the one hand or commercially published textbooks on the other. Their role as sources, agents and guides of school initiative in curriculum was not consistently worked out across the whole curriculum. The history of the Schools Council for Curriculum and Examinations for England and Wales, from its inception in 1963 to its closure in 1984, is a good illustration of this point, as there was no consistency of policy in respect of school roles and only a handful of whole curriculum projects (Skilbeck 1984c).

Thus far in this chapter it has been suggested that school-based curriculum development is but one of the various styles or modes of curriculum development, such as the national project team, the State committee or commission and the commercial publishing venture. Despite its attractions for some educators, it is by no means universally accepted or even understood either outside or within schools. Even in an educational system where schools have traditionally enjoyed considerable autonomy in curriculum decision making, other factors and forces in education itself and in the wider social and cultural environments shape or constrain the exercise of this autonomy. Even were it possible, it would not be desirable for schools to attempt a major role in curriculum making except by relating their ideas and activities to other educational institutions and agencies and by drawing upon the resources and talents available in curriculum development projects and other external bodies. In Britain, the transformations occurring in the roles and relations of central and local government, not only in education but right across the field of social and economic affairs, necessitate a rethinking of the concept of school-based curriculum development and the procedures to be deployed. It is as well to mention here another problem, which is a common misunderstanding about school-based curriculum development – that it is assumed to require of schools a significant curriculum materials production role. There was a period when, with school resource centres being widely sought, and new means of reproducing print materials being installed, the vision of the school as a centre of materials production was proclaimed. As Philip Waterhouse shows in the *Readings*, the central task of the school in respect of resources is *management* for educational purposes, not wholesale production. This is entirely consistent with and, I shall argue, necessary for effective school-based curriculum development.

All of this is, as it were, a reminder of the need to see the school situationally and to understand its actions in curriculum in appropriate contexts. None of it, however, is to be construed as a reason for the abandonment of the long-held progressive principle, that the curriculum of learners should be determined in an important measure by and through the agency of the educational institution of which they are members. Before proceeding further it may be useful for us to identify the major arguments for school-based curriculum development and to set against them several of the recurring doubts, criticisms and difficulties schools need to address in curriculum development.

In a project of OECD/CERI, which extended over several years and incorporated case studies, seminars, reviews and reports, the case for school-based curriculum development has been extensively debated and refined (OECD/CERI 1975, 1975a, 1978, 1979). I was closely involved in the project and will draw freely on its conclusions. In the light of such constraints – which operate differentially in the member countries of OECD – as legal, financial and administrative powers over school decision making, the capabilities of the teaching profession, and the need for school-based curriculum development to relate itself to other modes of development and the various types of organization of schooling, a case was ultimately made out on the following grounds:

1. Demands for the increased autonomy of the school in curriculum making are part of a wider movement in modern societies for greater participation in the control and management of all sectors of public life: the democratization of decision making and policy through direct involvement and not only via representative or legitimate bureaucratic structures. Schools, as a part of society where intellectual and professional freedom are a crucial concern, participate in this movement and must be expected to provide leadership at least to their own members including students, parents and local communities.

2. Descending models of control, such as centrally constructed (and nonparticipatory) curriculum policy or legislated or decreed changes in curriculum content and organization, have created dissatisfaction or resistance, or have resulted in indifference to the underlying ideas and values of the proposed changes. In addition, projects based on a centre–periphery model have usually been underresourced or inadequately designed as comprehensive innovations, and their limited impact has generated a widespread (if not entirely justifiable) belief in the 'failure' of large-scale project development. This argument holds true even of traditionally centralized systems like France where central governments have failed to enforce most of the large-scale postwar educational reforms (OECD/CERI 1983; Skilbeck 1984c).

3. The school is a social institution comprising people in active relation-

ships with one another: it is a living organism which needs to organize and manage its affairs in such a way that its primary purpose, the education of children and youth, can be achieved in the best possible way. It engages in complex, not one-way, relations with its environment, exchanging and interchanging ideas, people and resources; it communicates with that environment and both is influenced by and influences it. The conduct of its affairs including its responsiveness to that environment requires freedom, opportunity, capability and resources. We cannot expect a school to be a vital centre of education if it is denied a role of self-determination and self-direction: the curriculum is the central structural component of schooling upon whose reasonable control the educational vigour of the school and the success of its educational mission depend.

4. The content of the curriculum consists of learning experiences – planned, resourced, structured, organized, undergone, assessed and evaluated. These learning experiences have to be charted, drawing upon the fundamental resources of the broad, consolidated areas of human experience that we term culture, the knowledge structures that we term subjects, and the themes and topics of everyday life. In charting these experiences we have to draw inferences or make claims about individual learners' needs and this requires a close knowledge and appreciative understanding of them individually and collectively. The planning and designing of the curriculum, for given groups of students in particular institutions, is what schools can do best: the construction of and the teaching and learning of a specific programme or course are its essential curriculum tasks.

5. The necessity for adapting, modifying and adjusting plans, programmes and designs for the curriculum to meet unforeseen circumstances, or just the particular exigencies of teaching and learning, requires that at the very least, schools should be in a position to adapt curricula to local circumstances. Since learning includes variable types of group and individual activity, involving different rates and types of learning task and the differential use of resources, equipment and so forth, flexibility in managing the curriculum is essential for efficiency in school organization. These are minimal roles in curriculum; they can be more effectively carried out where schools have freedom and opportunity, in the form of designated responsibility, to design and construct as well as to vary and modify – a condition which, for example, external examination syllabuses make it difficult to satisfy.

6. The role of the teacher as a free and responsible professional person, cannot be fulfilled unless there is scope for direct participation in significant aspects of the curriculum including its planning, designing and evaluating. Teacher self-actualization, motivation and sense of achievement are integrally bound up with curriculum decision making which is the staple of teachers' professional lives. They are important qualities to cultivate in education and have a contribution to make to the maturity, freedom and sophistication of society at large. (OECD/CERI 1975, 1975a, 1978, 1979; Skilbeck 1974.)

7. With hindsight, we may now regard the school as a more stable and enduring institution for curriculum development than those regional, statewide and national research and development bodies which played so prominent a part from the 1950s to the 1970s in creating the modern movement of curriculum development. In the USA, few of the regional laboratories and university Research and Development (R and D) centres remain; the Schools Council has collapsed; many professional and teachers' centres in Britain have closed; the Australian Curriculum Development Centre has lost much of its independence; and many other national agencies are struggling for resources, under review or devoted very largely to producing syllabus materials within single subjects. The capacity of the educational system to sustain curriculum development as an institutionwide process embracing the whole curriculum is a function of several different parts of the system: teacher selection and training, in-service education, further professional development, well-framed national policies, earmarked resources and so forth. However, we have a most valuable resource for curriculum development in the school itself. Structurally (despite many organizational changes) it is stable and enduring; as a community it is characterized by a high degree of expertise and professionalism; substantial resources are concentrated in and can be mobilized through it.

These are, as it were, premises of the argument. All have been put to the test if not fully evaluated; but they have in general a hypothetical and forward-reaching character, since they are propositions for a policy and a programme, incorporating values. The aim is to define, strengthen and support schools in the role projected for them. Some schools, accepting the challenge and enjoying the freedom and resources, have responded, but we still know too little in any detailed, systematic way about how they have done so, including the difficulties they have encountered. Research has been relatively sparse, although there are studies available including one which analyses research findings partly in the light of the present author's concepts of and proposals for school-based curriculum development (Knight 1983).

Difficulties and challenges

The evidence of such research studies as have been made of school-based curriculum development, and of many of the contributors to the *Readings*, makes it perfectly clear that we cannot simply accept at face value a case for school-based curriculum development but have also to reflect upon the problems – and the possible alternatives. We should, then, note the kinds of difficulties that have been experienced or may be anticipated. These can be broadly grouped as follows:

1. *Capabilities and skills of teachers and others involved.*   The assumption of school-based curriculum development, that teachers will play a major (but not an exclusive) role in planning, designing, implementing and evaluating curricula, must be tested against what is known about the competence of the profession as a whole and in particular institutions. In one sense, this will always be found deficient in some respect; however, a policy for school-based curriculum development would identify this and indicate how, for example through programmes of professional development, in-service training etc., the need is to be met. This is a responsibility not only of educational systems but also of individual schools. (Crone, Evans in *Readings*.)

2. *Teacher attitudes, values, motivation; alternative value orientations.*   It cannot be assumed that the teachers of any system are predisposed to favour shouldering the responsibilities and demands of school-based curriculum development or that they will not have had experiences, perhaps of failed in-school projects, which have had a negative effect. As Colin Bayne-Jardine, Elsa Davies and others point out in the *Readings*, there is a responsibility falling upon school principals to foster a supportive climate for in-school initiatives. There may be more serious difficulties, including the active resistance of groups of teachers – for example some of those who are working towards examination syllabuses or who have been long settled in their ways – to becoming involved in review, evaluation and development groups, or covert scepticism about the likely results. (Saville, Russell in *Readings*.)

3. *Organization, management and resources.*   School organizational struc-

tures which are hierarchical and conservative in respect of decision making can easily inhibit or frustrate curriculum innovation. The organizational framework both inside and outside the school is a major factor in the take up and success of development roles (Lindblad 1984). Several of the *Readings* underline the difficulty of establishing sound organizational and managerial procedures to sustain and reinforce initiatives that might be started off with enthusiasm. One of the greatest resources for local development work is time, a precious commodity in the heavily timetabled school day. Skilful management of time is crucial, as Robert Crone points out in the *Readings*. Deployment of clear and well-tried procedures, such as GRIDS (Guidelines for Review and Institutional Development for Schools), as described by Agnes Mc-Mahon in the *Readings*, is another useful managerial contribution. But such problems as staff turnover, conflicting or demanding alternative priorities, the pressures on school management arising from such 'non pedagogical' demands as handling insurance, health, safety and other regulations, negotiating, office routines and maintaining relations with local education authorities – these are a potential inhibitor of significant local development work.

4. *The efficiency and effectiveness of school-based curriculum development as a general strategy.* Perhaps the most serious difficulty of all is the often unvoiced but very real administrative and policy scepticism about school-based curriculum development as a strategy for managing curriculum development. Costs have never been adequately calculated although in the OECD/CERI studies already referred to efforts were made at least to identify cost factors. The scale and variability of local development work do not lend themselves to systematic evaluation but in some informal evaluations school principals and administrators have questioned whether the wider and more ambitious functions of school-based curriculum development – notably in relation to whole curriculum planning and design – can be performed other than in a small minority of schools or in quite exceptional circumstances. Combined with the common – and rather superficial – criticism that school-based curriculum development by its nature will lead to varying standards and lack of uniform educational provision, this scepticism has been a powerful constraint in the extension of school-based curriculum development, at least in centralized educational systems.

5. *Localism, parochialism and conservatism.* Much that goes under the name of school-based curriculum development, while it may well

be a kind of highly practical and adaptive small-scale innovation in a particular part of the curriculum, lacks any significance for the overall curriculum of a school or a system of education. Sometimes, school-based curriculum development may simply mask a conservative resistance to a much needed general review, or serve as a diversionary measure to avoid challenge on more basic issues (Hargreaves, A. 1982). For these reasons and because of a feeling that schools cannot be expected to mastermind large-scale, comprehensive development of the curriculum, school-based curriculum development is sometimes regarded as an adequate device for tinkering with bits of the curriculum but quite inadequate in respect of policy planning. Consequently, in the minds of many, common or core curricula should be adopted by all schools, or we should ensure that there is a wide range of national, large-scale projects under way to serve as a constant stimulus and source of new ideas and practices. The challenge to the school is twofold: to show how it can plan and organize far-sighted, whole-school review, evaluation and development and not only limited theme or subject-based projects; to accept a role for itself in curriculum making which acknowledges a national or systemwide curriculum policy and process and specific curriculum-making school tasks that are related thereto.

These and other arguments against school-based curriculum development continue to be advanced. Better reporting by schools of their own experience, and more substantial comparative research studies will help in the clarification and analysis of problems which, in some form or another, are an inevitable outcome of innovation. The question must be whether we have the willingness and ability to respond constructively to difficulties, assuming that there are good grounds for wishing to extend and enlarge the school's curriculum role. In subsequent chapters, neither is the case taken for granted, nor are the difficulties evaded. By building in school-based curriculum development as a crucial component of a systemwide style of curriculum review, evaluation and development, we may find that the school's role in the curriculum becomes clearer and more manageable than it has appeared to many of its critics in recent years.

Summary

School-based curriculum development has a potential for the reform and improvement of education which has been only partly explored, either in the practice of schooling or in studies of educational R and D and strategies of change. It is not the same as teacher-controlled development – although teachers have a central role – since the school is a community in which many partners and interests interact. The school is an organic community, and curriculum is the comprehensive range of student learnings for which the school takes responsibility in the pursuit of educational goals and values. Accordingly, development must be a partnership and must focus on the whole curriculum and the whole child or youth. The case for school-based curriculum development rests on a mixture of arguments which include both the need for educational freedom and responsibility, and the inadequacy of top-down strategies of change. There are, however, problems and difficulties to face before the school can take its rightful place as a major curriculum centre. The processes of review, evaluation and development of the whole curriculum are not straightforward and impose demands which many education systems have yet to meet adequately. In performing its role as a central agent of curriculum construction, the school must seek new ways of understanding and relating to profound changes in national educational policies and structures, in the culture of modern society and in educational research and theory. Building up each school's capability to respond creatively to these challenges and to play its part in these larger movements is increasingly being recognized as a necessary condition for the growth and reform of schooling.

CHAPTER 2

DESIGNS FOR THE SCHOOL CURRICULUM

'Finally, this I account the worst of all, that when I have taken a great dele of paines, and have made my Schollers very ready in construing and parsing: yet come and examine them in those things a quarter of a yeere after, they will be many of them as though they had never learned them, and the best farre to seeke.'
(John Brinsley, *Ludus Literarius or the Grammar Schoole*).

Thus far in our discussion we have taken notice of some of the trends – the currents and counter currents – apparent in the modern movement of curriculum. The approach we are adopting towards school-based curriculum development has been indicated as, first, a proposal for delineating the school's role within a wider context – relating local developments to systemwide changes – and, second, a reaffirmation of an educational rationale for the school's engagement with curriculum policy as well as practice. It is necessary now for us to step back from the school's role and from curriculum development to consider some preliminary questions about curriculum itself. These must be addressed if we are to make sense of the curriculum field and of the kinds of action that might be taken within it.

Curriculum: changing meanings and definitions

What is a curriculum? With what kinds of questions and issues are we grappling in seeking to answer this question? What are the key concepts in the whole enterprise of curriculum making? From a purely formal standpoint, the answers to these questions may seem clear enough. That is to say, the term 'curriculum' has been and is used in a number of ways, indicated in the standard dictionaries and specialist encyclopaedias which can be readily consulted and – not such a straightforward task – in the writings of numerous specialists and commentators. But once we get beyond the mere listing and comparing of definitions we are faced with some interesting and challenging problems. By noting four definitions of the term 'curriculum' we may readily see what kinds of problems these are:

> all the experiences a learner has under the guidance of a school (Kearney and Cook 1960)
> the operational statement of the school's goals (Foshay and Beilin 1969, p. 278)
> a programme of activities designed so that pupils will attain by learning certain specifiable ends or objectives (Hirst 1974a, p. 2)
> an attempt to communicate the essential principles and features of an educational proposal in such a form that it is open to critical scrutiny and capable of effective translation into practice (Stenhouse 1975, p. 4)

'Curriculum', according to these definitions, denotes children's experience, school guidance, goals, actions to achieve goals, proposals and statements, principles, critical analysis, pupil learning and objectives. Other definitions would yield still more. Despite attempts made by some curriculum specialists, a precise and restricted definition has not been agreed (Johnson 1967). There are good reasons for this.

Naturally, it is not possible in a short definition to encapsulate everything that is to be referred to in an extended discussion. In this book our interest is primarily curriculum development, hence action to be taken in curriculum planning and design and the conditions affecting that action. *'Curriculum' will be used to refer to the learning experiences of students, in so far as they are expressed or anticipated in educational goals and objectives, plans and designs for learning and the implementation of these plans and designs in school environments.*

Because curriculum is such a commonplace term within education and is increasingly used in the wider public arena, definitions will just be a kind of shorthand for positions or viewpoints which can be quite varied and elaborate. In this respect, we have a number of programmatic definitions, which means that individual definitions will point to some preferred view of schooling or of action. Let us consider another definition, the traditional one that equates curriculum with the syllabuses of subjects to be taught. This presupposes a subject basis for schooling and, not surprisingly, suggests to some primary school teachers that 'curriculum' issues are not their concern (Kelly 1982, p. 7), since they don't see their teaching as the transmission of subjects. This definition does not suit others in education, either; they have introduced such qualifiers as the 'hidden' curriculum or the 'effective' curriculum. In the one case, it is not so much a programmatic definition that is being advanced as an attempt, in the use of the qualifier 'hidden', to unmask school realities, the deep structures, or perhaps the subtle manipulative intentions of teachers or administrators: the 'hidden' curriculum is the 'real' curriculum, the one that carries social messages, of status, dominance, valued and not valued knowledge, proper and improper ways of behaving and so forth (Bernstein 1977; Giroux 1980; Gordon 1982). In the other case, by the use of the qualifier 'effective', attention is being drawn to attributes of teachers, or conditions of the school environment, or the actual learning experiences of students. The 'effective curriculum' is what the student 'takes' from the learning situation, not necessarily what was planned or hoped for by the teacher and others (Schools Council 1981, pp. 42–43 ff).

The connection between 'hidden' and 'effective' is this: that in order to understand what is effective in the curriculum so far as student learning is concerned, we must go beneath the plans, intentions and aspirations and examine the curriculum as experienced. This takes us into observations, dialogue, assessment and evaluation – all necessary aspects of curriculum construction. References to 'hidden' and 'effective' curricula provide us with modern examples of how uses of the term 'curriculum' point to differences in educational perspectives and values. Perhaps a clearer indication of this is to be found in the shifts that have occurred over a period of some one hundred years both in English-speaking countries and more widely around the world.

The term 'curriculum' has a long history, yet it has come into regular use only during the last century, mainly as a consequence of the efforts in Western Europe, the older Commonwealth and the United States to develop a systematic or scientific pedagogy. This dates from the latter part of the nineteenth century. More recently, and especially as a result of the curriculum development projects and programmes of the past thirty years or so, we can observe widespread movements for curriculum reform as a strategy for educational development. What emerges from this historical perspective is a fascinating shift reflecting changing educational values and ideologies on the one hand, and research and practical experience on the other. (Brubacher 1947, pp. 249–317; Cremin 1961; Kliebard 1979; Seguel 1966.)

In a narrow, literal sense, curriculum means 'a course to be run'. This narrow meaning does point to something enduring and fundamental in the activities of schools: targets are set, there is an end in view, a course is to be completed. There is something akin to a race in the time-honoured notions of ground to be covered, timetables, competitive performance – and prizes to be gained by those emerging at the head of the field. Moving from the metaphorical to the substantive, the curriculum is a 'thing' – it has a structure, an organization traditionally derived from authoritative texts, which is potential curriculum; it is rendered into a pedagogical form by the production of a syllabus, or written outline of topics, themes and approved authors; and a standard of acceptable performance is specified in examinations. The curriculum is thus real and visible in these several steps or stages: in what is required to be learnt and in the performance of the learner. Both set or indicate a standard, hence the curriculum is a concrete expression of educational values (which can be stated as aims). Although the language used in the foregoing is a strong reminder of the traditional secondary school, all of the points made apply equally to primary schools in the period of the English Revised (Elementary) Code and its equivalent in other countries. The concept of curriculum has, of course, always been as relevant in primary as in secondary schooling.

In seeking an answer to the question, 'What is the curriculum?', we can find in the above account what is very probably still the commonsense, public notion of the curriculum. Until relatively recently, it was also the most common school or professional notion and it was not – and is not – at all unusual for schools to proffer timetables and syllabus outlines which were subject structured, as their curriculum outlines.

It is also from this understanding of the curriculum as subjects and subject matter to be taught in a formal way in schools that one of the commonest, if dubious, metaphors of teaching has emerged: the transmission of knowledge and skills. The curriculum is not simply a structure defined authoritatively as organized content for learning – it is a vehicle, a means of establishing a dynamic relationship between teacher and taught. It was dissatisfaction with that relationship in practice, together with better knowledge and understanding of the conditions affecting it, that prompted the beginnings of a very different view of curriculum. That change was also part of a much wider transformation of culture, whose ramifications take us far beyond this book. Suffice it to say that for varied and complex reasons a quite fundamental challenge to the concept of curriculum as structured, preorganized subject content to be transmitted emerged in the late nineteenth and early twentieth centuries. While it was not without precedents, what was distinctive about this challenge was that it became generalized as a corpus of widely discussed and highly influential ideas about pedagogy, under the generic title of 'progressive education'. (Connell 1980; Cremin 1961; Graham 1967; Selleck 1969.)

The progressive challenge

Progressive education has usually been thought of as a revolutionary set of doctrines about freedom in schools, resulting in more relaxed relations between students and teachers, a focus on student interests and activities in learning, and the introduction of more varied content organized by themes and topics rather than according to subject boundaries. Generally, but not always, emphasis was given to ways of integrating and otherwise interrelating student learnings both with one another and with life outside the school, for example through projects, themes and integrated studies. Whilst it is by now generally accepted that progressive education constitutes an ideology, not simply a shift in pedagogical practice, what is not so often noticed is that it denotes a shift in basic educational constructs and strategies including the abandonment of transmission theories of learning and subject-defined curriculum, and a resolute rejection of what are now termed the socially and culturally reproductive functions of schooling (Apple 1979; Skilbeck 1975, 1982b).

It is because this is so that the content and form of definitions of key terms in education, including curriculum, changed under the progressive influence. In passing, we may notice that whereas the direct impact of progressive ideas and doctrines on school practice – for example the English primary school – appears to have been quite limited, its influence on our language, ideas, and on the general climate of opinion about education has been profound:

> much more than a protest movement . . . [the progressive movement] was a creative educational effort by thoughtful, sensitive, adventurous men and women, alive to the importance of their calling and dedicated to its improvement. Nothing like it had ever previously occurred in the history of education. The progressive movement was an effort by many educators in many countries to come to grips with their perception that the new world of the twentieth century was causing substantial changes in social organization and in human relations . . . (Connell 1980, p. 119).

One of the consequences of the progressives' concerns – teacher-student relationships, student interest as a major factor in learning, and breadth and variety of educative activities in and out of the classroom – was that the term 'curriculum' itself had to be redefined. A definition was needed that would enable the older programmatic idea of subject-bounded content transmitted by teachers in authority to be displaced by the new kinds of programmes that the progressives were advocating and implementing. The new definition gave prominence to learning experiences, and to all of those experiences in which the school might take an interest for educative purposes whether or not it directly 'controlled' or 'provided' them. The literature of progressive education needs to be consulted for details but, as one of our definitions at the beginning of this chapter shows, the term curriculum had come to be defined as long ago as the 1930s, at least in the USA, as all the experiences a learner has under the guidance of the schools. This was the period when the influence on educational theory of John Dewey, William Heard Kilpatrick, Harold Rugg and other progressives was at its height (Cremin 1961, chapters 6 and 7; Schubert 1980, chapters 3 and 4).

A loose equation of 'curriculum' with the guided learning experience of children in schools spread throughout the English-speaking world. There were several consequences: first, the definition embodied, however elliptically, a powerful and challenging educational philosophy which provoked much debate and disagreement from those favouring narrower or more precise educational approaches; second, because the definition clearly enlarged the role of the school – in terms both of the 'areas' of human experience that might be explored and of the extent of the relations between school and other social agencies and forces – it invested the idea of 'curriculum' with a comprehensiveness which was to prove difficult for policy makers, developers and teacher education; third, the definition helped to draw attention to the context and conditions of learners' 'experience', the forces and factors working on it over and above those of the school with its avowed goals and purposes – hence the emergence of all the qualifiers, 'hidden', 'effective' and so on; fourth, the definition left open the relations between curriculum, teaching, learning, and their organization, giving rise to somewhat arid terminological debates about whether curriculum refers to the content of teaching programmes alone or to that content as taught and learnt – and assessed and evaluated (Johnson 1967).

Because of the wider social, cultural and educational references of progressivism, to which we have alluded, it is not surprising that from the early 1960s onwards, the progressives' programmatic definition took strong hold and in most books in English on the curriculum, of the past two or three decades, its use has been in evidence. There are good reasons for this, not least the changes that have occurred in school practice, and the inability of the older definitions to encapsulate them. Educators *are* concerned with children's learning experiences in schools; they *do* want those experiences, while incorporating subject matter learning, to have greater breadth and relevance to student interests and social trends; and they are conscious that whatever the school aims to provide by way of learning opportunities will be affected by a host of other in-school and out-of-school factors. Also, educators, like others, have been accustomed by powerful movements in modern culture to think and reason not in terms of linear causal sequences of individual, fixed entities (such as 'this fixed content, organized into these sequences of learning steps, will result in these measurable outcomes') but interactively and in nonlinear patterns. This means that key concepts in the world of educational practice – and curriculum is certainly one – will have about them an openness and looseness which, while it may inhibit precise usage, will foster and encourage the exploration of relationships and connections in the milieux of learning.

However, more recent advances in our understanding of the processes and concepts of curriculum have not come from the battle of the books that occurred between progressive educators and their critics but are a result of a combination of development and analytical activity which occurred, on an unprecedented scale, during the 1960s and 70s. We shall have more to say about this in later chapters. At this stage, we may note that in taking the definition of curriculum away from a course, a subject matter to be covered, towards experiences to be undergone, the progressives were undoubtedly shifting the emphasis away from the provision of something articulated, definite and preplanned and towards the nature of experience and the processes of experiencing. In this, they were following the lead of John Dewey, the most powerful of modern educational theorists (Dewey 1902a, 1902b, 1910, 1916, 1938). The different ideological underpinnings of these two positions notwithstanding, each has something valuable to contribute to an understanding of what we are referring to in the term 'curriculum'.

Always, in curriculum, there is a content of some description; invariably decisions have to be taken about how, where, when and by whom it is to be organized for teaching and learning, and, by whatever means, judgements have to be made by or about the learners with regard to how well that content has been learnt. We may, if we wish, distinguish educational aims as a separate domain, but once we start to think of those aims dynamically – as ends or directions or purposes to be realized through some kind of action – we have moved a long way towards the central concerns of curriculum.

Likewise, we may wish to distinguish the processes of teaching and learning and the ways of assessing performance from the heartland of curriculum, but in so far as our interest in curriculum has to do with a concern for the reality of those learning experiences, the distinctions will become blurred.

These are not merely observations about the problems of definition; how we define curriculum and use curriculum concepts and language will affect our views and actions in the matter of curriculum development. Any institution, school or otherwise, which takes an interest in curriculum development will be faced with the need to decide what are the foci, the scope – and limitations – of that enterprise. This decision is not simply a matter of stipulating what is 'practicable'; it must also show a sensitivity towards the interrelationships among the various elements of curriculum that we have identified. If we do not understand what these are we court the failure which is all too common in the implementation of curriculum proposals.

Review, evaluation and development

The three terms 'review', 'evaluate' and 'develop' will be helpful in carrying forward our discussion of changing concepts of the curriculum. Each refers to ways in which curriculum has been thought about and acted upon during and since the period when curriculum development projects were so often a feature of the educational landscape. Often treated as discrete, the subject of specialization, they can profitably be interlinked.

How do curriculum practitioners and theorists use the term 'curriculum' now, what is their frame of reference, and how, using these analyses, can we enhance our efforts as curriculum reviewers, evaluators and developers? Indeed, it is by thinking about what lies behind these definitions and concepts that we can build up a necessary part of the framework of curriculum action: solving curriculum problems, taking curriculum decisions, setting up curriculum action groups – all of these presuppose an understanding of relevant problems, decisions and actions, and processes of change. There is much more to this, as we shall see, than general concepts of the curriculum, but we can better develop our intervention strategies and procedures by first mapping the field of action.

Although there are many different ways of grouping and categorizing 'curriculum', two or three distinctions seem to be quite vital for reflective, evaluative and developmental action. First, there is the distinction between wholes and parts: a curriculum can be either the totality of the intended learnings, learning experiences and learning outcomes, or some defined part. The terms 'part curriculum' and 'whole curriculum' have been proposed to differentiate between these two. However, there is ambiguity here, since, as we have seen, curriculum can encompass, for a given range of learning experiences, a whole sequence from aims to assessed learning outcomes. Is the 'part' then one element or phase in this sequence, or is it the whole sequence but applied to just one area of learning? Let us suppose that a school declares its intention to 'review and evaluate' the curriculum, with a view to making such changes as the review and evaluation suggest are both desirable and feasible. Would this be understood to embrace concurrently all that the term curriculum, broadly interpreted, refers to? In principle, the answer would be yes, but the practical exigencies of institutional life are such that it is only relatively infrequently that anything so all-encompassing is attempted. Not surprisingly, when one approaches it thus, we have only a few examples in the literature of systematic research on whole-curriculum planning. The reasons for this are partly explained by some of the contributors to the *Readings* in terms of the realities of school life. There are glimpses to be gained from earlier studies, notably the American Progressive Education Association's Eight Year Study, and from occasional projects such as that arising from the Northern Ireland Schools Support Service (Aiken 1942; Crone and Malone 1983; DES 1977a; Galton and Willcocks 1983). For systematic analyses of what is entailed in whole curriculum review we have to turn to occasional theoretical essays, such as that by Broudy, Smith and Burnett (1964) or Lawton (1983).

'Whole curriculum' can be defined in the manner we have indicated, even where for purposes of action we are likely to focus on some part. But what does 'part curriculum' mean? Is this a particular content area of the curriculum across the school, for example reading and other kinds of language learning reviewed, evaluated and developed in all their aspects, or could we say that we were engaged in a curriculum development exercise merely because we modified assessment procedures, or substituted one set of materials for another?

There is no ready answer to these questions and they will not be resolved merely by juggling with definitions. As in other practical spheres, we have a range of actions open to us, from ones which are very limited and quite specific, to long-term, comprehensive and global strategy planning, whole-curriculum design and implementation. At what point does a *curriculum* analysis start? For the purposes of this book and given our focus on developmental activities in schools, that analysis is directed towards:

1. the sequence of review, evaluation and development processes and activities extending from a consideration of the purposes of the teaching to its outcomes or results in student learning;
2. deliberate efforts to relate work done on some particular area of content to other areas, to school organization of learning situations and management procedures in the school curriculum;
3. the context of system changes and theories of whole, common and core curricula.

This means, in effect, that 'curriculum' is here being given a 'whole-curriculum' and a school orientation. If this is our perspective we can nevertheless fully acknowledge that any particular process or enterprise of curriculum development for practical purposes will very likely focus on parts of the whole, treating the patterns of relationships with other parts as secondary or for later consideration.

We have linked in a sequence, to which we shall return throughout this book, three kinds of activity: review, evaluation, development. A *review* is a reflection on practice, depending perhaps on an organized scrutiny, with an oral or a written report on what is observed (although some 'School Reviews' are more comprehensive than that, veering towards evaluation – see, for example, those required by the Victoria (Australia) Department of Education (Halpin 1982; VISE 1981). An *evaluation* requires that whatever is observed and reported is examined and judged in the light of criteria, goals, values or standards of worth for which a justification is offered (Eraut 1984; Skilbeck 1984c, Introduction). *Development* means enabling, or undertaking, action to modify or change what is reviewed and evaluated; it is the culmination, in whole-hearted action to achieve certain goals or purposes, of the events set in train by the reflective and critical phases. Through development, we seek to resolve or provide the means of resolving the problems or shortcomings identified in these phases, to give practical expression to the values and aims that are brought to full awareness as much by the determination to act as by reflection and criticism. An interesting example, in the area of school–work transition, is provided by a report to the Victoria (Australia) Institute of Secondary Education (Kemmis et al. 1983).

A curriculum is, in one sense, a programme *design for learning* that satisfies certain criteria and is structured according to selected principles. Mention has been made already of the interest now taken in the notions of 'hidden' and 'effective', referring to the contexts and conditions in which curriculum designs are used in curriculum review, evaluation and development, and to their effects on student learning. Designs for human action, in use, become quite varied and may lose much of their original sharpness of outline or conceptual distinctiveness. Recognition of this fact is a necessary part of understanding curriculum implementation; it is a mark of our awareness that curriculum change is a social and environmental affair in which human relations, organizational factors and institutional politics all play their part. Nevertheless, just because there are distinctive and different views in our society about the purposes of schooling, debates continue about what ought to be taught and how it might best be organized for learning. There are different and conflicting conceptions of the curriculum, hence different 'design briefs' as a consequence. Some draw attention to cognitive processes as curriculum 'organizers', others to personal fulfilment and personal integration, to socially useful skills, the academic disciplines and so on. Connell (1980) and Eisner and Vallance (1974) show how such conceptions influence curriculum planning, and there is a useful historical overview in Schubert (1980).

In accordance with these different viewpoints a number of distinctive general briefs for curriculum designs or design models have emerged. We cannot attempt to review them all, but turn now to four which, taken together, will give us insight into the range and nature of the tasks to be undertaken in curriculum development:

1. Curriculum as a structure of forms and fields of knowledge
2. Curriculum as a chart or map of the culture
3. Curriculum as a pattern of learning activities
4. Curriculum as a learning technology

Curriculum as a structure of forms and fields of knowledge

A long-held tradition in education treats the curriculum as a body or corpus of knowledge to be organized, communicated, acted upon and in some sense reproduced by students. Strenuously criticized during the progressive era, as pedagogically and epistemologically unsound, socially divisive and restrictive in a science-based democracy, and unsuited to a mass school system (Dewey 1916, 1938), this view nevertheless survived criticisms and indeed was skilfully reaffirmed, for example in the Norwood and Crowther Reports on secondary education (Board of Education 1943, chapter 3; Central Advisory Council 1959, chapter 25).

It was not, however, the impact of these Reports that kept this particular cognitive theory alive. Rather, it was a combination of professional assumptions, values and skills of teachers, external institutional structures, notably secondary school examinations, and a new factor, the major subject-defined American and English curriculum development projects. Amongst the earliest and most influential were those in mathematics (primary as well as secondary) and science – two subjects where it seemed at the time to be relatively easy to reach firm conclusions about crucial theories, facts, learning sequences and methods of demonstrating proof or testing hypotheses (Goodlad et al. 1966, sects. I and II; Heath 1964; Rosenbloom 1964). In addition, two highly influential theorists vigorously and persuasively advanced the thesis that in talking about the curriculum we are in fact talking about clear-cut structures of knowledge and how to organize and communicate them: Paul Hirst and Jerome Bruner. Their writings and commentaries on them are well known and widely available (Bruner 1960, 1966, 1972; Hirst 1974a).

It is therefore not necessary here to do more than pin-point crucial elements in the position they have advanced, as they relate to forms or structures of knowledge within curriculum design. There are important differences in their respective positions but it is not misleading to identify some common or overlapping propositions:

1. That a liberal or general education should be grounded in systematic study of clearly defined areas of knowledge: not subjects necessarily, but domains individualized and differentiated by (i) concepts; (ii) a logical structure of propositions; (iii) criteria for truth (Hirst 1974a, p. 85).
2. That the relationships – such as partial integration – that might, for curriculum purposes, be attempted to be built among these forms of knowledge need to take close account of their distinctness (ibid. p. 191).
3. That the curriculum ought to be clearly defined by cognitive objectives leading to specified or specifiable learning outcomes that have some definite relationship to the forms of knowledge (ibid. pp. 147–151).
4. That knowledge structures should define the curriculum, a structure being defined as a clear pattern of relationships, of concepts, processes and items of information within a discipline (Bruner 1960, chapter v).
5. That a theory of instruction can be constructed for curriculum purposes, comprising specifications of (i) experiences which implant a predisposition in students towards learning; (ii) ways in which distinct fields of knowledge should be structured; (iii) learning sequences; (iv) the nature

and pacing of rewards and punishments (Bruner 1966, chapter 3).

6. That knowledge structures of the 'established' disciplines should be defined and differentiated and taught to bring out their central concepts and themes, methods for testing knowledge claims and the social processes by which knowledge is generated and communicated (Bruner 1960, 1966).

7. That learning is developmental in human beings, proceeding from concrete, nonverbal experiences through visual and other sensory organization involving images, diagrams etc. to symbolic (Bruner 1966, chapter 1).

8. That logical structures in the forms of knowledge ought to be distinguished from, and take precedence over, psychological processes of learning (Hirst 1974a).

For both Hirst and Bruner the primary function of education can be stated in cognitive terms – the growth of the mind. A curriculum, therefore, is in all essential respects a plan or programme for the enhancement of cognitive powers through the identification and application of the most powerful intellectual strategies available. As Bruner put it, 'the curriculum of a subject should be determined by the most fundamental understanding that can be achieved of the underlying principles that give structure to the subject' (Bruner 1960, p. 31). Notice that, for Bruner, subjects are the building blocks of the curriculum, on the argument that there are to be found within the academic disciplines not only structures but traditions of inquiry, bodies of experience and communities of authoritative specialists to be drawn upon for purposes of curriculum construction. The analysis of the structure of the discipline is held to be the primary source of a learning strategy; drawing upon its cultural and human capital is the way to get curriculum development going.

So far from this being a form of cultural imperialism, the engagement of scholars and researchers in the analysis, design and development of school curricula was seen as a way of ensuring, ultimately, a unity between all forms of education, social cohesion and cultural integration. However, like many of the early advocates of curriculum construction through small, expert teams of scholars, researchers and theoreticians, Bruner later had cause to abandon at least one of his principal theses:

Interviewer: 'But if you could change the structure of the educational system now, given that the classroom is an unalterable entity, what would you do?'

Bruner: 'One thing I know is that when you're in trouble, you
                 should diversify and see what works. I have given up on
                 these great top-down schemes!'
(Tetroe and Woodruff 1980–81, p. 35)

Through the writings of Bruner and Hirst, a cognitive view of the
curriculum has gained ground. It is basically a structural view, even
Bruner's well-known adaptation of the Piaget stages in learning, although
some attention is given to functions in the form of individual student
learning strategies (Case 1978). Bruner's work, in part an outcome of his
own involvement in the 1950s and 60s in project-based curriculum development, has been taken up in subsequent projects and in teacher education
programmes both pre-service and in-service, around the world.

Hirst's concept of the curriculum may be simplified, without being
distorted, in terms of a constellation of seven distinct knowledge areas.
Even though Hirst is careful to say that they do not in and of themselves
constitute a curriculum map or plan, they are presented as a principal
source of ideas about the general structure and content of the curriculum of
general education. The areas have never been definitely stated, despite
several attempts, and it remained unclear just how prescriptive Hirst would
wish to be about them after he had reviewed his well-known 'Liberal
education and the nature of knowledge' (1965) essay, in 1974 ('The forms of
knowledge revisited'). However, the trend of his thinking is clear from the
original list, of mathematics, physical sciences, human sciences, history,
religion, literature and the fine arts, and philosophy (Hirst 1965). There can
be no doubt that the forms were intended to provide the substance for the
intellectual objectives which Hirst believed should have primacy in the
curriculum.

Hirst's proposals were picked up in England and Wales by Her Majesty's
Inspectorate whose writings on the curriculum from the mid 1970s onwards
have shown a distinct preference for areas of experience (DES 1979c):

aesthetic and creative
ethical
linguistic
mathematical
physical
scientific
social and political
spiritual

The HMI areas, of course, go beyond the intellectual and cognitive domains of Hirst's analysis but there is a similar concern for structure and breadth in the whole curriculum.

These kinds of statements are often thought of as models. That is, as a simplified outline of elements to be included in a design for the curriculum. In a sense, they are, but we must also see them as basic definitional and conceptual moves not only because, as models, they are at best only partial, omitting many of the fundamental elements needed for designing an action programme, but also because they predispose the reader to view curriculum per se as a working out, in planning and design terms, of the forms and areas as cognitive structures to be acquired and developed through systematic teaching. Curriculum is, on this count, not simply 'guided experiences' or any set of subjects: it is *these* forms, *this* structure, with an emphasis on an orderly progression through the forms, areas or structures of disciplines. This gives a strong intellectualist colouring to curriculum development undertaken along these lines – a marked feature also of Hirst's and Bruner's views.

Curriculum as a chart or map of the culture

From a social perspective, education is a means of inducting people into the norms, values, modes of conduct, belief system – broadly speaking, the way of life – of a people. Richard Peters spoke of education as initiation, meaning a process of induction into preestablished ways of life (Peters 1964). Elsewhere, he gave more emphasis to the relationship of education to reform and to a notion of achieving desirable aims and events which might lie well beyond present social or personal circumstances (Peters 1972b) Thus, induction can be, at one and the same time, a process of joining or assimilating, and a means of projecting aims and values not yet realized.

Other writers, taking their cue from anthropological ideas of culture, have focused on curriculum as itself a derivative and a representation of culture. The American curriculum theorists, B.O. Smith, W.O. Stanley and H.J. Shores, writing in the 1950s and under the influence of the anthropologist Ralph Linton, said:

> The people of every society are confronted by problems of inducting the immature members into their culture, that is, into the ways of the group. The individual at birth is a cultural barbarian, in that he has none of the habits, ideas, attitudes and skills characterizing the adult members of society . . . In literate societies . . . a sequence of potential experience is set up in the

school for the purpose of disciplining children and youth in group ways of thinking and acting. This set of experiences is referred to as the *curriculum* . . . To understand the structure and function of the curriculum it is necessary to understand what is meant by culture, what the essential elements of culture are . . . (Smith, Stanley and Shores 1957, p. 3)

As to what these 'essential elements' are, there can be no conclusive answer, partly because culture is a constant flux, partly because different ways of analysing and interpreting culture yield different results. Smith, Stanley and Shores, for example, adopted the 'culture as a total way of life' approach of the nineteenth-century anthropologist, E.B. Tylor, with its emphasis on culture acquired through membership of society and taking in the ideas, ideals, beliefs, skills, tools, aesthetic objects, methods of thinking, customs and institutions of a social group (Bidney 1967, p. 28). Even when classified, after Linton's scheme (Linton 1936), into 'universals' (accepted by all members of society), 'special' (subcultures such as youth culture, vocational skills) and 'alternatives' (divergent or counter-cultures), their definition of 'culture' takes in the whole of life and selections must be stringently made. However, that *selections* have to be made gives us a lead, and Denis Lawton, defining curriculum as 'a selection from the culture', argued that this means a key role for schools and that they would be helped in this by having a general chart or map of culture to provide guidance (Lawton 1983).

Curriculum, for Lawton, consists of a selection made by schools of studies from each and all of the following structures, or subsystems of the cultural system, as he puts it:

social structure/social system
economic system
communication system
rationality system
technology system
morality system
belief system
aesthetic system

As an advocate of common curriculum, Lawton's view is that all students should encounter all areas, in a systematic way and through well-organized and sequenced study. His interest is primarily in whole curriculum: curriculum is a selection, made by schools, for all students and from the eight areas indicated. Thus his proposals are focused on the school's role in whole-curriculum planning. We discuss this in more detail in Chapter 7.

There are several features of these conceptions of curriculum as a map or chart of 'domains of culture' to which attention needs to be given if they are to become the basis of workable designs. In making selections, procedures, rules, guidelines and indicators are needed to avoid arbitrariness and to achieve something like a coherent framework. Lawrence Stenhouse (1975) was alert to this problem when he drew attention to the following features of culture:

1. that the domain can be thought of as the society's intellectual, emotional and technical 'capital';
2. that the capital may be characterized as 'public traditions';
3. that communication is a basic cultural process;
4. that subject disciplines exist both 'in' culture and in their own right;
5. that propositions about culture are, from a pedagogical standpoint, hypotheses to be carefully formulated and tested in practical situations.

The last point led Stenhouse to his definition of curriculum which we quoted at the beginning of this chapter. Curriculum embodies the essential principles and features of an educational proposal in such a way that both critical scrutiny and practical testing become possible.

Concepts of culture, however, as Raymond Williams shows, have a remarkable elasticity over time and in accordance with the viewpoints and preferences of those advancing them. It is a good example of a word whose many meanings cannot be elucidated except by an ideological analysis which would disclose the interests, values and organizational structures underlying those viewpoints and preferences (Williams 1981). This point is also discussed in its relevance to curriculum in some of the present author's writings on the subject (Reynolds and Skilbeck 1976, chapters 1–3, 7; Skilbeck 1982b).

Have we not, then, got ourselves into a tangle from which extrication may be possible only by adopting a more straightforward or direct approach? Perhaps – but once we start to probe a little into even the most simple statements about curriculum, such as that it refers to 'what teachers teach', or 'what and how pupils learn', or 'essential knowledge and skills', we discover long chains which connect the phenomena of schooling with the society and its culture. There are two ways, at least, out of the difficulty. The first is to accept that there are in fact many ways of analysing, schematizing and categorizing cultural systems and processes just as there are different ways of schematizing knowledge systems. When it comes to curriculum review, evaluation and development as tasks to be undertaken in and by schools, it will be helpful to know that there are different ways, that there is value in knowing what some of them are, that choices among them can be and have been made, and that cultural analysis can be used in a very practical way. We return to this point in Chapter 7.

Secondly, if we treat the curriculum as a cultural map we need not suppose this to mean that the school has to construct a kind of overview of culture which it then transmits to students. Such overviews have a very limited educational value; moreover, 'transmission' is an unsatisfactory metaphor. Let us think instead of the curriculum as itself a process of mapping – the means whereby students and teachers jointly structure, and restructure, selected aspects of the culture. This is not as grandiose as it sounds, since what it refers to is a set of procedures for selecting learning experiences, organizing them, and reviewing the process in which teachers and students collaborate: the curriculum is thus not something 'out there' to be mastered but a set of relations between teachers and taught focused by themes, questions – and domains and areas of experience and knowledge. Culture is, as Whitehead remarked, from an educational perspective an activity of mind; it is not an inert system to be assimilated. We return to this point also in Chapter 7.

Curriculum as a pattern of learning activities

In the preceding paragraphs we saw that the idea of curriculum as a cultural map can be approached both substantively – a culture to be mapped – and as a process: the central curriculum task is one of mapping the culture in which the student as well as the teacher is deeply involved. This sounds rather like a high-order intellectual activity. Is it not, after all, the business of sophisticated adults to be charting the frontiers of knowledge, understanding and experience?

As we have seen, the early progressive critics of stereotyped and passive methods of learning inert subject matter by rote proposed a curriculum of activities. Elegant and memorable expression was given to this concept long ago, by the authors of the Hadow Report – a report not on the education of mature and sophisticated scholars but the primary age child. The curriculum, it was said:

> is to be thought of in terms of activity and experience rather than of knowledge to be acquired and facts to be stored. Its aim should be to develop in a child the fundamental human powers and to awaken him to the fundamental interests

of civilised life so far as these powers and interests lie within the compass of childhood, to encourage him to attain gradually to that control and orderly management of his energies, impulses and emotions, which is the essence of moral and intellectual discipline, to help him to discover the idea of duty and to ensue it, and to open out his imagination and his sympathies in such a way that he may be prepared to understand and to follow in later years the highest examples of excellence in life and conduct. (Board of Education 1931, p. 93)

Romantic and idealistic (and admirable) as these sentiments may seem today, in an era of mass schooling many parts of which suffer from social problems, economic pressures and the insidious undermining of educational values by other forces in contemporary society, they nevertheless draw together and crystallize a distinctive and powerful movement in curriculum theory. This movement has always aimed to define the curriculum through a consideration of human experience and as much from the child's standpoint as from that of the world beyond the school.

The thought and the wording of this passage in the Hadow Report echoed the American philosopher, John Dewey, and were very much in tune with the English philosopher and mathematician, Alfred North Whitehead, neither of whom can be regarded as oblivious of the social purposes of schooling. Definitions of the curriculum which draw attention to the world external to the learner, whether this be the world of forms of knowledge or domains of culture, run the risk – however unintentionally – of projecting a view of education in which the learner is to be led, drawn, pushed, filled or otherwise treated as the object, not the subject. The progressive movement aimed to correct this bias. Doubtless those who use terms like 'initiation', 'induction' or even 'inculcation' (which, unfortunately, denotes in its Latin root 'grinding in by the heel'!) intend these to serve as processes in which the learner is engaged, interested, active, participatory. But, as Dewey said, there is something peculiar in the idea of first defining a 'something' which it is important for the learner to know and then searching for ways of interesting him or her in it. This, for Dewey, raised insurmountable difficulties psychologically and pedagogically, difficulties which, in spite of the antiquity of this 'push-pull' thesis in the commonsense experience of mankind, would have to be resolved if educational programmes were even to connect with the inner forces of the human person (Dewey 1916, chapter X).

For Dewey, the resolution of these difficulties lay in a lifetime's work to elaborate, explain and justify to his numerous critics a view of education as 'growth': of pedagogy not in the form of an imposed order or discipline but grounded in the activity and interrelationships of persons; of the curriculum as an interaction between the learner and the world; of experience as the interplay of acting, being acted upon, reflection and experimentation. As for how the curriculum was to be defined, Dewey by no means dismissed knowledge structures or cultural domains. The curriculum was to consist of planned and ordered experiences, worked out through studies of the culture, drawing on knowledge domains, and devised as topics, units and projects. For younger children, these were to be derived mainly from the fundamental 'occupations', or the socio-industrial arts of mankind as they have emerged in history. At the secondary stage, subjects were to be treated as reservoirs of human experience, to be drawn upon in problem-solving and practical forms of learning – but not treated as distinct logical entities. Dewey, by contrast with Hirst, accepted no scheme for the logical differentiation of subjects (Dewey 1902a, 1902b, 1916). Logic, the theory of inquiry, and scientific method enable us to unify and integrate knowledge and experience (Dewey 1920, chapter vi).

Dewey's most celebrated disciple, William Heard Kilpatrick, took up the themes of activity learning (project method) and the unity of inquiry in the curriculum (problem solving, inquiry methods), working out their implications especially for the public elementary school in America in the first half of this century (Kilpatrick 1929, 1951). In Britain, the influence of this way of thinking was felt both through a growing – but always relatively small – interest in Dewey's writings and in the spread of progressive educational ideas as in the writings of Edmund Holmes, A.S. Neill, Nora and Bertrand Russell and others in the progressive camp, and through the perhaps more unexpected source of the two national committees, Hadow and Plowden. Perhaps above all others it was the Plowden Report that gave clearest voice to a belief that not only must the starting point for curriculum analysis be the child in school but the meaning of curriculum will be first sought in the child's experiences in relations with others – children and teachers:

> Underlying all educational questions is the nature of the child himself . . . Part V, 'The Children in the Schools', is the heart of the Report. (Central Advisory Council 1967, introduction)
>
> The school sets out deliberately to devise the right environment for children, to allow them to be themselves and to develop in the way and at the pace appropriate to them . . . It lays special stress on individual discovery, on first hand experience and on opportunities for creative work. It insists that knowledge does not fall into neatly separate compartments and that work and play are not opposite but complementary. (ibid. p. 187)

Curriculum as a learning technology

We have been considering views of the curriculum which are distinguished by a distinctive orientation towards either the activities and experiences of the learner, or the way of life of a society including, and quite conspicuously, the way forms and structures of knowledge have crystallized into particular disciplines.

Curriculum in all of these cases refers to some pattern of areas of human experience, whether it be perceived in a way that is personal and unique to the child or as the accumulation of group experience which is susceptible to some kind of logical or systematic analysis. One of these areas of experience is technology which, while it has its origins among the earliest tool-makers and users, has only become a dominant force in culture on a worldwide basis in the twentieth century. Given the prominence of technology and its close relations with two other great driving forces in the modern world, namely science and industrialization, it should not surprise us that technology has itself become a kind of model for the design of the whole curriculum.

Technology is primarily a way of organizing the environment, either in the form of applying to everyday problems an apparatus of knowledge and skill usually but not necessarily with a science basis, or in the form of managing organizations, institutions and social processes according to certain design principles. It is not an independent process in society but derives its content and mode of operation from culture as a whole, and, in turn, has a pervasive impact. It may be put into the services of large-scale scientific, research and organizational enterprise, or remain a simple set of procedures supporting self-reliant or small-scale activity.

Such a summary statement scarcely does justice to the immense range, power and pervasiveness of modern technological processes. But it does pick out some essential points relevant to an understanding of the curriculum. Our concern here is not with technology *in* the curriculum or a technological perspective *across* the curriculum, desirable as they may be, but with *the curriculum as itself a technology*: a tool for problem solving, a way of structuring learning tasks and of organizing social relations and situations through the systematic application of certain criteria, principles of action and practical techniques. One striking claim of the technological approach, frequently contested, is that a single model can be used across a great diversity of situations and a wide range of subject matters. The notion of the curriculum as itself a technology, to be applied in the quest for a solution to the problems of what is to be taught and learnt, and how, seems somewhat bizarre. Perhaps behind it lies not only an exaggerated rationalism but also an unduly narrow view of types and styles of technology. Nevertheless, we have witnessed over several decades the growth of a view of curriculum planning and design which consists, essentially, of the application to the whole potential field of human learning of a relatively simple, unitary device. The best-known example of curriculum conceived as technology is the Tyler rationale. This is a process model for designing the curriculum, which we have already touched upon, in Chapter 1 (see the section: 'A context for school-based curriculum development'). We need to go into a little more detail.

The Tyler rationale is a curriculum process model; that is it sets forth the steps and stages of a process of curriculum development in such a fashion that the logic of the sequence is clarified, the reasons for each step are given, and the tasks to be undertaken at each step are enumerated. It may be regarded as a rational, technological model for use in designing a curriculum – at any level and for any given area of study. The Tyler rationale has not only been used and applied in its original form; it has had a wide influence. One well-known writer, Hilda Taba, elaborated the model in such a way as to give it a more detailed treatment than Tyler attempted. She elaborated his and Herrick's steps into the following (1962, p. 12):

Step 1 – Diagnosis of needs
Step 2 – Formulation of objectives
Step 3 – Selection of content
Step 4 – Organization of content
Step 5 – Selection of learning experiences
Step 6 – Organization of learning experiences
Step 7 – Determination of what to evaluate and of the ways and means of doing it

We may appreciate better the claim that this amounts to a view of curriculum as a technology, a structure of interrelated tasks, by studying Taba's more detailed model of Steps 2–6 (Table 2.1).

What is usually overlooked in discussions of and commentaries on Tyler's rationale and its various elaborations, such as Taba's, is that the rationale was used initially, as Tyler himself makes quite clear, to help his graduate students at the University of Chicago understand what is meant by 'curriculum'. The model, in a curious sense, *is* the curriculum or, more precisely, a curriculum is a design for learning, a structured pattern of tasks that satisfies the requirements of the rationale. This helps to explain its

Table 2.1 A model for curriculum design

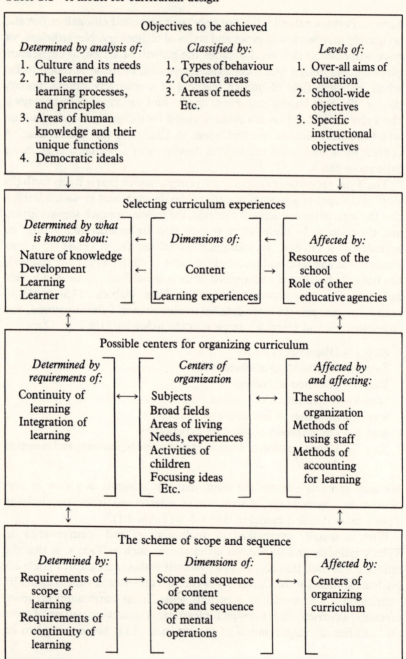

Source: Taba (1962)

great practical appeal. It is interesting, too, that Tyler was the evaluator for one of the most famous of all educational experiments, the Eight Year Study, sponsored by the American Progressive Educational Association in the 1930s (Aiken 1942). This experiment, amongst other things, led to the development of innovative curricula in a group of high schools and traced the careers of students in these innovative programmes including their performance in colleges which gave them entry on the basis of accreditation of the experimental programmes instead of conventional tests and examinations. Thus Tyler had had a close involvement with the progressive movement in which the concept of curriculum as a structure of student experiences had been so prominent. It appears, however, that Tyler had also been associated with another strand of American curriculum thinking out of which what many would regard as an alternative view of the curriculum has emerged, namely the behavioural objectives movement. We discuss this in greater detail in Chapter 8.

What, then, is meant by curriculum as a learning technology and what is the significance of the Tyler rationale? To explore these questions fully would take us far into the recesses of twentieth-century educational theory. This is not necessary, however, since by inspecting the model and relating it to the objectives movement we can see clearly enough the technological links. The model illustrates a design sequence: curriculum is a sequential design for learning; curriculum originates in a statement of learning objectives; it proceeds through tasks and activities which are designed as operations for the realization of those objectives (both observable and ascertainable learning acts and conditions/materials/resources needed for those learning acts to occur); and it culminates in performances or student behaviours which may be assessed against the objectives. The objectives, by being operationalized, specify two kinds of behaviour: first and foremost, student learning behaviours and, second, the action taken by teachers to facilitate those learnings. Tyler was, in the spirit of the progressive movement, concerned about the activities of students: their learning experiences were what the curriculum should be addressed to. Moreover, the objectives at one and the same time include 'both student behaviour and content'. The model is capable of further refinements such as those Tyler himself made (the 'derivation' of objectives from philosophy, psychology etc.) and those he did not (such as the location of the model in particular cultural milieux) but these need not detain us here. The Tyler rationale is thus what he *meant* by curriculum, not only how to *design* a curriculum. As the city is a machine for living, so the curriculum is a machine for learning. Also, we may see it as a solution to a problem:

Question   – How do you define curriculum?
Answer   – By defining your objectives in the recommended
              fashion and proceeding as indicated to the assess-
              ment of student learning.

Although not presented with the flair and elegance of Tyler, the objectives model has been promulgated by numerous curriculum theorists. One of them, W.W. Charters, who preceded Tyler, is of particular interest because he tried – unsuccessfully in the event – to draw up a complete task analysis derived from the enumeration of adult life tasks: these were to form the substance of discrete objectives for general and specialized education. His formidable lists ran into hundreds and then thousands and could never as it were 'catch up' (Charters 1923). There is indeed something farcical about such an attempt quite apart from the educational objections that must be made to the uncritical relationship he drew between school and society. This was based on a notion of the school as a kind of factory, processing children as if they were raw material, which Charters had derived, it seems, from Franklin Bobbitt. The following passage from Bobbitt well illustrates a view of the curriculum which is at the centre of many of our contemporary controversies:

1. As a foundation for all scientific direction and supervision of labor in the field of education, we need first to draw up in detail for each social or vocational class of students in our charge a list of all the abilities and aspects of personality for the training of which the school is responsible.
2. Next we need to determine scales of measurement in terms of which these many different aspects of the personality can be measured.
3. We must determine the amount of training that is socially desirable for each of these different abilities and state these amounts in terms of the scales of measurement.
4. We must have progressive standards of attainment for each stage of advance in the normal development of each ability in question. When these four sets of things are at hand for each differentiated social or vocational class, then we shall have for the first time a scientific curriculum for education worthy of our present age of science.
(Bobbitt 1913, p. 49)

Despite the crudities of this analysis, including its deterministic concept of science and its readiness to submerge the living experience of education beneath a class-based, intricate yet rigid assessment system, Bobbitt was anticipating in these remarks a great deal that is now familiar in practice if not always put so explicitly in policy.

But our purpose here is not to elaborate or evaluate these rather mechanistic approaches to curriculum design. Bobbitt's and Charters's work is of interest in this chapter because, like Tyler, they viewed the curriculum as a technical device, a kind of machine which administrators, teachers and students alike could learn to operate. Questions therefore of content, induction, experience and the others we have touched on in this chapter in reviewing the first three positions were subsidiary: the problem in curriculum was to get the system right and then, having done so, to learn how to operate it.

Educational technology, including programmed learning and the extension of computer-managed instruction, are other examples of this way of thinking. While they are of course important in a wider consideration of the 'what' and 'how' of curriculum it is not necessary to dwell on them in order to bring out a neglected feature of the objectives model. Whatever its uses and limitations may be, it has introduced into curriculum analysis a very challenging set of constructs.

It has sometimes been argued that the deficiencies of the objectives model are such that it must be replaced, for example by a 'process' model which avoids prespecified objectives and adopts an educational approach based on broadly defined areas of knowledge and understanding guided by criteria and 'procedural principles' (Stenhouse 1975). We shall consider this argument in Chapter 8. 'Process' and 'objectives' are not such obvious alternatives. It should be clear from the foregoing that the objectives model is itself a process model and that it draws attention to a most important fact about curriculum: that it is dynamic, a set of relationships. We need, therefore, concepts and definitions – a curriculum language which presents curriculum not as some fixed structure but as transactional, as a flow, a dynamic pattern – in short, as a construct. The term 'curriculum development' seems to suggest the need for all of these things but there are pitfalls: development, as many critics have pointed out, can be reproductive or it can give scope to ideas and forces the very opposite of those advanced as goals and purposes.

Summary

The problems of curriculum development are of different kinds. While some are practical, to do with resources, the interests and capabilities of the education profession, experiences in classrooms, and the multiplicity of interests that need to be satisfied, others arise from diverse and sometimes conflicting conceptions of curriculum itself. In order to address these problems and to respond to new social challenges, educators need a clear understanding of what kind of enterprise curriculum development is and how it is viewed from different educational perspectives. This is not an easy matter, given the variety of usages of the term and the rival schools of educational thought. The meaning of the term curriculum has changed in the twentieth century, in response to enlarged views and expectations of the school and its role in society. Perhaps the most profound challenge to older, fixed and narrow definitions, such as 'a course' or 'a syllabus of study', has come from progressive education with its elevation of the principles of children's interests, activities and experiences as central in any education-ally worthwhile curriculum. Other challenges result from social changes, including the impact of science, technology and industrialization. 'Curriculum' has become a dynamic concept, referring to actions embodied in plans, programmes, designs, processes. It is unsatisfactory to treat it as a fixed 'thing' to be transmitted.

Curriculum design is a way of organizing knowledge and experience for teaching and learning. Some theorists represent this pattern of knowledge and experience as discrete forms of knowledge, each with its own structure; others see it as a more loosely interrelated set of cultural systems, or areas of experience. These elements, often represented in ways quite external to children and youth, need to be treated as a resource: the curriculum is experiential and should be designed around the closely observed personal experience of learners.

With the emergence of an objectives model, what has come to the fore is a concept of curriculum as a kind of technology – a pattern or design comprising clearly specified tasks for teachers and students. The development of the curriculum thus becomes a matter of using this design or pattern according to a mixture of criteria in which educational values may or may not be conspicuous. The potential value of this systematic approach to curriculum development is obscured partly by its origins in crude behavioural manipulation. There is need for it to be reconstituted and more closely related to what are often seen as alternative views of the curriculum and processes of curriculum design and development.

CHAPTER 3

DEVELOPMENT AND CHANGE
IN THE CURRICULUM

'The element of complacency which is never far beneath the surface of English education deserved to be shaken by the profusion and variety of American experiment.' (Stuart Maclure, *Curriculum Innovation in Practice*)

Development is a species of change implying purpose, structure and goals or end-states. It may be thought of as a process of planning and organizing change on a rational basis whereby ends are determined and means defined and mobilized to meet them. As we shall see, the matter is not quite as simple as this in the curriculum. Other kinds of change may be just as important and have a greater effect on what happens in practice than any planned intervention. The sequence – of an existing structure which is ascertained, processes of planned change or guided evolution and anticipated outcomes – is subject to chance, accident, the impact of environmental forces – and mismanagement. Thus, changes in the size and composition of school populations, technological innovations in communications, the advent of war, revolution or economic depression, and movements of resources and personnel may all have profound effects on curriculum. These can counteract intended changes, and pose new problems for curriculum developers to address. Several decades of 'curriculum development' have taught us to be more cautious in approach, more flexible in planning, and more ready to accept less than optimum results.

As for 'development', it would be misleading to imply that the term refers to a single, unitary set of activities, conveniently foreshortened by the conjunction of 'curriculum' and 'development'. Such a conjunction is useful, but we must be careful that the shorthand does not distort our awareness of the numerous tasks and activities of quite a diverse kind involving different agencies and personnel by no means all of them pursuing educational ends. 'Development' has a wide range of connotations both within and outside education and we need to be alert to these in order to get clear about curriculum development as the kind of change process in which we have a particular interest. Let us consider a couple of examples, from psychology and social change theory.

The nature of development: psychological, social and moral issues

In developmental psychology, processes of development include both genetic and historical or environmental factors and they are susceptible to analysis into sequences, phases and patterns which can be, to a degree, predicted as well as described. Piaget's 'genetic epistemology' and Kohlberg's derived analysis of stages of moral development are good examples of psychological theories of cognitive and moral development where noticeable and regular structures, in what is said to be an invariant sequence, provide a key to understanding growth in individuals and groups. In an educational setting theories of this kind need to be extended and elaborated through the consideration of a planned sequence of environmental changes (such as the introduction at a particular point in time of concrete apparatus in teaching mathematics or the teaching of values like 'justice') which are required in order to reinforce or stimulate the emerging intellectual, moral and other structures in the personality. Straightaway 'development' becomes more complex: the patterns are not a consequence of some inevitable unfolding but of interaction with a carefully organized and managed environment which draws upon our knowledge of areas of experience, forms of knowledge and human development: hence Piaget's interest in the processes whereby children assimilate and cognitively reconstitute parts of their environment (Ginsburg and Opper 1979). However, as Peters points out in an essay on human development in education, these stage models of development are normative not merely descriptive, requiring us to posit and to justify values, standards or criteria (Peters 1972b).

Development takes in more than mere interactions between individuals (whether they be persons, like students, or institutions, like schools) and environments. In human and social terms, development implies structures and purposes which have a profound relationship with culture, requiring us to specify types, forms and qualities. One of the topics of dispute among eighteenth and early nineteenth-century students of human behaviour was the extent to which fundamental processes of human growth, for example language development in children, are dependent on a certain *quality* of environment. Genuine or fabricated evidence, including the 'discovery' of children raised by wolves and other wild animals, or deserted in woods (for example, Jean Itard's 'Le Sauvage de L'Avreyon') was invoked in support or rejection of one or other hypothesis about the learning of language, morals and social behaviour. To be developed meant to have attained something of value, to be civilized or made 'human'. From these studies and debates there emerged the late nineteenth and twentieth-century empirical interest in the relative weight to be accorded genetic and environmental factors in various aspects of growth, notably intelligence, and more recently the theories of Piaget and his followers.

The issue of development thus is not reducible to gross concepts of environment and heredity and the respective weight to be given to them. Theories of development do not take us very far unless they address qualities sought or achieved and criteria for judging performances. It used to be fashionable to talk about these as attributes of civilization. Was the wolf-child capable of being civilized or was he dehumanized; could he become truly human; are certain conditions of growth necessary for civilized behaviour? Development, by being linked thus to 'civilized' was shown very clearly to have a reference to standards or norms in the arena of personal and group psychology. Do we not talk about the standards – or expectations – of civilized life? Development then, as a normative concept, is to be thought of as betterment, improvement – a change for the better or towards some goal or ideal. Historically, development has been associated with the idea of perfectibility in the sense of having or setting ideals and is hence tied in with the notion of moral progress (Passmore 1970). This makes it necessary for us to build in a purposive dimension to our discussions of development, in the form of both criteria or conditions to be satisfied in the process itself and an end or ends towards which the process is directed.

In considering development in relation to persons, we are thus referring to a quite complex process, which involves an interplay of hereditary and environmental factors and the invoking of criteria, norms, standards and goals or values. 'Development', I have indicated, suggests 'progress', 'improvement', the striving for or achieving of something worth while, as in the development of one's musical talent, or one's relationship with other people. Sometimes, of course, as in the activities of 'property developers' or 'first world development policies towards third world countries', the word is used pejoratively but always, then, with the idea in mind of something attainable or desirable not being carried out in an approved fashion. We can have too much, or the wrong kinds of, development; what is done under its name fails to satisfy certain standards. It has sometimes been a criticism of school-based curriculum development that, as a way of improving the curriculum generally, it is faulty or inadequate: a case, if the criticisms were valid, of a particular procedure falling short of a larger view of development.

There is another perspective on development which is relevant to our understanding of the concept of development in the curriculum. This is the Marxist theory which treats social change as a process of development over which individuals and even whole societies have only a limited kind of control. This is that part of Marxism which treats history as a conflict of forces or a dynamic field. Large historical events occur, as a result of which, over a very long timespan, certain kinds of social order emerge. There is, it is said, a pattern to all this, a necessary sequence. The theory suggests an inevitable progression: the liberation of humanity through an irreversible, sequential process in which capitalism and the dictatorship of the proletariat are but phases, although progressively more 'advanced' phases. There is considerable emphasis on conflict in the social dynamics, leading ultimately to some universally desirable state of human affairs. This theory of development plays down human intervention except in so far as people can discover the forces of history and get behind them. ('Development' has its own logic which it is incumbent upon us to understand if these minor interventions available to us are to be successful, i.e. effective in 'moving things along'.)

In a famous passage, Marx summarized the economic and social determinism of his theory of development: 'The mode of production in material life determines the general character of the social, political and spiritual processes of life. It is not the consciousness of men that determines their existence, but, on the contrary, their social existence determines their consciousness' (Marx 1904, preface). His collaborator, Engels, in discussing another great developmental theorist of the nineteenth century, Hegel, relates these processes to an inevitable succession of events in history: 'in the course of development all that was precisely real becomes unreal, loses its necessity, its right of existence, its rationality and in the place of moribund mentality comes a new, viable reality – peacefully if the old has enough intelligence to go to its death without a struggle, forcibly if it resists this necessity' (Engels 1969, p. 238).

Materialism and determinism are not the only features of these statements: what they point towards is the need to understand social dynamics. Successive revisions of Marxism, including the discovery of a 'young Marx' whose ideas were much less deterministic, have yielded a scenario for social change wherein actors have important roles. We can and ought to plan for change, and aim to take charge of social forces; development is not necessarily linear, nor is there only one criterion, the economic: development can become a matter of practical intelligence applied to social issues and problems, and even the larger sweeps of historical change are susceptible to human intervention and modification. This is part of a general repudiation of deterministic and fatalistic theories of change, or of resistance to change (Schaff 1970). In educational theory, for example, the until recently popular left sociological view that the principal function of schooling in a capitalist society is to reproduce preexisting 'relations of production' – loosely speaking the prevailing socio-economic order – is giving way or has been substantially modified. In place of the blind forces of reproduction we have the possibility of education as itself a potential force for change in society and culture.

Whatever may be revealed by sociological research and analysis about the functions and effects of particular schooling practices, it has never been popular among curriculum theorists, policy makers and researchers to treat the curriculum as simply reflexive of the existing social order. The curriculum has frequently been singled out as an object of policy, or instrument or means whereby desirable changes in education could be made and wider social reform thereby fostered. In the aftermath of the Bolshevik Revolution of 1917, following decolonization in the 1950s and 60s, and in many other historical and contemporary settings, planned curriculum change has been proposed as a method of advancing new social and cultural goals and establishing new kinds of social order (Connell 1980).

This aspect of curriculum change is neatly symbolized by one of UNESCO's programmes where, in Asia and Oceania, under the auspices of the Bangkok-based Asian Centre of Educational Innovation for Development, a major innovation goes under the name of 'curriculum *for* development'. Here, curriculum development is explicitly related to nation-building programmes as is shown in the following extract from a regional consultation meeting: 'the new concept of development, as is reflected in national development policies of many countries in the region, needs to be carefully studied for its implications for educational development in particular. The new concept of development lays special emphasis on enhancing the quality of life of the general mass of the people, and on meeting their basic and fundamental needs relating to health, education, social living, environment, earning a living and cultural expression, without which national development cannot be promoted on a self-generating basis' (UNESCO 1978, p. 55).

How do these assorted proposals, theories and beliefs about development help us to understand the process of curriculum development? Several general points arise, which we may treat as general propositions helpful in understanding and initiating development programmes. First, development is dynamic and active, a process of actualization with an inbuilt pattern or order. Second, development contains an element of deliberation, planning, forecasting, rational calculation – but it is a process which involves forces and factors over which there may be little scope for control. Third, development is a qualitative concept: not merely does it describe something, it calls into play criteria, standards, values. Concepts of the good and of the ordering of human life and social affairs in a quest for the good may not be articulated, but they are inferred by development plans and programmes. Fourth, development is relational, in that it presupposes or aims to set up and use linkages across systems, usually in the form of an arrangement or intervention to achieve desirable ends. Fifth, development has concrete social and individual aspects; it infers, or applies to, particular social and historical settings – it is not reducible to an abstract system. Sixth, development calls into play and involves the manipulation of materials and resources. Seventh, development is a form of growth and in some measure is irreversible: it is ongoing if not always continuous and it always has a reference to some future as well as a past state of affairs. A development process has a life of its own and cannot be manipulated or controlled regardless of its own character. Development does not equate with power.

In the course of our discussion of curriculum development, we shall illustrate and seek to justify these general propositions about development. Their purpose is to suggest a way of thinking about change and also to show that in considering processes of curriculum development we are not merely applying techniques. Psychological, sociological and philosophical accounts are useful as ways of sensitizing us to dimensions of developmental processes. We must be alert, however, to two extreme positions which characterize certain development theories. One is an outgrowth of the inevitability view: change in education is directional, the tendency of change is to serve existing interests; change is essentially manipulative and reproductive; development is an organic process over which individuals and groups can have little or no real influence; development of the curriculum is a government 'plot' to dominate and control. The other view is a derivative of the unfolding or sequential theory of development: that development is an irreversible progression comprising a fixed sequence of clearly identifiable stages, each of which needs to be passed through. This is the fallacy of using insights and approximations derived from limited empirical investigations, as if they predicted and prescribed universal patterns and desirable norms of behaviour. In pedagogy the mistake was evident in the early treatment of Piaget's developmental stages as firmly age-fixed and as an invariant sequence. In educational planning (including curriculum planning) a similar fallacy was evident in the notion of a fixed set of stages which an educational system or subsystem might seek to bypass or fore-shorten at its peril. Planning, it was said, needs to designate actions appropriate to each of these stages, in a correct sequence. This position was argued in a book that influenced development agencies in the 1960s and 70s: Cyril Beeby's *The Quality of Education in Developing Countries* (1966). Beeby claimed that there were stages in the evolution of teachers' and administrators' capabilities and understanding and that the latest (and most 'perfect') in the series, that of the autonomous, mature professional, has been reached by few if any societies. Again, the notion of an invariant sequence is advanced as if it were a law of culture whose character can be determined once for all, and from a particular standpoint. We have here a reversion to the 'natural order' point of view. Its value lies not in its rather tidy-minded sequencing of stages with an assumption of a natural pro-gression but in its reminder that there are wider social, cultural, economic and political forces and factors at work in curriculum change which must be understood – and skills which must be mastered – if development is to be successfully undertaken.

Thus far in this chapter we have seen how development is perceived in some psychological and political theories. The interweaving of factors and conditions in the environment, in personality and in 'history' with the deliberations, intentions and plans of individuals and groups should pre-pare us for the uncertainty of outcomes of particular forms and types of development. Prediction and control, if sometimes of a quite limited kind, are possible, but they depend on analysis of the processes of development and attempts to understand the conditions affecting development in par-ticular situations and circumstances. We have already, in Chapter 2, referred to the efforts made by educators to construct and apply designs for the purpose of developing the curriculum. Our discussion of wider views and theories of development should help to explain why these efforts so often meet with difficulty. Curriculum development is itself a complex social process whose operation calls into play other social factors which may help or hinder the changes being sought. Moreover, our understanding of the processes of curriculum development is still quite limited. We must therefore treat claims to have found the 'right' or 'best' way to effect curriculum development with scepticism. Curriculum development is still at the experimental stage where hypotheses and testable programmes for action are preferable to blueprints and prescriptive models. There is no 'right' way though there are criteria and guideposts.

Sources of curriculum change

Turning now to the more general educational question of how and why the curriculum changes, and recalling that development, conceived as a process of deliberate, planned intervention, (a) is only one kind of change, (b) will be affected by other factors in the environment, (c) is normative or value-oriented, and (d) is not inevitable but requires purposive action, how can we attempt to understand such a large and amorphous topic as curriculum change? Any attempt to reach understanding requires us to simplify, and is bound to result in omissions and distortions. But the situation here is no different from any other area of social life where we attempt to understand what is happening by categorizing a multiplicity of individual incidents and generalizing about them. The remedy lies not in avoiding or denouncing all this, as do those theorists for whom power dominance pervades all relations and all knowledge (Foucault 1970, 1977), but in treating the categories and generalizations hypothetically and heuristically: how much do they encompass and explain and what can we do with them? The evidence for what follows is scattered widely in modern educational and social science literature, some of it indicated, to which reference needs to be made for further detail.

Let us first of all divide the *sources* of changes in the school curriculum into four groups:

1. Changes in society at large (and let us not overlook the fact that the education system itself and the curriculum subsystem are integral to 'society at large') which impinge upon or implicitly challenge existing curriculum practices and policies. These are indirect in their effect and curriculum decisions are often made in ignorance of them. Nevertheless,

they can be crucial, for example declining birth rate, economic crisis.

2. Responses to changes in society which explicitly and deliberately enlist curriculum policy and practice as a means of achieving stated goals and ends. These include, for example, attempts to encourage schools to show greater awareness of industry, or of problems of peace and war.
3. Changes within education which impinge upon or implicitly challenge existing curriculum practices and policies. The reorganization of secondary education or multicultural or equal opportunity education policies are examples.
4. Changes made or sought in curriculum policy and practice to promote certain ends or achieve particular goals in the education system.

In using this classification of change we must exercise care. We have noted already that educational changes are themselves a form of social change. No hard and fast distinction can be made between changes originating within education and those in other sectors of society. Nor is it always possible to be clear whether particular curriculum changes result from ends sought for the curriculum or from moves elsewhere in the education system. Finally, policy–practice distinctions are not clear-cut since one person's policy is another's practice and we find examples of policy and practice at all levels in the educational system, from the individual classroom to the office of the Secretary of State for Education and Science.

These difficulties are not crucial here, however, for our interest in curriculum change is not in how to schematise it but in getting an understanding of the kinds of changes that are occurring and might occur in so far as they seem to have relevance for school-based decision making. The four types of changes outlined above can be further divided into changes in policy and changes in practice. This distinction becomes of greater significance where an educational system is so structured that specific educational changes are sought in response to social policy planning.

Although curriculum change can be effected by change in any of the four cells in Table 3.1, it is only in one (cell 4) that there might be what we can call a self-initiated, a self-determining curriculum change. Even here, however, given that the school is but one of several agencies with a direct role in and responsibility for curriculum change, the scope for specifically school-initiated change is relatively limited. This does not make it unimportant. On the contrary, the better that schools understand and work out their relationships with the wider environment, the more likely are they to be able to organize and manage curriculum development as a successful change strategy. For example, social change may bring scope and opportunity

Table 3.1

1	changes in society (indirect effects)		3	changes in education (indirect effects)	
	Policy	Practice		Policy	Practice
2	changes in society (direct effects)		4	changes in education (direct effects)	
	Policy	Practice		Policy	Practice

for schools, access to resources, new freedoms as much as unwelcome constraints. Again, individual schools can learn from the experiments and projects of other schools, or benefit from an interpretation of local or central policy changes. Other changes may test the school's capacity to adapt and modify its curriculum; for example, in response to urban renewal programmes, population shifts, or changing patterns of employment. These illustrate the need for creativity and energy in the school staff so that they are ready to take up opportunity, and for improvements in schools and education systems in their knowledge of social change.

This becomes clearer if we make a further breakdown of the fourth cell (change in education: direct effects). In contemporary Britain, within the education system there are several major forces and factors for curriculum change of which the school itself is but one (Table 3.2). In order for the school to undertake development work in the curriculum it must establish a web of relations and learn to use the educational environment as a whole, as a resource.

Tables 3.1 and 3.2 may seem to indicate that in respect of curriculum change schools may have, at least potentially, a very large and varied *responsive* role but a very small role in *initiating* ideas and undertaking new developments. Many have reached this conclusion and it may be that it is a fitting one given the power of many of the forces and groups identified in the tables to impinge upon schools regardless of their needs and wishes. Yet it would be quite wrong for us to conclude that curriculum development at the school level must of necessity be largely responsive or reflexive. Planned curriculum development by schools requires that they address their wider environments, responsively, where that is appropriate, and constructively and creatively design programmes to meet the needs they define. In this, they ought to have access to and be using the best possible information

Table 3.2 Changes in education (direct effects)

Agencies with a major role in promoting curriculum change

- Individual schools and groups of schools
- Educational research and development institutions and programmes
- Examination boards
- Committees of inquiry
- Inspectors, advisers
- Secretary of State for Education and Science/DES/advisers and other government departments and agencies (e.g. Manpower Services Commission)
- Local education authorities; Education committees
- Education publishers, broadcasters etc.
- Teacher educators (pre-service and in-service)
- Professional associations

about changes elsewhere in the education system and society at large. However, schools are often poorly organized and resourced to undertake this kind of social scanning. School-based curriculum development requires more than amateurism and enthusiasm.

We have yet to consider either the kinds of changes in the curriculum that have occurred, or the opportunities available to schools, provided they know their way around the curriculum world, to do serious curriculum work. In the remainder of this chapter we will look a little more closely at the first of these – some of the changes in society at large, in education generally and in the curriculum. We shall come to the second point, the opportunities available to schools, in later chapters.

Social change and the curriculum

Throughout the world, in practically all societies, rapid change is occurring in roles and relationships, economic conditions, mores and values, religious and political beliefs, relations between nations, ways of everyday life and so on. These and other changes in society at large implicitly and explicitly challenge us to rethink the curriculum. They often result not in a searching, reflective analysis but in superficial reflexive changes, adaptations and adjustments on a greater or lesser scale. The rate of change, its scope, and the attendant transformations in culture profoundly challenge the conservatism of schooling. Yet schools must attempt to come to terms with change which is often ill-understood. Curriculum development provides a focus for these attempts.

Among the most salient of contemporary changes are an avowedly ideological shift from monocultural to multicultural perspectives and the phenomenum of massive youth unemployment, and we shall discuss these as examples of significant social changes with implications for the school curriculum as a whole. Other changes in Britain of a comparable kind are the applications of new technologies in the manufacturing and service sectors of the economy, the changing roles of women, the emergence of leisure industries, mass tourism, rapid changes in communications or the changing pattern of the country's international status and relations. Social change is pervasive and continuous, a defining characteristic of modern culture, even in what are often thought of as the more stable and traditional societies. Multiculturalism and youth unemployment are a useful choice for us, because they have had a visible impact on British education and they are particular instances in this country of the interactions of several basic social forces and relations in the contemporary world. They illustrate four of the fundamental aspects of social change:

1. ideological, normative (changing values, belief systems)
2. institutional, organizational (changing social structures and institutions and their relations)
3. personal and interpersonal behaviour (changing patterns of behaviour in small and large groups)
4. interacting, dynamic forces (processes of interaction among different aspects or forces of society)

In the course of only two decades, there has been official acceptance of cultural pluralism in Britain which incorporates legislation, the establishment of a regulatory or monitoring agency, programmes of positive discrimination, and vigorous campaigns locally as well as nationally to change widespread attitudes and practices. Similar, and sometimes more far-reaching, changes can be found in other societies. Perhaps the best examples come from the USA, where the issue is focused by long-standing inequalities between black and white communities, Israel, where a new nation has had to be forged out of very different groups and nationalities, and Australia, where immigration has been for almost two centuries a major element in national development. In each of these instances, there have been striking contrasts between proclaimed, official policies, widespread community attitudes, and the values and aspirations of different interest groups expressed in conflicting ideologies (Australian Ethnic Affairs Council 1977; Banks 1981, 1984; Craft 1982; Smolicz 1979; Stent et al.

1973). As Alma Craft points out in the *Readings* volume, pluralism in the field of multiculturalism is both descriptive and normative: the society is culturally diverse (descriptive); the goals of tolerance, mutual acceptance, respect for diversity, and diversity in unity have been proclaimed and officially – although not generally in society – adopted (normative).

It is a feature of pluralist societies that there is tension and at times open conflict among ideologies. In respect of multiculturalism defined as ethnic multiculturalism, or relations among distinct ethnic and linguistic groups, alternative or critical ideologies exist, to challenge such norms as appreciation of diversity, or the fostering of ethnic traditions and languages, and to try to promote another kind of change in society by making it less diverse, for example by population shifts (resettlement of black groups) or assimilation policies. Schools are caught in this conflict. On the one hand, they give allegiance to normative multiculturalism as a policy goal – sometimes, in fact, they are required to do so by local education authorities (ILEA 1983). On the other hand, in some schools – and perhaps they are a majority – significant numbers of students and teachers do not subscribe to the normative multicultural philosophy and in many parts of the country they have no direct experience of ethnic and linguistic diversity. Here is a case of changes in the wider society which involve the school but where there is no general agreement, official policies notwithstanding, about appropriate curriculum responses. One solution, that of Local Education Authority Guidelines, does provide a pointer to schools, but not a sufficient one for purposes of curriculum review, evaluation and development. The gap between the school and the wider societal arena where these ideological debates and movements are occurring is probably too wide for the typical school to be able to bridge it by taking heed of the admonition to 'make your curriculum more multicultural'. For this reason, national, regional and local curriculum programmes and projects are needed: at an intermediate level detailed work needs to be done on the kinds of responses schools can and might make to a profound shift in a sensitive area of social life. Schools will need to identify and ally themselves with other social groups and forces if the normative goal of multiculturalism is to be achieved, and, within the school, only whole-curriculum policies would suffice given the complexity and obduracy of the issue at stake.

Our second example comes from the economic sector: long-term economic decline and youth unemployment. It raises problems of a similar nature to multiculturalism but here there is already evidence of substantial – if controversial – activity at the intermediate levels and confusion in schools as to what would or could be an appropriate curriculum response. As with multiculturalism, there is already a substantial literature which it would be impossible to review here. One of the consequences of government intervention through education, training and subsidized employment for adolescents and young adults is the funding of information services on the rapidly changing policy environment and of the numerous projects and studies under way. One of the most useful is the Australian National Clearinghouse on Transition from School, where Abstracts and Newsletters provide an excellent résumé of trends and ideas not only in Australia, but, selectively, in other countries (Australian National University 1981 onwards).

It is not our purpose to try to examine and assess trends in employment and changes in government policy but to suggest that important social changes are occurring which are very directly impinging on education and fostering or even forcing quite substantial curriculum changes. Long-term economic decline in Britain combined with government policies to reduce the scale and proportion of public sector spending constitute one kind of challenge to education: gaining resources for the maintenance of the existing structures in secondary, further and higher education, and for personnel and programmes including the existing curriculum provision. It is argued that these cannot be sustained, due to falling school populations as well as cost cutting. The need for greater efficiency is also argued. Altogether, education is under great pressure to restructure.

The provision of school curricula is a cost, and like all costs, it is one that can be, in principle, reduced. The claim on resources that curriculum development makes must be supported by strong arguments if it is not to be ignored. Developments of the curriculum can be more easily discarded on the one hand, or avoided on the other, than changes in school organization. Thus the move from the 1950s onwards to broaden and enrich the curriculum could be reversed and probably would be if it became necessary severely to curtail the purchase of books and materials, provision of specialist staff, maintenance of teachers' centres and advisory services and the conduct of curriculum-supportive educational research and development. In fact, in Britain in the early 1980s it appears that such a curtailing is occurring. A concomitant, if not a direct outcome of economic difficulty, is the threat now posed to broad-based curriculum development in schools. In the maintained sector of education, there is relatively little scope for individual or even combined school initiatives to resist the effects of reduced public funding, except in relation to vocational training. Whatever small-scale enterprise might be shown there is very little room for manoeuvre over such costly items as salaries and plant. Curriculum development in such circumstances is likely to be largely reflexive and defensive in character unless very determined efforts are made, within existing resources, to rethink and replan curricula according to well reasoned educational principles. Fortunately, many schools are prepared to do just this. They will need to if we are ever to achieve a comprehensive system of general education for all.

The issue of youth unemployment is separate from economic decline; on the other hand, a return to high levels of youth (i.e. 16–19) employment, if it is possible at all, seems dependent on substantial economic growth and that raises questions of political ideology, and international relations as well as economic and fiscal policy. Our concern here is with the manner in which government response to the fact of youth unemployment and to trends and forecasts has brought about a realignment of school curricula. Two or three illustrations will suffice. First, there has been a quickening of criticism of the supposed or real inadequacies of schooling: school curricula and teaching procedures are criticized for not producing skilled, articulate, adaptive and 'industry-minded' young workers. The employability of school leavers, especially low attainers, in commerce and industry has been questioned. This puts schools on the defensive, and occasions doubt and anxiety about established curriculum practice. Second, specific, heavily funded interventionist programmes have been introduced, with a strong bias towards training and vocational preparation. These now exist in schools as well as further education colleges and at selected industrial and commercial sites. This is an example of the introduction of new curricula, largely bypassing the conventional education channels, and structured very precisely according to a socio-economic analysis of manpower training requirements (Holt 1983a). Schools are poorly placed to challenge these programmes even where their educational (and social) value may be questionable.

Third, despite the specific nature of the criticism of schooling noted above and the vocational and training initiatives, changes made or contemplated in school curricula may not be very far-reaching and they are unlikely to address the deeper structural problems of the economy. The cause of this is not far to seek: the focus of effort is the middle and upper secondary school and further education curricula. By this stage, action is of necessity largely remedial. If there are problems in basic skills and attitudes, there will need to be a reassessment of curriculum for the first years of schooling and it would be more reasonable, if politically unacceptable, to devote the bulk of resources and energies to a restructuring of curriculum for early childhood education and onwards. It is also obvious that if school curriculum reforms do have a part to play in arresting or reversing long-term economic trends, and that is a question which has never been seriously addressed, changes could not be confined to the vocational aspects of curriculum or to particular groups of students, namely low achievers. Here is an example, then, of a very prominent and widely publicized economic and social problem to which school curriculum changes of a fairly limited and – in relation to the depth of the problem – superficial kind are being directed. Political programmes and unfriendly ideological assessments of general education in schools are being made as a substitute for a more searching analysis of the curriculum and of the social role of the school.

Thus far we have briefly reviewed two large and controversial areas of social and economic change with indirect as well as direct implications for the school curriculum. The curriculum policy adaptations that have been made, although vigorously presented and supported with special funding, have addressed only parts of the problem, in general the most obvious, widely publicized and politically significant. Much more profound changes are needed in school curricula – and in government policies – to meet the challenge. The two areas of change fall within what John Dewey, in his major study of educational theory, *Democracy and Education*, defined as the two most decisive forces for change in the modern world: science and technology, and democracy.

Multicultural education is not only a response to changing social realities, it is also a declaration of the need to act upon the democratic goals of equality, shared experience and social solidarity and of the rights of individuals and groups including the perceptions, values and interests of previously submerged subcultures. Large-scale education and training programmes in response to youth unemployment are a consequence of a number of changes in modern society and one of these is the impact of technological change on the world of work: the application of science to society has had many consequences, one of them being significant technological and structural unemployment. Of course, it has had other consequences too, of a more positive kind and of equal significance for education, and calling for other curriculum changes. The point is that issues and trends such as multiculturalism, far-reaching changes in economic trends and policies, and youth unemployment are not resolvable in curriculum terms by guidelines, expenditure reviews, 'increased efficiency' and vocational training programmes. Granted the need to work directly on these as they manifest themselves in specific problems and demands, we must also look for their wider implications, seeing them in the context of fundamental changes in society which affect or challenge the curriculum in numerous and varied ways.

When it is suggested by governments that the curriculum ought to be 'more relevant' or 'better related to the needs of industrial society', or when special interest groups agitate for the school to respond to their preferences and needs, the problem arises of how the school is to survey the wider social landscape, identify the fundamental forces at work in society and assess the numerous claims made for this or that change. The movement towards core curriculum, which we examine in Chapters 6 and 7, is one attempt to answer these questions. As Richard Slaughter argues in the *Readings*, a future orientation, in which we deliberately seek out and use ways of scanning society, is needed if we are indeed to take seriously the question of how to relate the curriculum to social change.

We have considered two changes belonging in the first two cells of Table 3.1: changes in the wider society which for one reason or another impinge on the curriculum, both directly and indirectly. We turn now to cells 3 and 4 in Table 3.1 and to Table 3.2: changes in the education system which do or might affect the curriculum, and policies, agencies and programmes specifically set up to engender and foster curriculum change.

Education system changes and the curriculum

As an example of changes in the educational system which, on the face of it, would seem to have far-reaching consequences for the curriculum, let us take, first, the abolition of the 11+ examination at the end of primary school and, second, the conversion of selective secondary education into a more or less comprehensive system.

The effects of the abolition of the 11+ have not been fully charted and it is not possible to say with any certainty just what its specific curriculum consequences have been. What is now clear, however, is that the widespread adoption of more open, freer, child-centred, exploratory and innovatory curriculum approaches hoped for by many advocates of abolition has not occurred (DES 1978b; Galton et al. 1980; Galton and Willcocks 1983). The criticism that the examination restricted the curriculum at least in the upper years of primary schooling may have been valid, as the criticism of the inadequacy of the examination for the purpose of selection related to long-term progress in school certainly was. It would not follow, though, that the removal of constraint and the provision of opportunity for new curriculum initiatives would result in schools actually doing what it was now open to them to do. Curriculum change entails more than response to opportunity: what is necessary is not merely this negative freedom. New goals need to be set, new programmes thought out and implemented and new resources and materials brought in; teachers need support, encouragement, guidance and new skills. Curriculum change is neither merely reflexive – an automatic response to some shift or demand for change in the wider society – nor is it spontaneous in situations where constraints have been lifted. One of the difficulties for primary schools, following the abolition of the 11+, is that a clear and definite goal and accompanying structure were removed without anything definite being put in their place. The philosophy of the Plowden Report might have seemed the basis for a new orientation, except that it was very quickly subjected to criticisms and its educational aspirations became absorbed into the arguments of the 1970s over standards of performance and the clamour against progressive education. Despite the publication in the late 1970s of Her Majesty's Inspectorate's review of primary education and, more recently, of the Schools Council's *Primary Practice*, there is still, in Britain, no clear set of national guidelines for the primary school curriculum and there remains a lingering resistance to such an approach, on the grounds that it would impede the development of individualized curriculum at the school level (DES 1978b; Schools Council 1983b).

In the case of the national policy shift from selective to comprehensive secondary schools, what is most striking in terms of curriculum is the absence of any planned programme or policy for comprehensive curriculum. The change here was organizational, first at the macro-level of the conversion of existing schools and the establishment of new ones and, second, at the micro-level of restructuring within schools. Hence new roles were created; there were new staff groupings and new processes of decision making. From these, it was perhaps assumed new types of curriculum would emerge. But, as Alan Hodge and others show in the *Readings*, things can easily go wrong. Commitment, skills, resources may all be lacking. Unless there is a national move towards a policy for a comprehensive curriculum and, locally as well as nationally, examples are given and ways shown of constructing such curricula, it cannot be expected that schools will consistently move towards a comprehensive curriculum (however that may be defined). Her Majesty's Inspectorate observed that the structural and organizational shift to comprehensive schools in Britain had not been accompanied by the design and implementation, nationally, of comprehensive curricula. Instead, they said, all too often the old curricula for selective schools were somewhat modified and inserted into the new institutions (DES 1979b).

What neither HMI, nor central government, nor indeed local authorities as a whole, have done, however, is to produce policies and guidelines for the comprehensive school curriculum. It is thus quite unclear what a comprehensive school curriculum is, in policy terms, as distinct from what comprehensive schools actually provide through their individual curricula. Here, as with the abolition of the 11+, is a case of a national policy left incomplete because only structural and organizational aspects of schooling, and not curricular ones, were addressed. This does not confer freedom on schools but confusion and uncertainty which inhibit whole-curriculum planning and development, fostering sectionalism and parochialism.

In the removal of the 11+ examination and the introduction of the comprehensive schools, both important national policy changes in the structure of schooling, we have good illustrations of one of the central difficulties in the curriculum field in Britain and perhaps other countries as well. This is the uncertainty and inconclusiveness of relationships between curriculum decision making and shifts in broad educational policy, administrative and organizational arrangements. In Britain, this has been justified as a fundamental freedom for schools or as professional autonomy (Morrell 1963; Skilbeck 1984b). However, teacher autonomy and school freedom need not be abrogated – and may in fact be enhanced – by the establishment of coherent national curriculum policies. Is it not desirable that curriculum change be systematically related to broad policy and structural changes – which themselves incorporate considered responses to the kinds of social and educational changes we have been discussing in this chapter? In Britain, such policies were at least implied in the Reports of the Central Advisory Council until the distinguished line came to an end by central government decree, with the Plowden Report. Despite recent efforts by the DES to affirm policies, which we discuss in subsequent chapters, there remains something of a vacuum and this is a source of difficulty for school curriculum development.

Can or should we really treat the curriculum as if it were a largely independent, school-determined domain? The desirability question will be argued at length. The question of the school's independence in the curriculum in practice is, however, a spurious one. The neglect of thorough-going policy analysis of the curriculum implications of the abolition of the 11+ and the introduction of comprehensive schooling was just a failure of national policy and not an acknowledgement that it is to the school that we must turn for creative and constructive curriculum thinking. It was precisely during the 1960s and 70s, when these structural changes in the educational system were occurring, that we witnessed an array of new agencies, programmes and initiatives for the curriculum, almost all of them outside the school itself and many at a considerable remove from the school. It was also during this period that the authority of the school in curriculum matters came under challenge, notably from critics of what were thought to be widespread innovations in pedagogy (Black Papers 1969–1977).

Agencies for curriculum change

In our discussion of how and why the curriculum changes we must now bring into consideration those agencies which aim to foster and promote curriculum change by working directly in and on the educational system. In Table 3.2 some of the most prominent of those agencies are identified. How do they effect or try to effect curriculum change and what do we know about the results of their activities in the practice and processes of schooling? Taking the last question first, the answer is, surprisingly little. There have been research studies on curriculum change at the school and classroom level, relating changes to the intervention of outside agencies. This research has shown how the outside agencies formulate plans, construct and implement programmes and attempt to disseminate them. What it has been more difficult to establish is the actual effect on teaching practice and especially student learning. The reasons for this lie partly in the relatively small amount of research on implementation of change in the curriculum – more of a problem in Britain than the United States, though, where there have been large-scale studies of this type (Fullan 1983; OECD/CERI 1982).

A more decisive consideration is the difficulty of showing just how particular changes in teaching and learning, and in school policies for the curriculum, embody and reflect outside interventions. As a former director of studies at the Schools Council, Jack Wrigley, said of the Council's own research and development projects the principle of operation had to be 'an act of faith plus trial and error' (Wrigley 1970, p. 22).

Wrigley had in mind the way the Council's projects used research; we can take his comment to include the procedures for extending curriculum innovation into schools through the agency of the Council itself – advisers and inspectors, committees of inquiry and the follow-up work they usually engendered, and even the reasonably well-funded programmes launched by central government to bring about some shift in school practice.

While we cannot be sure about the effects in practice of the numerous proposals for changes in the school curriculum essayed by outside agencies, or about the consequences throughout the educational system of the pressure they exert, we can and do know about their proposals, and there is one group of agencies whose pressure on the curriculum does seem to produce very direct results: the secondary examination boards. Such is the power of the latter, at least in the secondary sector, that their supporters sometimes argue that, if we want specific curriculum changes, we should devote our energies to the syllabus committee and the boards (Dines 1984).

We will conclude this chapter by sampling the kinds of changes sought and the strategies for change employed by several of the key agencies over the past two decades. The choice of two decades is not arbitrary for Britain: it was in 1964 that the Schools Council for Curriculum and Examinations for England and Wales was established, to undertake research and development in school curricula and examinations, and in doing so to try to sustain the principle of teacher freedom, expressed in its Constitution thus:

> In the execution of the provisions of this Constitution and in the exercise of all functions conferred hereby, regard shall at all times be had to the general principle that each school should have the fullest possible measure of responsibility for its own work, with its own curriculum and teaching methods based on the needs of its own pupils and evolved by its own staff. (Schools Council 1978, p. 1)

Taken from the 1978 (and last) revision of the Council's Constitution, this principle had originally been stated in the Report of the Lockwood Committee upon whose recommendations the Council was first established (Ministry of Education 1964).

The Schools Council was but one of a large number of varied curriculum agencies established in different countries during the 1960s and 70s. In the United States, these included a national network of regional educational laboratories and university-based education R and D centres; in Scotland the national committee model has been used; in Ireland, there are nationally and locally funded units; in Australia, state and federal curriculum divisions, units and centres came into existence; and in many countries in the developing world, national ministries have established curriculum development groups or units (Skilbeck 1984c).

Many different styles and approaches to curriculum development have been adopted by these national and regional agencies. Yet there are some common elements which we can illustrate from the activities of the Schools Council. Like most of the agencies mentioned, the Council adopted the project team style, whereby a group of specialists, including classroom teachers, is assembled to work on a specified area of the school curriculum. Generally, 'area' was defined in subject terms and the practice of the team was to undertake some research, develop and trial materials and teaching strategies, modify and publish them and then undertake some form of dissemination through workshops, teacher in-service courses and so forth. Over the years, modifications to this mode of operation were made, alternative strategies proposed and adopted by some teams and, eventually, a more school-problem orientation was attempted through the Council's work programmes which were adopted after the 1978 Constitutional revision (Schools Council 1982, 1984). The Council's impact on curriculum thinking and practice was undoubtedly considerable and certainly went beyond teacher awareness and utilization of specific projects materials. The Council served both as a focal point for modern curriculum development in Britain in the 1960s and 70s and as the training ground for developers, evaluators and others. Its closure by unilateral central government action in 1984 marked the end of an era – the era when curriculum was seen as a proper object for large-scale research and development projects and when views about overall policies for the curriculum were thought to be best derived from a partnership of central and local government and the teaching profession. Whether the movements set under way by the Council will continue and grow under the new, separate, government-appointed agencies for curriculum examinations (the School Curriculum Development Committee; the Secondary Examinations Council) it is too soon to say.

The Schools Council never saw its role as promulgating overall aims, policies and strategies for whole-curriculum development: its focus was distinct areas of the curriculum and themes like raising the school leaving age. A more interventionist curriculum policy role, since the late 1970s has been assumed with increasing confidence by the Department of Education and Science. For the first time in decades, the Department in 1981 issued a general policy statement on the whole curriculum – actually the government's policy statement. Entitled *The School Curriculum*, this short document, together with follow-up circulars, initiated school and local education authority reviews and reports, the returns for which are likely to continue to come in for several years during the 1980s (DES 1981a, 1981b, 1983a).

A well-tried method of bringing curriculum and other educational issues to the fore is the *national committee*. For many years the Central Advisory Council was convened periodically, under a succession of chairpersons, to examine and report on aspects of secondary and primary education. Influential reports following these inquiries include the Crowther and Newsom Reports on secondary education and the Plowden Report on primary schools (Central Advisory Council 1959, 1963, 1967). With the publication of the Plowden Report, the Central Advisory Council went into abeyance, for reasons never fully explained but probably because central government officials were unenthusiastic about a Committee which had the necessary authority to conduct wide-ranging reviews but was under no obligation and in fact had not the means to take responsibility for implementing recommendations made. This type of boat-rocking was not readily accepted! Government in Britain is now more interested in reports on topics it chooses, by committees it convenes as one-off, special-purpose exercises. These include the Bullock Committee on language and the Cockcroft Committee on mathematics (DES 1975, 1982c). The Secondary Examinations Council and the School Curriculum Development Committee, which have succeeded the Schools Council, might seem like a return to the older committee model of initiating change. It is not clear, however, despite their determination to act independently, whether they will enjoy the scope and freedom of the Central Advisory Council to make far-reaching policy proposals. In Scotland, the Consultative Committee for the Curriculum and in Northern Ireland, the Northern Ireland Council for Educational Development are examples of committees working in the closest possible association with department officials and inspectors in undertaking research and development projects on particular topics or in areas of policy nominated by government.

What is the function of these national committees; do they provide a major impetus for curriculum renewal; and how can they assist in school curriculum change? A committee of review has certain advantages: a considerable budget for investigation, a varied membership which can draw on wide experience, access to decision makers locally and nationally, a high measure of credibility and professional confidence – at least while it is conducting its inquiries – and the opportunity to make recommendations which cannot be completely ignored or dismissed. On the other hand, a committee may serve as a convenient buffer, or be a way of postponing decisions and delaying actions. On the completion of its inquiries and delivery of the report both the members and the staff disperse. It is left to government departments, the profession and perhaps interested community pressure groups to assess the recommendations and carry them through to implementation. The committee method certainly helps to maintain diversity and a kind of pluralism whereby national policy debates on the curriculum are not dominated by government and officials. Yet, because of the way members are selected and the effective management of committees by professional departmental administrators, it is seldom that really striking or bold proposals emerge. More often, as was the case with Plowden and Bullock, a crystallization of ideas and practices already established occurs. Of course, for school curriculum making this can be extremely useful, as a summary and documentation of forward-looking and professionally accepted thought and practice.

The foregoing remarks apply in the main to the special-purpose national committee. When a *standing committee or council* is established, with a budget for research and development, a professional staff of its own and some prospect of continued existence over the long to medium term, several of the disadvantages listed above are overcome. Thus, in Scotland, the Consultative Committee on the Curriculum, in which teachers as well as local authority and departmental representatives play a prominent role, has been implementing a major reform of lower secondary school curriculum and assessment procedures, along the lines proposed by the Munn and Dunning Committees (the former was itself appointed by the Consultative Committee on the Curriculum). From a school perspective there are advantages in this committee style, where action on reports is given high priority and where a partnership between schools, the local authorities and a national body which sets a framework can readily occur.

In this brief overview of agencies and bodies responsible for stimulating and supporting curriculum development, mention must be made of LEA *inspectorate and advisory services* which have, even when understaffed and underresourced, an increasingly important role. As Ron Letch points out in the *Readings*, the local inspectorate is part of the linkage between the individual school and national-level agencies in a period of intensive policy making. Since the mid-70s, HMI have progressively extended their role as surveyors of the national educational scene (as distinct from inspecting individual schools) and expounded a general philosophy as well as detailed programmes of curriculum review, evaluation and development. For detailed examples of both HMI and local inspectorate or advisory service roles in promoting curriculum change, reference needs to be made to the specialized literature including the local advisers' and inspectors' journal, *Inspection and Advice*. In general, it can be said that they not only help to

promote and disseminate policies of employing bodies and central government but also contribute, often in a quite individual way, to professional
development and interchange. Their role is complicated by a duality of
function: professional advice and support on the one hand; supervision,
assessment and reporting on the other. There must always be an ambivalence within the teaching profession towards an area of the service which
combines what can so easily be contradictory roles. This ambivalance has,
at times, resulted in teachers' unions preventing inspectors from visiting
classrooms and has led towards systems of peer assessment for purposes of
review and promotion: these trends became apparent in parts of Australia
during the 1970s.

Such difficulties do not apply to *professional associations*, which are
usually teacher dominated, or to teacher education institutions. Yet, as
sources of change in the curriculum these bodies are usually obliged to work
indirectly. It is uncommon, although not unknown, for professional associations to be involved directly in substantial programmes and projects of
curriculum development. One case in point is the Association for Science
Education which joined in partnership with the Schools Council and subsequently with the School Curriculum Development Committee to fund
and conduct the Secondary Science Review.

Finally, in this brief review of agencies involved in or affecting curriculum change, we must mention a group of the more enduring and
commonly underestimated institutions: those involved in pre-service and
in-service education.

The impact on the school curriculum of *teacher education institutions*
occurs through their role in building up professional skills, influencing
attitudes and values and defining areas and topics of study in pre-service
and in-service courses, their involvement in research and development
projects, advisory and consultancy roles, and committee and professional
association membership. Research studies have suggested that teachers are
less influenced by this (and indeed by any groups outside the school) than
by immediate peer contacts and head teacher roles within the school (Ross
1980). Does this indicate a lessened role in the future for professional
development (in-service as well as pre-service) as a source of growth and
change in the school curriculum? Not if teacher education can become more
school based and classroom oriented, for example in the ways discussed by
Glen Evans and Jean Rudduck in the *Readings*, or more capable of using
the research and development strategies associated with action research,
the teachers as evaluators and teachers as researchers movements which

are discussed in others of the *Readings* and in the author's volume on curriculum evaluation (Skilbeck 1984c). If these orientations can be sustained, professional formation and continuing development of the teacher must be regarded, potentially at least, as perhaps the single most important source of influence on curriculum development as a planned, deliberate process in the school (National Inquiry into Teacher Education 1980, chapters 3 and 4).

Summary

Curriculum development is a process of planned and organized change arising from particular environmental or organic conditions, directed towards end-points, which may be of a general or specific kind, and characterized by particular patterns or styles. Development cannot be completely controlled but it can be informed and guided. Those undertaking curriculum development need to be alert to trends in society at large as well as within education. But taking all of this into account can be a problem for the school due to the scale and diversity of change and the school's limited resources for planning and developing curricula.

Changes in society at large have their own momentum and can have a more powerful impact on the school curriculum than the deliberate planning efforts of teachers and others within the school. This calls for a careful appraisal of the school's social roles and relationships, with emphasis on finding ways of utilizing the resources of the education system in school-based or school-focused developments.

Theories of development in philosophy, psychology, social and political science indicate that development is neither a natural unfolding nor an externally directed or environmentally determined change but is interactive. It does have discernible patterns, can be structured and planned, and incorporates values or qualitative standards which have to be defined and justified. Development is a normative concept presupposing something of worth or value both within the process itself and as a goal or outcome.

The need to have a well worked out theory of development for the enterprise of school-based curriculum development is underlined by the scale and pervasiveness of change in modern society. The phenomena of multiculturalism, youth unemployment and problems of national economic performance and longer-term trends, such as industrialization and technology applications, illustrate how changes in the environment can influence schooling. Schools will either perceive these changes as constraining their own ideas and planning, or as providing challenges and opportunities for new kinds of curricula. Schools have often responded to these wider changes, in a reflexive and adaptive way. This is scarcely sufficient since the changes themselves need an educational appraisal and their significance for the curriculum needs to be drawn out. To assist with these difficult and time-consuming tasks, agencies like curriculum development centres and national committees have been established. They can provide a focus for large-scale development programmes or needed changes in policy. Schools can use their materials and proposals in their own development work. Other institutions and bodies in the education profession can also be a significant source of support for schools in curriculum development. Teacher education and programmes of professional development are a vital adjunct to curriculum development, and are among the several key professional agencies that need to be mobilized in support of the school's curriculum role.

CHAPTER 4

THE DILEMMA
OF THE SCHOOLS COUNCIL

'Instead of blending naturally with the country's own established traditions, all these sudden innovations had a dislocating effect.' (Max Hayward, *The Russian Empire*.)

In the previous chapter we saw how change in the curriculum is a response to many different kinds of forces and pressures. An overview of some of the agencies in education also showed that there is a considerable resource that can be drawn upon by schools in undertaking development work. Looked at from another viewpoint, there are numerous pressures of one kind or another on schools, seeking to influence or inform their curricula. Of all of these agencies, however, those most explicitly and directly concerned with the systematic review, evaluation and development of school curricula are the national-level bodies which have been established to foster, stimulate and fund curriculum development.

Sometimes criticized as remote from schools and ineffectual agencies of school development, these agencies are nevertheless of singular importance in any assessment of modern curriculum development. By selectively reviewing the work of one of them, the Schools Council for Curriculum and Examinations for England and Wales (Schools Council), and drawing on the experience of several others, we can see more clearly what curriculum development entails, the issues to which it has given rise and the methodological solutions that have been found to the problem of determining effective curriculum development strategies.

The modification or renewal of curriculum content and organization have always been high among priorities for school reform or in the adaptation of schools to changing social circumstances. Yet it is only during the past three decades that planned curriculum development on a large scale and using systematic procedures of research, development and dissemination has become a prime focus in educational policy, planning and research. Together with the in-service education of teachers and experimentation with different types of school organization, it has been, at all levels of the education system, singled out as a key to educational improvement. The relative recency of this interest must be taken into account in attempting to assess its usefulness as a potential or actual support for school-based curriculum development. It is largely through the influence of these specialized agencies that curriculum development is so often seen as a clearly identifiable, fairly homogeneous process of upgrading or modifying content and producing new teaching and learning materials and techniques.

Strategies of curriculum development

Despite differences of opinion about what are the needs in and best ways of carrying out curriculum development, we can virtually define the modern period of curriculum development as one where strategies for change were planned and systematically applied to specified content areas and the modes of teaching and learning deployed within them. This approach has not precluded whole, cross-disciplinary or thematic curriculum development nor does it necessarily treat the school as having a lesser role than the specialist agency, but emphasis undoubtedly went towards the subject or area-specific project. Thus, although the concern for *strategies* and *models* of development was a major new factor, their applications were quite commonly to established subject areas in the curriculum: the 'disciplines' and the 'basics'. In this respect, there is a continuity between the more recent trends and those apparent in the late nineteenth and early twentieth centuries, when investigative national committees concentrated on the 'basics' or tool subjects in elementary schools and mind-training, civic, morality-building and skills subjects in secondary schools (Connell 1980, part 1; Cremin 1971; Good 1956, chapter XIV; Gordon and Lawton 1978).

The concept of curriculum development as a strategy or set of strategies for improving content and methods essentially on a subject-by-subject or area-by-area basis undoubtedly has value within individual schools and for a whole educational system. I shall argue later that, notwithstanding their advantages, these strategies do not provide a sufficient basis for effective and educationally sound school-based curriculum development. It is necessary, however, for us to understand the strategies, how they work and the difficulties they have encountered. In this chapter, by drawing mainly upon the Schools Council's work over two decades from 1964, I shall seek to elucidate these strategies. Although they have never been analysed in the way the American reforms of the same period have been, the Council's studies and projects over two decades are perhaps the richest single source anywhere for knowledge of content-specific strategies of curriculum development.

A word needs to be said at the outset about the term 'strategies of curriculum development'. As used here, it refers to those procedures for modifying or renewing the curriculum where systematic use is made of research and development, problem solving, planning and similar rationally derived techniques for managing or guiding change. We shall have to qualify this definition later, not least in order to take account of critics who have argued against the prevalence of rationalistic assumptions and techniques in education. However, it will serve us adequately at this juncture and as a way to understand strategies of curriculum development as conceived by the Schools Council and similar bodies.

Unlike school organization changes (e.g. the introduction of comprehensive secondary schools or destreaming in primary schools following abolition of the 11+ examination), or the expansion and diversification of INSET (in-service teacher education), curriculum development in Britain has been provided for some twenty years with the backing of a major central agency. It is not an exaggeration to say that for a decade or more curriculum development at or through the Schools Council and in Britain were largely synonymous and that the Council was esteemed by educationists around the world.

Through the Council's practical work, we can observe major trends in curriculum policy and uses and applications of strategies and models for design, development and evaluation. The Council operated through a network of regional and local groups and institutions. Some of them, including both schools and local education authorities, had their own separate interests in curriculum development and we cannot hope to trace those in any detail. This influence and recognition resulted not so much from the Council's useful examination work as from the numerous research and development projects fostering and supporting guided curriculum change. As we shall see, in practice its performance of this role was to prove much more difficult than had been supposed and despite its influence and status it ultimately failed to survive its critics in and out of government. We can, however, learn as much from these problems and difficulties as from its successes.

The reasons for the widespread professional interest in planned curriculum change as a major educational strategy, that grew up so rapidly in the 1960s and has continued ever since, cannot be easily unravelled: they are not confined to the educational sector but, as we have seen, are in part a reflection of wider social and cultural changes. By giving detailed attention to the *content* of teaching, the Schools Council, together with the Nuffield Foundation, in the early mathematics and science curriculum development projects was following the American lead by responding to some of these changes, namely in scientific and mathematical knowledge and, to some extent, their social and technological applications. Yet, content changes are only part of the story. Teaching methods and student attitudes and interests attracted more attention in later projects (Schools Council 1973; Stenhouse 1980). As we look more closely into curriculum development, we shall see that it is a portmanteau term entailing a response to a perceived context as much as modifications of teaching content and the organization of learning through new materials and methods. These changes in materials and methods have often arisen from direct and acknowledged social concerns. For example, the US beginnings of large-scale, team-based project development in mathematics and science seem to lie as much in growing concern over the prospect of declining superiority in the military and industrial sectors as in changing mathematical and scientific knowledge (Goodlad 1964; McClure 1971). These concerns were being freely voiced by public figures in America in the 1950s, whereas the curriculum theorists' interest in the structure of knowledge did not begin to show until after the publication of Jerome Bruner's *The Process of Education* in 1960. It is against this background that the Nuffield Foundation and then the Schools Council commenced project development in Britain in the early to mid-60s.

However mixed its ancestry, curriculum development rapidly became a definable and recognizable set of processes under the aegis of central governments and national agencies. In its most characteristic form, it was a pattern of study-inquiry-research, materials construction and trialling, evaluation, further development, publication and dissemination. There were many variations on this, the 'project' model, as we shall see later in the chapter. Under its influence, theories of curriculum development have emerged, been challenged, and modified. They all refer to the role of the school but there is no consistent line of opinion about just what that role in curriculum development might or ought to be. Sometimes, the school was seen as recipient, a 'site' in which projects were to be 'trialled' or 'field tested' and 'installed'; at other times, the project itself consisted of a network of schools and the process of the project consisted of school action in reviewing, evaluating, developing – sometimes in producing and printing materials as well.

Since they have often been put forward by people directly involved in or offering commentaries on curriculum projects or agencies, we can regard modern theories of curriculum development very largely as outgrowths of, or commentaries on, efforts to change the curriculum in practice. This may be more the case in Britain than in the USA, where on the one hand the role of the school other than as a recipient has often been quite obscure in high-powered government-funded projects or large-scale commercial publishing of curriculum materials and, on the other, commentators have been sharply critical of curriculum theorizing for its disregard of practical issues in schooling (Jackson 1968; Schwab 1969, 1971). Allowing for this, the central role of large-scale development projects in shaping curriculum theory and discussions and studies of school roles in curriculum development is indisputable. Parallel with this, and increasingly in all countries, curriculum theories have had to begin to recognize emphatic central-government policies towards the curriculum, and social policy generally. We may find evidence of this in the sociologically inspired theories of control and social reproduction and in the preoccupation of several leading curriculum writers, not only in Britain, with increasing centralization of power over the curriculum (Anyon 1980; Apple 1979; Becher and Maclure 1978; Lawton 1980; Lundgren 1983).

Much of the discussion of curriculum control reflects a divergence between centralizing trends and policies, school curriculum practices (and views) and some of the most popular assumptions about why and how curriculum development should take place. These divergences are not simply a matter of participation, localism and school initiative versus central, national priorities and school responses to external directives, although there are in the curriculum landscape many examples of such straightforward conflict. The locus of decision making is changing and with it new roles and relationships are emerging.

We have, now, an accumulation of experience of curriculum development, the deployment in practice of many different modes and styles, acknowledgement of a multiplicity of influences on the school and rapid changes in the external environment which are impinging on education. Where does all this take us in working out curriculum strategies? It is necessary to try to sort out the distinctive roles of different groups, local and national, professional and public in curriculum development given that curriculum is now a vast arena in which there are many, diverse interests. Yet it would be misleading to reduce all this activity and the issues arising to two polarized, conflicting stances: localism versus centralism, with school-based curriculum development identified with the former and government policies, plans and interventions in the curriculum with the latter. That is, 'grass roots' versus 'top-down' strategies, in the popular jargon.

It would be consistent with a centrally coordinated and even a centrally initiated curriculum policy that individual schools and school authorities should undertake curriculum review, evaluation and development, that resources for this purpose should be centrally allocated and that the results should, in turn, be used in future modifications of central roles. On the other hand, unless those central roles were carefully defined to ensure that local initiatives and activity themselves contributed to policy formation, the charges of manipulation and dominance might well be valid. This point applies equally to relations between individual schools and local authorities and to central government–local government relations.

By reviewing two decades of curriculum development, we shall see better what the positions and the arguments are, and come to a more concrete realization of the kinds of decisions that schools and professionals in and out of the classroom can – and ought – to make in the curriculum in this kaleidoscope of changes, pressures and new possibilities.

A national development agency: the Schools Council (1964–84)

The significance of the Schools Council as a factor in modern curriculum development is of several kinds. *First*, the Council was established, funded and staffed in order to give a focus to school improvement through research and development work in both curriculum and examinations. *Second*, the Council was intended to be close to teachers, directly involving them in its work. *Third*, the projects of the Council, which covered practically every subject area at all levels of schooling and included many theme-based, cross-disciplinary, integrated projects, were intended as a practical contribution to school curricula. *Fourth*, the Council joined actively in contemporary educational debate and discussion, sponsored research on a range of contemporary educational problems and organized a small number of whole-curriculum studies. *Fifth*, the Council was instrumental in numerous local initiatives. *Sixth*, the Council's influence has been the major single factor in promoting a professional literature of the curriculum. *Seventh*, the Council has encouraged or sponsored pre-service and in-service curriculum courses for teachers. *Eighth*, the Council has been studied as a model both for curriculum development projects and programmes and for the establishment of new curriculum development agencies in many parts of the world. *Finally*, the Council has generated a great volume of materials and resources and provided an information service about these and other developments in education. There have been, unfortunately, relatively few analytical studies of its general approaches to, and understanding of, curriculum development. As yet, we have had mainly descriptive or critical essays – or encomiums – and research into individual projects, notably by the Council's own evaluators (Bell and Prescott 1975; Harlen 1978; Lacey 1984; Skilbeck 1984b; Tawney 1973, 1976).

Some twenty years after its inception, the Schools Council was formally disbanded in 1984, following withdrawal of funding by its major partner, the Department of Education and Science. Its contribution to curriculum development was not thereby brought to an end. Its ideas and work will be to some extent continued through the two new agencies, the School Curriculum Development Committee and the Secondary Examinations Council. Due to the circumstances surrounding the Government's withdrawal of funds from the Schools Council, the establishment of these bodies in the wake of the Council's collapse has not been warmly welcomed, nor have they been given a broad remit or the kind of resources needed for comprehensive research and development. It is therefore all the more important that the initiatives and contributions of the Schools Council should be sustained through continuing use and progressive improvement of the materials and ideas it set in motion and by other research and development work in that tradition. It could very well be that an even greater role in curriculum development will be secured for this tradition after the Council's closure than was achieved before. This is because the Council's work was in many respects seminal and because it evolved and developed through its own experience. What its later work was pointing towards is increased local initiative and development within a well-defined framework. This is directly in line with the kind of broad-fronted strategy being proposed in this book, although the Council in its last years was still unable or unwilling to define its role in relation to the new DES-sponsored national policies in curriculum.

Does this broader, school-based and school-focused, strategy preclude roles for the large-scale team-based projects which the Schools Council in its early years fostered so actively? On the contrary, this national team type of curriculum development is of its nature long-term; it has a pervasive effect on the educational system as a whole which is often unnoticed at the time and is by no means confined to the direct usage of its project materials. Thus, much of the examination reform proposed by the Council in the 1970s – practically all of it rejected or pushed aside at the time by governments, and examining bodies and higher education institutions – is the basis of several of the changes under way in the 1980s, including the movements to build examinations (and syllabuses) around defined subject criteria and experiments with school profiles or records of student achievement. Similarly, the efforts by the DES and LEAs to foster school review, evaluation and development depend directly on the experience gained through Council projects, drawing upon strategies, procedures, techniques and even the concepts and language of the Council's development work of the 1960s and 70s. Thus attention to some of the basic strategies adopted by the Council, specifically in curriculum research and development helps us to identify many of the issues which are central to school-based curriculum development.

It was just because the Council sustained such a large, varied programme of research and development, encouraging and supporting numerous talented and hard-working teams that it created a substantial pool of ideas and techniques. This is not to say that the Council ultimately succeeded as a national development agency. In an assessment of its strategies we shall see that there were major problems and unresolved confusions. We can learn as much from these for school-based curriculum development as we can from individual project successes.

The Schools Council for Curriculum and Examinations for England and Wales – to give its title in full – was established in 1964. It has been remarked that its establishment is evidence of central government's bid to increase its own influence on the school curriculum (Salter and Tapper 1981, chapter 6; Skilbeck 1984b). Certainly, the initial move, to set up a Curriculum Study Group within the Department had to be abandoned as a result of LEA and teacher union protests. A committee, under Sir John Lockwood, proposed a publicly funded, independent Council to be established outside the Education Department and representing teachers (in a majority) and LEAs as well as the Department. These recommendations were promptly accepted by the Minister of the day, Sir Edward Boyle, and the constitution proposed by the Lockwood Committee was adopted (Ministry of Education 1964).

The question of who should control the curriculum, a continuing motif in debates ever since and a question that arises with every effort to develop the curriculum, thus surfaced at the very beginning of the Council's life. It appeared in the Council's constitutional principle that power and responsibility should be shared between the defined major partners, in the tacit recognition of the Department's funding role, in the placing of a department official as *primus inter pares* in the curious system of three joint secretaries (one each representing the Department, LEAs and schools) and in the adoption in the constitution of the principle of teacher choice. The foregoing qualifications notwithstanding, that principle reads like an unequivocal affirmation of the ultimate prerogative of teachers in the curriculum. As phrased in the Lockwood Report, the principle is:

> The objects of the Schools Council for the Curriculum and Examinations are to uphold and interpret the principle that each school should have the fullest possible measure of responsibility for its own work, with its own curriculum and teaching methods based on the needs of its own pupils and evolved by its own staff: and to seek, through cooperative study of common problems, to assist all who have individual or joint responsibilities for, or in connection with, the schools' curricula and examinations to co-ordinate their actions in harmony with this principle. (ibid. p. 12.)

Later refined to a single 'object', this principle of 'each school its curriculum' was reaffirmed in all of the changes including two major constitutional revisions that the Council passed through. It could be regarded as the curriculum equivalent to the Ark of the Covenant, with its roots well back in English progressive educational values. There are similar sentiments in the Hadow Report of 1931, and in the Norwood Report of 1943. There is, too, a remarkably similar passage in Whitehead's *Aims of Education*: '. . . the first requisite for education reform is the school as a unit with its approved curriculum based on its own needs, and evolved by its own staff' (Whitehead 1932, p. 11).

The principle was to prove something of a problem although, after the early days, this was rarely acknowledged openly. Choice could mean rejection of the Council's ideas and products, which was all very well as a principle but difficult to accept cheerfully when dissemination strategies became an issue in the late 60s and into the 70s, and questions began to be asked about uptake of materials. The principle was nevertheless retained virtually intact, surfacing yet again in the final official review of the Council, that carried out on commission from the then Secretary of State for Education and Science by Mrs Nancy Trenaman (DES 1981d).

Enhancing school curriculum development

We have noted that the principle of each school's determination of its own curriculum has an ancestry in professional and official views going back into the past. How was the principle to be interpreted and why did it constitute a problem for the Council? To answer these questions adequately we would need to penetrate deep into the Council's affairs. Such a detailed inquiry is not appropriate here, yet several points are of interest. During its twenty-year existence, the Council carried through hundreds of projects – many of them subject based and on a very large scale, extending over a decade or longer – and research studies, organized innumerable workshops and conferences, was instrumental in establishing a nationwide network of teachers' centres, and published voluminously. In practically all of this work it avoided prescription or even firm direction (it had not in any case the authority to require schools to do anything). Its answer to the question of schools' choice of curricula was very largely given by making available (at a cost) a multiplicity of materials for teaching and learning, and suggestions for methods provided through publications, conferences and workshops.

Availability of resources is one thing, but the positive exercise of freedom by schools is another. Schools would need *access* to materials, resources, strategies; they would need curriculum development *capability*; and they would need to be working in *conditions* where what was in principle possible and desirable, for example selection and adaptation of published resources, could occur in practical and productive ways. The generation of a large and varied set of projects, focused on defined needs and issues in the school curriculum, may be a necessary but it is certainly not a sufficient enterprise to ensure the positive exercise of curriculum freedom by each and every school. The Council would have to collaborate and cooperate, relating its work to numerous other initiatives and structures. But in a system as large and diverse as English and Welsh education, this was to prove a frightening-ly complex and ultimately impossible task. As some of its sharpest critics pointed out, the Council's strategies were to prove only a moderately effective way of effecting change or influencing practice. The Government's 1976 Education 'Yellow Book', wherein the Council was given an official thumbs down, is a good illustration of the critical tendency, and a par-ticularly damaging one, given the power of central government over the Council's affairs:

> The Schools Council has performed moderately in commissioning develop-ment work in particular curricular areas; has had little success in tackling

examination problems, despite the availability of resources which its predecessor (the Secondary Schools Examination Council) never had; and it has scarcely begun to tackle the problems of the curriculum as a whole. Despite some good quality staff work the overall performance of the Schools Council has in fact, both on curriculum and on examinations, been generally mediocre. (DES 1976, paragraph 50)

The Yellow Book went on to make some agreeable noises about the 'valuable contributions to the development of the school curriculum' of some (unspecified) projects. The immediate impact of the leak of the Yellow Book was outrage, on the grounds that, first, as participating partners in the Council, Department officials were themselves implicated in any shortcomings it might have and could not fairly and in supposedly confidential documents undermine it in this way; and, second, the criticisms themselves were tendentious – weakly argued and documented and showing malice (Lawton 1980, chapter 5).

It is not our purpose here to discuss criticisms of the Council's performance. Setting aside the one-sidedness and superficiality of much of the criticism directed at it, including the Yellow Book, it was true that the Council had not really thought through the practical implications of its project development work for school curriculum change. The sheer production of a large and varied volume of interesting and high-quality materials in separate subject areas, even when we add all the associated activities of workshops and conferences, the designs for learning, the evaluation and research reports, does not in and of itself constitute a strategy for school curriculum development. Nor does it necessarily strengthen the school's curriculum capability in practice to have available kits of materials, though it could be argued that schools as much as the Council were at fault in not taking the trouble to organize themselves to cope with the great changes that were needed in their curricula, or with the Council's resources for use in planning such changes. Later in the chapter we shall look at steps taken by the Council towards the end of the 1970s to take up anew the problem of school action. For the present, it is necessary to bring in another of the Council's principles: its declared interest in research and development and its interpretation in practice of existing models for research and development in the light of its declared object of school autonomy or choice in the curriculum.

On the face of it, research and development projects spread across all major curriculum areas or subjects would seem to be a possible way of enhancing school curriculum making. Yet we have seen already that materials may be produced but if they are not in a real sense available to schools to incorporate in their own planning and teaching, they may be a weak means of helping schools. This certainly was a criticism, and it was strengthened by the by now commonplace (but still controversial) opinion that too many of the Council's materials were overvoluminous, jargonistic or in a less than easily used format (DES 1981d). We need to see what was entailed by the Council's proposal that the school evolve its own curriculum, and how this principle was to mesh with nationwide, large-scale sponsored curriculum development undertaken by selected, specialist research and development teams.

One vision of the relationship between the national research and development agency and the school is that of the high-powered centre producing resources of such quality and persuasiveness that the role of the school will be largely confined to selection and modest adaptation. In what now reads as a strange miscalculation, the American David Clark wrote, in 1967:

> The look of the future in educational research will be composed of large, inter-agency centers housing large R and D operations . . . Centers of research and development will emerge on a scale beyond anything presently in existence. And these centers will be in a position to influence and affect educational practice directly through constituent agencies and indirectly through the pressures of their quality production. (Clark 1967)

In fact, the grand strategy, in the USA, of a national network of regional educational laboratories and university education R and D centres fell upon hard times in the 1970s and, with the concurrent decline of the large-scale funded curriculum project, that model of change *for* schools had to be abandoned. The British situation was rather different, in that there never was quite such an enthusiasm for a grand strategy, even in the minds of the sponsors of the large-scale projects. There was, nevertheless, sufficient interest in national research and development, with national projects covering most if not all curriculum areas, for the curriculum role of the school to become quite problematic.

Returning to the Schools Council's conception of curriculum development, we may note that, at one and the same time, the Council adopted the large-scale project model, and declared the legitimacy of the school as the principal element in deciding on the curriculum. The conditions of schooling, however, are such that the individual teacher and school are never entirely free to make curriculum choices. Nor, on the other hand, are strategies likely to succeed if they assume that schools can be, on purely professional grounds, enlisted as receiving units, along the lines presupposed by the more extreme version of research and development as outlined by Clark. In other words, neither the extreme version of school autonomy for curriculum making nor the equally extreme notion of a grand strategy based on professional research and development will suffice. This is apparent if we think for a moment about the many pressures on schools, and changes they are obliged to make, including curriculum changes, that are not the result of their own deliberations or designs. The freedom of the school also entails the exercise of their prerogatives and responsibilities by the several legitimate interests over and above the teachers (e.g. parents, students, community groups, local and central government). The professional model, whether school based or external research and development based, has also to be qualified with reference to constraints, such as secondary school examination and job entry requirements, and legal considerations as, for example, the obligations in the 1944 Act to provide religious instruction and in the 1980 Act to give parents more definite rights. The 'objects' of the Schools Council, as proposed by the Lockwood Committee, did not directly acknowledge any of this, but there was reference to the need for the Council to cooperate with and assist 'all who have individual or joint responsibilities for, or in connection with, the school curricula and examinations' (Ministry of Education 1964, p. 12). The belief persisted in parts of the Schools Council that the school could be the decisive unit, freely accepting or rejecting whatever was made available by way of projects. In other parts, and notably those where interest began to be taken in utilization of Council's publications, another theme emerged, that the Council actually had a responsibility not just to assist and cooperate, but to *promote* the products of its own large-scale projects.

To summarize a rather tangled mixture of beliefs and assumptions: the principle of maximum teacher choice was enunciated and at times seemed like a unilateral declaration of teacher or school rights in the curriculum against all others. At the same time, large-scale projects were launched which ultimately yielded materials that the developers wanted teachers to use – not merely select or reject. The need for teachers to be professionally engaged with the curriculum at the school level – in making choices appropriate to local and individual needs and circumstances rather than simply passing on some given body of information or responding mechanically to outside forces – was constantly affirmed. Yet it was unclear how far, or in which ways, teacher freedom in the curriculum would be reconciled with either the Council's own materials and its research and development programmes or other forces and pressures in education. These matters were given a political cast when early Joint Secretaries of the Council proclaimed the principles of liberty and pluralism: the State and its arms or agencies should not infringe on the professional exercise of judgement by professionals and others, just because the State felt it had some better way of doing things. It is particularly interesting that two civil servants who were instrumental in establishing the Council, Derek Morrell and Geoffrey Caston, publicly upheld these principles.

They regarded the Council as fundamentally an instrument for the support of the teacher in the school. In an article on the Schools Council written some years after he had left, and citing remarks by Morrell about 'the describable curricular reality' lying in a 'positive reciprocity of feeling between teachers and taught', Caston declared that curriculum development essentially happens in the school and is 'the mutual responsibility of teachers and pupils'. 'The system', he continued, 'must be organized to support and reinforce that responsibility, and not to diminish it' (Caston 1971, p. 77). Caston was convinced that the way to do this was to assemble teams of researchers, developers, evaluators and teachers, and to publish their findings and products 'so that professionals can choose to use them or not to use them, as they wish' (ibid.) He believed, too, in the need for regional in-service and research centres, such as were established for humanities at the Centre for Applied Research in Education at the University of East Anglia and for science at Chelsea College, University of London, an early indication that perhaps, after all, dissemination was being seen as an issue to address by structured means. His overarching principle was, nevertheless, the individual teacher's and school's responsibility for the curriculum. Take-up of Council projects was therefore quite a secondary consideration.

These declarations of the principle of school autonomy raise the question, 'Who is best fitted to make choices and decisions about the curriculum?'. For reasons that should by now be obvious, this question can no longer be answered, as perhaps Morrell and Caston hoped it could be, by invoking a sacred principle of teacher liberty. Our task, now, is to interpret single principles (e.g. teachers decide the curriculum) by interrelating and reconciling the different perspectives and viewpoints of the several interests involved, and by taking full account of contextual, environmental and situational factors, including the availability and potential of educational research and development projects in the curriculum. The processes of curriculum review, evaluation and development must themselves provide scope for participation and mutuality, with roles for several more categories of participant than were identified in the famous 'reconciliation' of 1964, when the Schools Council partnership of teachers, LEAs and DES was established. The quest must be for a new consensus, and for a more rational use of scarce planning, research, design and development resources than was evident in the Council's early days. These resources were not in fact available to schools on the policy of 'let the schools take or leave the projects'. (Many schools scarcely even knew about the projects and were in no position to make rational choices.) Nor were these resources effectively utilized in the grand strategy approach, whereby researchers and developers produced solutions for schools to adopt. (Many of the solutions were inadequate and, in any case, the schools would not accept the role of adopters and implementers, a role which was inconsistent with a cherished faith in professional autonomy.)

Applying the principle of 'schools choose'

Choice in the curriculum, whether referring to the decisions made by teachers (and others) about the what and the how of teaching, or to the choices students make among all the things potentially available to them in the curriculum, depends on information, skill, understanding and a disposition to exercise the choices that may be available. Lacking commitment to principles of choice, lacking knowledge of what could be done, lacking effective access to a wide array of courses, materials and strategies, lacking sophistication and competence in curriculum decision making, teacher choice would be nothing but an empty formula. The Schools Council was very much aware of this and, having declared its commitment to the principle, proceeded to the series of moves already mentioned – assembling project teams, publications, workshops and conferences, establishing local and regional teachers' and information centres. In retrospect we can detect a strategy but at the time, strategic considerations were frequently submerged beneath the politics of committee decision making – a problem at any level from the single institution to the national system (Lacey 1984).

There are two aspects to highlight in our further analysis of teacher and school choice as goals to be achieved through the activities of national agencies such as the Schools Council: first, choice means items from which selections are to be made; second, choice implies skill in decision making. To meet the first requirement, the Schools Council did indeed produce a splendid array of rich and varied materials. The second requirement called for something that was to prove rather more difficult and indeed was scarcely within the Council's province and certainly beyond its resources: new styles of teacher education both pre-service and in-service.

Let us consider each of these problems of choice more closely: neither was to prove susceptible to successful Schools Council intervention; both have been frequently raised in curriculum thinking and must be addressed by any institution involved in curriculum development. The idea of choice as dependent on a wide array of course materials and teaching strategies sounds straightforward. But is it? Two or three considerations quickly show how difficult it is to equate teacher autonomy in the curriculum with the exercise of choice among professionally developed materials. The Council was not the only agency involved in materials production. In fact, this was traditionally the preserve of commercial publishing and the Schools Council quickly found itself involved in the most complex relations with commercial publishers as a result of which, while numerous publications appeared, there was a very definite commercial assessment made of projects and very difficult, often long drawn out, negotiations were entered into between publishers, editors, Council officers and project teams. Materials had to be sold: neither LEAs nor central government consistently sponsored the uptake of materials by schools and, in the market, Schools Council materials had to compete (sometimes with rapidly assembled commercial imitations). The cost of materials was undoubtedly a consideration in their purchase and use (DES 1981d). Since projects were usually participatory in the sense that trial schools and networks of educators were directly involved and were themselves expected to change as a direct consequence of participation, it could not be assumed that materials found to be unsuccessful would simply be dropped: they were, in trial form, already in use and this was a further complication. In passing, we may note that this is a general problem with any kind of action research (curriculum development included): what is to be evaluated is already in use.

To bring the Council's materials into the commercial publishing arena with all the attendant complexities and pressures became inevitable and, some say, was ultimately beneficial. It was not, however, quite what was meant by the original doctrine of a curriculum evolved by the staff of each school. The reason for this is not that each school in constructing its own curriculum necessarily designs and constructs all of its materials. As Philip Waterhouse demonstrates in the *Readings*, that is an impossible expectation and not at all what is required for school-based curriculum development. The difficulty, rather, is the distance between sophisticated, costly, expert-produced materials published nationally and the circumstances of the individual schools and classroom. That distance was not to be breached, as we shall see, by more and better dissemination strategies.

We have been considering the problem of choice by teachers of externally produced materials from the standpoint of a producing agency which was also a publicly funded research and development centre. The problems we have identified are important in trying to understand the tensions and contradictions of national agency work where different and sometimes conflicting principles concerning teacher freedom, professionalism, dissemination and the pricing and purchasing of materials operate.

Viewed from a school perspective, there are other kinds of problems in relation to the selection of resources and materials. Many practical aspects are discussed in specialist books on resource management (Waterhouse 1983). One of these, to which we now turn, is the problem of ensuring that schools and teachers can make choices on a basis of knowledge about what is available and its relevance and suitability for the designs and plans they have for the curriculum. This is a significantly different matter from simply choosing a suitable textbook for an examination syllabus, or a composite reading scheme, since the curriculum is itself constructed in part by the selection, and adaptation (not merely adoption) of what might well be a large and varied array of materials.

We have already observed that the principle of school choice in the curriculum cannot be exercised unless information is available and there is genuine access to it. Within a single, large school it is often difficult to ensure a free flow of information about policy or curriculum practices throughout the several departments and faculties, to say nothing of what is happening in other schools or in the LEA. In all schools, the selection of appropriate materials and resources requires good information sources and sound organization. In a national system of some 30,000 primary and secondary schools and some 400,000 teachers (the figures changed considerably over the 1960s and 70s, but were of this order) it proved beyond the capability of the Schools Council to get information through in such a way that it became a normal school practice to consult Council *Project Profiles* and other informative publications in designing courses. When surveyed in the mid to late 70s, a disturbingly high proportion of teachers claimed to be unaware of much of the project material produced by the Council and directly relevant to their subject or pupil-age specialization. (Steadman et al. 1978–81). In addition to these difficulties arising from the principle of teachers exercising responsibility for the curriculum by choosing from available materials, there was also the problem of finding ways of helping teachers to develop and improve their curriculum skills. This point is directly relevant to school-based curriculum development, which requires a minimum competency in curriculum review, evaluation, design and implementation, and a readiness to deploy these understandings and skills. That kind of readiness is not only a matter of factual knowledge and discrete skills, such as materials analysis, the mounting of small-scale experiments and the evaluation of results; it also entails a situational readiness: the educational environment has to be of a kind where these skills can be realistically exercised. In turn, this means a supportive or at any rate not a hostile climate, resources, scheduled time and so forth. Schools have a responsibility to ensure that curriculum change, whether internally or externally initiated, is approached realistically, in the light of these considerations (see *Readings*, Sections 3 and 5).

It is a valid criticism of many of the Council's projects that they made too many optimistic assumptions about school climate and conditions, a common failing of innovators inside as well as outside schools. Furthermore, it was not within the Council's power to support or undertake the kinds of professional development programmes whereby the teaching force as a whole might become 'tuned in' to curriculum development. Precisely the same point arises in respect of in-school development (Crone and Malone 1983, chapter 4). While individual Council projects normally involved large numbers of teachers, in trial schools, writing teams, workshops and so on, they were still only a small minority of teachers overall. Ironically, the great stimulus, given mainly by the Council, to curriculum studies in pre-service and in-service teacher education, has now begun to take effect, showing results up and down the country only after the Council had itself reached its peak and gone into decline, through its abandonment by central government. The lesson, not lost on schools and local authorities, is the need to assess conditions for change and to foster and support professional development as a necessary component of a curriculum development strategy.

Thus far, we have seen how the idea of teachers' building curricula through the choice and selective use of Council materials proved to be complicated and, ultimately, beyond the power of the School's Council to implement. We must now turn to another dimension of development. In its early project work the Council followed, not a grass roots style of supporting local initiative, but a different set of procedures, derived from earlier American and Nuffield Foundation projects in mathematics and science.

These closely resembled a currently popular theory concerning the inter-relationships of research, development and diffusion (RDD). More than any other consideration it was this use of the RDD model, through central site teams, that produced unmanageable tensions in which school-based curriculum development became obscured, despite the good intentions.

Adoption of the Research-Development-Diffusion (RDD) model

How did adoption of a version of the RDD model conflict with teacher and school responsibility for the curriculum, and what does that conflict have to tell us about curriculum development in the school? We can answer these questions and draw some conclusions for curriculum development gener-ally, by tracing in outline the Council's approach to research and develop-ment and seeing how an initial enthusiasm for RDD came to be supplanted or diluted by other beliefs and practices.

In the early 60s, when the Schools Council was established, there was relatively little experience available, anywhere in the world, of strategic intervention in development of the curriculum. Planned, large-scale research and development projects, of the type used in industry, agriculture and the military, were to prove seductive. Up to shortly before that time, the methods or devices in common use in education were:

1. the syllabus or curriculum committee, usually a national-level body often tied in with examination boards and producing recommended or required syllabuses and recommending or requiring specified teaching and learning materials (common in centralized systems and whenever external examinations were in use);
2. the 'blue-riband' committee, which took up or was assigned some curriculum problem or area of schooling to investigate, comment upon and make recommendations about, for future action (in Britain, the Hadow Reports, and those of the Crowther and Newsom Committees are examples);
3. commercial texts and other materials usually produced on commission by specialist text or resource book writers;
4. ad hoc and mostly small-scale reviews and experimental projects in individual schools or education authorities;
5. occasional large-scale experiments, such as the American Eight Year Study (Aiken 1942);
6. the programmes of experimental schools, such as the pioneering in-

dependent progressive schools in England, Continental Europe and the USA, and the American Laboratory schools and school district small-scale projects (Connell 1980; Cremin 1961);

7. and finally, notably in the USA, a well-established if still fairly small body of academic researchers and theorists who were involved either in psychologically oriented experiments in school learning or in teaching and writing at the level of university degree programmes in curriculum development. A good account of Hollis Caswell, a typical member of this community in the between-wars years, is given by Mary Seguel (Seguel 1966, chapter 6).

The foregoing list points to significant and under-valued achievements in curriculum practice, research, development, study and theory. Despite the limitations of scale, poor follow-through and a lack of systemwide dynamics, they are sufficient to refute the belief that curriculum development 'started' with the large-scale projects of the 1950s and 60s. There is, certainly at the school level and in the academic study of and research into curriculum, a continuity within which the project-based development movement eventually will itself find a place – and not perhaps the dominating one it assumes now. Allowing for all this, a quite radical change did occur in the 50s and 60s, the Schools Council was part of it – although it did not originate it – and that change in some fundamental respects is the main driving force behind curriculum development as we now know it.

We have already discussed some of the forces and factors making for curriculum change in the preceding chapters. It was partly dissatisfaction with the results and effects of the methods and devices just mentioned, partly a realization that something on a much larger scale was needed, that led to the search for new ways of regenerating the school curriculum. Direct application to the curriculum of the schools of the apparatus of scholarship and research and development procedures; investment of considerable sums of public money; and the creation of specialist agencies and programmes: these seemed the way ahead in the 1950s, the principal new means of encouraging and fostering change in the schools themselves.

For quite understandable reasons, that many subsequent critics of this general approach to change overlooked or quickly forgot, it came to be believed that the school curriculum was susceptible to large-scale planned, strategic intervention through the assembling of small specialist teams applying the research, development and diffusion procedures which had been successfully employed in spreading innovations in agriculture, and certain branches of industry. Determining needs and priorities, assembling and funding the teams and generally organizing the multiplicity of discrete enterprises was seen to be a large enough task to justify the establishment of specialist, publicly funded agencies at the national level. What was initially thought to be a suitable action model consisted of a sequence of clearcut steps: undertake research, develop procedures and products through that research, and diffuse or disseminate them throughout an appropriate environment (RDD). This logical sequence of events is one key element in the process; the other is the assembling and deployment of specialist, expert teams to undertake the specified activities, the grouping and support of these teams through large-scale funding (so-called 'soft' R and D money) and their location in specialized departments or agencies. Critics of RDD have usually concentrated on problems or weaknesses in the technical processes of research, development and diffusion, and the locating of teams in remote 'centres', neglecting the equally important social dimension of funded, institutionalized, collaborative development and the resulting organizational issues (Kelly 1982, chapter 5).

We must keep these (1) technical (2) control and (3) organizational/institutional dimensions clearly in view since one of the most serious problems arising from this whole new style of curriculum development was the technologizing and institutionalizing of the processes and the personnel and their separation and distance from school sites. The problems of dissemination and implementation about which much has been written, are, as I shall argue later, an inevitable consequence of a particular way of looking at curriculum research and development. They cannot be solved simply by better designed techniques, the dispersion of 'centres', or more attention to dissemination and more funding – frequently advocated remedies within the specialist agencies.

Let us now examine in rather more detail the RDD model as it has been applied to curriculum development. In doing so, we shall discover that its limitations and weaknesses in practice have by no means rendered it useless. Its elements, critically assessed, reassembled and strengthened through the experience of local small-scale development work, will yield us better ways for the future including school applications and uses.

In one of its early publications, reporting its first three years, the Schools Council briefly adumbrated what it took to be the processes of curriculum development with a heavy emphasis on materials production:

a)   investigation, including surveys and definition of needs

b) creation of new materials
c) trials
d) diffusion including courses and conferences
e) evaluation

'Not all projects', it was said, 'pass through every stage in exactly the same manner which is outlined, but this is the pattern to which the Council tries to work' (Schools Council 1967b, p. 6). Noteworthy here is the assumption that the typical project is a materials-producing one: the *type* of product sought is known in advance and this is a particular interpretation of RDD. Philip Halsey, one of the Council's early curriculum officers made the point quite explicitly late in the 1960s:

> The typical staffing of a project consists perhaps of three or four full-time staff, mostly teachers, with appropriate secretarial supporting staff. The main work of the team itself is the creation of new materials. These may include teachers' guides, pupils' material, information resources and all sorts of visual aids. An essential feature of development is the experimental trial of draft materials at an early stage in the school . . . (Halsey 1969, p. 28)

Somewhat later, one of its most searching critics, John Nisbet, commented on the Council's commitment to this version of RDD. He brought into play the ideas of Donald Schon (1971), the prominent critic of the practice of innovations intended for systemwide use being generated at central sites:

> The weakness of the 1960s style of curriculum development was that it was based on a 'centre–periphery model' of curriculum change. This model assumed that innovation must start at the centre, and should 'diffuse' to the periphery – that is, to teachers in the schools. (Nisbet 1979, p. 53)

Instead of centrally generated, more or less research-based packages of materials, Nisbet said what was needed from central agencies was short discussion papers on issues and their implications. The problem, as Nisbet saw it, was the alienation of the teachers by professionalized development work conducted away from the classroom – even if classrooms were used for trialling purposes (Nisbet 1976).

We have seen that, on the matters of school autonomy in curriculum making and the propagating of its own products, the Council followed different principles which, even when they did not conflict or compete, led to ambiguities. There is a similar problem in relation to its apparent commitment to the RDD model. It is true that the Council sustained a large number of central teams (although most were located away from the

Council in colleges and universities so it was more of an administrative and coordinating than a research and development centre) and that it subscribed to the steps and stages of the RDD model. Yet it did have a very wide repertory of types and styles of development. As if to prove its eclecticism, in a booklet outlining samples of its own work, prepared for an international conference on curriculum innovation in 1967, the Council included excerpts from a wide array of discussion papers: Working Paper 12, 'The Educational Implications of Social and Economic Change'; Working Paper 10, 'Curriculum Development: Teachers' Groups and Centres'; Working Paper 11, 'Society and the Young School Leaver'; Working Paper 7, 'Science for the Young School Leaver'; Working Paper 5, 'Sixth Form Curriculum and Examinations'; Examinations Bulletin 1, 'The Certificate of Secondary Education: some suggestions for teachers and examiners'; Curriculum Bulletin 1, 'Mathematics in Primary School'. In many cases, these discussions invited readers to enter into a reflective dialogue, to assess their own professional practice. They also, in most cases, reported on preliminary investigative work, feasibility studies and small-scale projects which were to have a strong RDD flavour. Thus we must not overlook the Council's long and varied interest in fostering discussion and reflection on current curriculum issues – precisely what some of its critics charged it with neglecting.

Having given a preliminary account of the Council's interest in RDD in the context of its wider range of concerns, let us turn now to how one of its leading American exponents, R.N. Bush, Director of the Stanford Educational Laboratory, defined educational research and development. Bush's account, like other American analyses that might be cited, is both more precise and more uncompromising than what we find in the Schools Council. It shows us both similarities and differences between the American educational laboratory and the Schools Council approaches. According to Bush (1976), in the ideal situation a specialist research and development team is assembled and undertakes:

– needs assessment
– specification of objectives
– analysis of alternative strategies and treatments
– choice among alternatives
– construction of partial or tentative systems or prototypes for testing in field situations
– continuing evaluation and refinement

– production
– dissemination and installation

Although Bush's version, by the use of the word 'production', implicitly at least envisages materials production, his outline applies equally to new action strategies and different kinds of developmental processes; for example, the 'needs assessment' might show that a skills training programme or new leadership styles were most needed.

For reasons that have never been made clear, but must be closely connected with teacher demand for classroom materials, the early British – and much of the American and other nations' – work in curriculum development turned to new materials as the greatest need. The teacher demand was real, but was it ever evaluated in comparison with other demands and needs? In a speech given before the Schools Council was founded, Derek Morrell, one of the first joint secretaries, used the odd expression 'a "package" of knowledge about the curriculum, and about teaching methods', assuming thereby a particular meaning of curriculum development (Morrell 1963). This kind of assumption, together with the American and Nuffield materials-based projects and the rapid growth of low-cost print technology, may very well be what led to the belief that curriculum development is enshrined in the production of a package of materials for teachers and students. Whatever the explanation of this overwhelming emphasis on materials, it proved to be unsatisfactory if only because the producing agency was unable to bring about acceptable change through their dissemination and utilization.

There has been a great deal of criticism of the RDD model, in the form we have been examining, applied to curriculum development and educational reform generally. This ranges from dissatisfaction with its apparent neglect of school utilization of new resources and the implementation of change (as distinct from product diffusion) and its confusion of diffusion (a 'natural' spread) with planned dissemination, to criticisms of the assumptions about the sequence, research-develop-diffuse, about the role of central teams of experts, and the very idea of educational change as the uncritical acceptance of any other person's view of things (Skilbeck 1984c).

It is one of the unfortunate results of using the RDD model that it over-simplifies events. Moreover, it is often unclear in the literature whether it is being used retrospectively to try to explain a process of planned curriculum change – and to make it seem more orderly than perhaps it was in practice, or as a recommendation for future action, or as a description of how projects are in fact designed. One of the most trenchant critics of RDD in curriculum studies, the late Lawrence Stenhouse, drew attention to some very real weaknesses; he was troubled by its inadequacies as an explanation of change processes and its defects as a guide to curriculum action. Stenhouse believed there is a better way of thinking about teachers in relation to research and development than as recipients of other people's – even other teachers' – curriculum materials. Research, for Stenhouse, is every teacher's responsibility and what a national project team can best do is generate hypotheses about teaching and learning, with perhaps exemplary materials, for teachers to test in their classrooms (Stenhouse 1975, chapters 9 and 10).

This may not be quite how Stenhouse's own Humanities Curriculum Project started off, since it was a Schools Council materials production enterprise (structuring diverse print and visual sources for use as 'evidence' in discussion) but it is how it evolved and came down into the educational literature. Moreover, even if generating testable hypotheses were the most distinctive achievement of a national project, it is at least arguable that the generation of significant hypotheses and teachers' engagement with curriculum issues as a means of testing those hypotheses is a justification for the large-scale, central-team project. In other words, there is here a mutuality between the teacher-as-researcher concept and that of the RDD model, which is too easily glossed over in the tendency to treat RDD as a 'production' model. We shall have more to say about the virtues of teacher engagement with, as distinct from receipt of, research and development later. But, there is a prior question to ask. Did the curriculum agencies, Schools Council included, not only advocate but in their practice actually use the RDD model? Were things quite as clearcut as that? In other words, how much experience of large-scale, planned RDD do we actually have in curriculum making in Britain?

Earlier in the chapter, I observed that when the Council was established in 1964, there were available to it on the one hand forms of curriculum intervention of a fairly traditional kind and, on the other, the promising model of RDD, which had enjoyed such success in the production of new pharmaceuticals, fertilizers, weaponry systems and new production techniques in heavy industry as to be regarded as the typical mode of innovation. All of these used RDD in the sense of research-based products developed by specialist teams and made available (and actually sold) on specified markets. The Schools Council, as we have seen, established as its principal mode of operation, the small, specialist, development team, and produced materials, yet these teams seldom followed any straightforward and recognizable sequence of research to development to diffusion. There was, in fact, no large and powerful research centre; instead projects were widely scattered and all were a form of temporary system, with relatively short life spans in most cases. As Jack Wrigley put it in a retrospective impression of his role in the Council's research and development in the late 60s to mid 70s:

> The concept of 'research and development' was taken over from engineering and it was immediately apparent to me that in the field of curriculum innovation the concept needed considerable modification. The development phase more often than not did not follow from a particular research phase. So I conceived the idea that in education, research and development should interact with each other, that in some projects the development would begin first based upon hunches, ideas, ideals, and thoughts of creative people . . . in some cases we would begin with the development aspect and eventually carry out research projects. Similarly with regard to evaluation it was very clear to me that the Council committees, and indeed the mood of the whole nation, at that time, was not seeking for elaborate independent evaluations of the curriculum innovations being planned . . . there was the need for ongoing or formative evaluations rather than final or summative ones. So we created a group of critical friends, we appointed to most of the projects an evaluator who would not pretend to be independent of the project but sympathetic to it, would organize the feedback for the curriculum development projects in such a way as to make them more effective. (Wrigley 1981, p. 6)

This passage not only shows the readiness of senior Council staff to handle with great flexibility what in textbooks often seems like a rigid approach, it also brings out an interest in ideas and initiatives from whatever source they might come, whether or not part of a systematic research design.

Research as understood in the physical and social sciences, academic institutions and specialized research agencies was given a relatively minor role in the Council's affairs, although there were many investigations and inquiries into current curriculum practice. If we are willing to allow that there is, in practical affairs, another kind of research, loosely defined as action research, then practically all of the Council's projects may be treated as extended pieces of research.

By action research in education I do not mean, necessarily, small-scale, in-school projects focused on the solution of particular problems or the illumination of immediate issues. Action research includes small-scale studies of the kind undertaken by John Elliott, Stephen Kemmis and others who have been influenced by the concept of individual teacher as researcher in the school setting (Elliott 1982; Kemmis et al. 1983) but may be on a very large scale as well. What defines action research is not scale, or teacher involvement, but the construction of action programmes to solve problems or meet defined practical needs, their careful observation, analysis and evaluation, and the use of the insights and experiences thereby gained for constructing theories and building up knowledge including experiential knowledge and practical skills for future use. Epistemological and methodological foundations of action research are to be found in the American philosophy of pragmatism as expounded by Pierce, James and Dewey and their followers (Ayer 1968; Schilpp 1939).

The growing appeal of action research in its different forms consists very largely in the fact that in the field of curriculum action the life of the school is decisive, that teachers are necessarily participants in school-level action projects and that some of the difficulties arising for large-scale research and development might be overcome through small-scale, in-school projects. There is, moreover, an affinity between action research in the curriculum and studies of classroom and school life – the curriculum in action – which was recognized long ago in the curriculum literature (Caswell 1935, 1937; Corey 1953; Jackson 1968). It should be apparent that action research in the curriculum in Britain owes a great deal to Schools Council projects. Its evolution may be traced through many of them, including the Mathematics for the Majority Continuation Project, the North West Regional Curriculum Development Project, Geography for the Young School Leaver, the Humanities Curriculum Project and others (Stenhouse 1980).

Much of the Council's research in the more usual sense of systematic observation and assessment of specified changes came out of evaluations; that is, it either contributed information and ideas for use by projects in progress or it reported on their achievements and, to some extent, effects. The Council evaluators played another role, in exploring and trying out new procedures for observation such as case study and synoptic accounts of situations and events, thus contributing towards the apparatus of school review and institutional self-evaluation and action research, all of them related to school-based curriculum development (Harlen 1978; Tawney 1973, 1976).

If research – as a front-end activity providing a knowledge base for development – was often rather scanty or even disregarded altogether, dissemination was recognized as a problem, but fairly late in the day and never in a way that could be regarded as satisfactory. The Council was seldom criticized for weaknesses in research of the kinds we have been discussing, or even development, but was often under attack, including self-criticism, for weaknesses in dissemination (Lacey 1984; Parsons et al. 1983).

But much of the criticism either made invalid assumptions about dissemination as an activity in, or related to, the processes of curriculum development, or failed to address the dilemmas facing any national agency which proclaims the school's right to choose its own curriculum, selecting from a wide array of materials. To see why this should be so we need to turn towards a problem inherent in large-scale curriculum development work and likely to occur whenever there is a project with the expectation that its findings will be extended to situations other than the one in which it was undertaken.

The whole point of RDD as a form of innovation is that problems can be identified, research can be undertaken, possible solutions identified and the results generalized. Let us take an example, from outside education. In industrial terms, suppose a paint manufacturer finds that his product has poor weathering characteristics in a wide range of climatic conditions. He is in business to manufacture and sell paint, at a profit. Here is a research issue of a problem-solving kind, in that he needs to have a sound product, knows that it is faulty – and that his customers know it is faulty – and yet doesn't know just why the paint is not weathering well. What is needed, then, is identification of the precise nature of the problem, sustained research to establish the contributing conditions, and both theoretical and practical exercises to find satisfactory variations in his basic materials or their combination. Also needed are research into conditions in the market, and knowledge of competitors' products and marketing. But this is only the beginning; there is also development: paint technology. Development of the new product must include a production programme, perhaps new equipment, training of personnel, trials of the material, and a financial appraisal. Supposing all this to meet quality and other criteria, the product must be a contender for the third stage, diffusion. With the new product coming on line, research and development costs to be recovered, competitors to contend with and consumers to be persuaded to buy the product, a marketing strategy is needed: the product has to be sold, profits made. I am indebted to ICI for part of this analysis (Imperial Chemical Industries 1984). Admittedly, it is a simplification, but a couple of points raised are useful for our discussion. Leaving aside the manufacturer's ability to pinpoint a problem in a product compared with the educator's difficulty of addressing qualitative problems in learning and teaching, we may note:

1. a new product (paint) developed on one site has to be diffused to a very large number of different sites (shops, purchasers);

2. provided certain criteria are satisfied, the success of the operation will be determined at least in part by sales of the product compared with the cost of the RDD.

It may be that, philosophically, the paint manufacturer believes in choice in the market; he may also be a great believer in do-it-yourself and he may, privately, feel that his paint is not better than his main competitors'. But, as a manufacturer, he does see them as competitors and he is in no doubt that his job is to get the paint marketed and sold: that becomes his primary concern at this stage of proceedings. His philosophical musings, if any, do not inhibit his efforts to sell his product. In his more reflective moments, perhaps he has certain reservations about the nature and impact of scientific research and technology in the world at large – and a kind of distaste for crasser forms of marketing – but he has a very definite interest in keeping all this to himself and mobilizing all his resources to produce and market his product: that is how he justifies his research.

Returning to education and curriculum development, research has never been seen in quite this light, nor indeed has it ever gained this kind of acceptance. For whatever reasons, the Schools Council did not succeed in bringing research as a basis for action centrally into its affairs, and it certainly did not see curriculum development as culminating in the installation of its numerous products in the nation's schools. The Council not only believed that teachers had their own choices to make, their own curriculum to construct. It could not, and would not, commit itself either to the systematic generation of educational knowledge or to a market-type dissemination strategy: it could not, and did not, wish to treat teachers as commodity receivers and users. Equally, it was unable to conduct the kind of alternative strategy, whereby teachers nationwide would become active participants in the whole research and development process, thus rendering dissemination of commodities unnecessary. The RDD model was therefore scarcely applicable either descriptively or prescriptively to the kind of curriculum development the Council believed in or wanted. Its focus was neither research, nor diffusion, but development. Unfortunately, however, it allowed itself to be caught in the tail of the model, dissemination, and became increasingly troubled about its inadequacies in that respect. Only very late in the day did it begin to undertake the kind of research that might have enabled it to work constructively on the solution of its problems.

This is not the place to go into the dissemination issue in curriculum, important as it is, even for local development. Suffice it to say that in the case of the Schools Council the problem was very largely of the Council's own making: by never resolving the issue of teacher choice or the all-out promotion of its materials and ideas, by vacillating over the applicability or otherwise of the RDD model, the Council became enmeshed in insoluble problems over the utilization of its work. There are important lessons here for local curriculum development, especially where it is collaborative and long term. First, clarity about goals, processes and techniques is essential. Second, the choice of action strategies is important and the role of research has to be defined, if we are not to proceed with a great jumble of isolated and miscellaneous initiatives.

Some of these issues were finally recognized in the Schools Council when, in the review that took place in the late 70s, following the very damaging criticisms made in the Yellow Book and elsewhere, the Council proposed to strike out in rather different directions. It is not necessary for us to follow through the ensuing Programmes of Work, which in any case collapsed with the Council's closure, at a stage in their evolution when it was too soon to say how successful they might have been. The new strategy is of interest to us, though, since it seems to have picked up many of the difficulties of the earlier periods in such a way as to point directly towards school-based curriculum development as a likely pattern for the future.

A field orientation towards curriculum development

The new strategy adopted at the end of the 1970s by the Schools Council had three dimensions. First, there were constitutional changes in the Council: to bring in more community representation and better liaison with parents, employers, further and higher education; and to attempt to translate a vertical and hierarchical committee system into a lattice of 'different but equal' groups. Second, there were changes in management and staffing, with a more unified structure, the replacement of the troika – or joint – secretary system by a single chief executive, and (following the review) the introduction of more permanent posts into the Council. These changes are summarized in the Trenaman Report (DES 1981d). Third, a new orientation towards 'the field' was declared. This was presented in a slender and little-known document 'Principles and Programmes' (Schools Council 1979) soon after the new constitution was adopted. Reiterating its original partnership thesis, the Council said that 'the base for development will be strengthened and much more achieved if it works in partnership with other central and local, public and private agencies'. But how? And in what ways was this to be different from what had gone before? 'The Council', the paper went on, 'is also ready to adopt new methods of working to support local education authorities and schools more effectively, building into LEA management support and development systems, and helping schools to clarify and achieve their aims. In particular, the Council is committed to supporting local curriculum developments, and to working more closely with advisers, in-service trainers and HMI in developing and disseminating better practice in education.' Reference also was made to the Council's intention to strengthen its information and clearing house roles.

Personalities and roles cannot be separated from development programmes. In the post-1978 environment in the Schools Council the Chairman, Secretary and Deputy Secretary were, for the first time in the Council's history, all local education authority people. This symbolized, if it was not immediately responsible for, the progressive shift towards local development groups and small-scale enterprise, away from the large-scale, small-team projects (but we must keep this in perspective: even as late as 1983 these still constituted something like half of the Council's research and development effort in the curriculum). An example of this shift is to be found in Agnes McMahon's article in the *Readings*: the project known as GRIDS (Guidelines for Review and Institutional Development for Schools).

Within the five new programmes of work, there are many examples of local initiative, supported and focused through small-scale projects. The titles of the Programmes revealed a new interest in the constituent elements of the curriculum development process, as distinct from either applications through subject-centred projects or general curriculum policy issues – such as core or common curriculum. The programmes designated in 1979 were:

1. purpose and planning in schools;
2. the competence and effectiveness of individual teachers;
3. subjects and themes of curriculum for a changing world;
4. meeting the needs of individual students; and
5. assessment of students and improvement of examinations.
   (Schools Council 1979, 1982)

Further outcomes of the emphasis on within-school development are the three publications on processes of school review: *The Practical Curriculum*, *Primary Practice* and *Planning One-Year 16–17 Courses* (Schools Council 1981, 1983a, 1983b).

Together, these three papers present a unified view of planning, designing, developing, implementing and evaluating curricula which the Council regarded as relevant to all levels and stages of schooling. In each document, it is assumed that schools and colleges are, or need to be, engaged in systematic review, evaluation and development of their own curricula following a broadly common set of aims and adopting a common procedure. The processes are briefly outlined and guidance given in their applications and uses in different kinds of school and college situation.

It is ironic that only in its closing years was the Council able to bring together, in a single coherent set of linked documents, its proposals for how and why schools should undertake curriculum review, evaluation and development. Although individual projects, in many cases, attempted this for particular curricular areas, it had not previously been attempted across the whole curriculum, although there were the whole-curriculum policy papers produced by the Council in the mid-70s, and particular projects, such as the one dealing with aims in primary education, which gave advice on how teachers might think about aims and plan classroom work accordingly (Ashton et al. 1975a, 1975b; Schools Council 1975).

Reference was made, in the Council's 'Principles' statement of 1979, to 'better practice' in education. Since 'good practice' has become such a cliché in official statements on the curriculum we should ask not only how was 'better practice' to be disseminated but how were we to recognize it if we encountered it. A reflective analysis of 'good practice' requires us to relate action observed to purposes, effects and contexts, and to draw out and justify our criteria, our values and aims. The 'goodness' of any practice is neither self-evident nor uncontroversial. Is it good practice so to teach as to achieve high scores on reading tests and in external examinations? Does 'good practice' necessitate fieldwork, workshop experience and other kinds of explorations and applications across the whole curriculum? Is expository teaching bad practice? How are we to decide whether inquiry methods give good long-term results, or better – or worse – short-term gains than learning through didactic methods? One of the best sources of incipient, partially disclosed criteria relating to 'good practice' in the curriculum is the body of literature emanating from HMI since the mid-70s (DES 1977a, 1977d, 1978b, 1979b, 1979c, 1980b).

'Good practice' is not, however, only a matter of reflective analysis. What is crucial is the capability and the disposition to act – not only 'knowing the good' but 'doing the good'. Are projects and programmes of work intended to be examples and models to be adopted or, as Stenhouse suggested, proposals to be tested? School development groups will find the necessity to address this question, and a single institution faces a similar difficulty to that of a whole system: if 'good practice' is to be diffused throughout the school, there must be procedures for observation, close interchange of ideas and experience and a sense of a community with shared aims and aspirations. The staffroom of a large school may well contain, in miniature, the divergence of opinion, indifference or resistance to change that constitute one of the barriers to the spread of 'good practice' in the educational system as a whole.

The Schools Council, in adopting the 'good practice' cliché (which it did quite early in its history) may have provided many incentives to it and in its projects many examples of it – but, despite its intentions it was not very helpful to teachers in sorting out the aims, values and criteria upon which affirmation of good practice ultimately rest. For this a certain style of research and scholarship is required and development agencies and groups are usually too impatient for results to provide for this kind of reflectiveness and detachment. In the school setting, adequate time is needed for discussion and consideration of the purposes of the school and the relationships between action now and results later.

From the activities of the Schools Council over some two decades, much is to be learnt about curriculum development in all its facets and in many different settings. In this chapter, we have used the Council's aims, aspirations, achievements, and problems – its experience – to throw light on the evolution of curriculum development as a national enterprise. The intermingling of research and evaluation ideas, models and processes, of a team-based approach to development, of beliefs about correct sequences in a curriculum development process, and of alternatives to the prevailing wisdom has produced what is perhaps the most comprehensive single illustration of the challenges of curriculum development. The Council's own recognition of its difficulties and the need to change direction provides further elaboration of the development process: the pressure of events leading to a reassessment of style and approach, and experimentation with new approaches. But the Council was not the only performer on the national curriculum development stage with a major part to play in encouraging, supporting and guiding school-based curriculum development. After a long period of relative quiescence in curriculum matters, the officials of the Department of Education and Science, and Her Majesty's Inspectorate, have returned to their traditional powerful, if indirect, roles in school curriculum. As the Council declined in power, status and influence, so they have risen to prominence. In the next chapter we turn our attention directly towards the part they have come to play in the school curriculum.

Summary

In contemporary curriculum development, initiative, energy and resources have been concentrated in specialist agencies, usually of a national or regional dimension. The formation and funding of these agencies is itself a recognition that they have a key strategic role to play in identifying problems and needs in the educational system and in endeavouring to resolve the problems and meet the needs through planned action programmes undertaken on a large scale. Theories of change and development were drawn upon in establishing agencies; in turn their work in research, development projects and evaluation studies has generated rich experience from which ideas and theories about how to develop the curriculum have emerged.

The contrast often drawn between centralized, or 'top-down', and local, or 'grass roots', initiatives in curriculum development is oversimplified, or at least needs to be reassessed in light of the experience of curriculum development through national agencies. This and many other issues in curriculum development are illustrated in the work of one of the most active and influential of all national curriculum agencies, the Schools Council. Establishment of the Council gave rise to a variety of initiatives and dilemmas, central to which was an unresolved tension between school autonomy and freedom of choice, and large-scale research and development projects. The Council's partial adoption of the RDD model in its early years exemplifies the tension, which resurfaced in many different ways, between those who wanted schools to use and adopt the products of projects and those who saw the schools as themselves the primary agents of curriculum, using or ignoring Council projects at will. Successive attempts were made, both to reformulate the problem, as in the case of the Stenhouse Humanities Curriculum project, and to strengthen one or other pole: dissemination of procedures and products; enhancement of teachers as researchers and developers. Although the main arena in which these questions have arisen has been the Schools Council, its research and development projects and programmes of work, the issues themselves are not specific either to a research and development centre or a national-level agency. They have parallels and counterparts in curriculum decision making within the school.

CHAPTER 5

MOVES TOWARD A NATIONAL
CURRICULUM FRAMEWORK

'Wher-ever we come, and which way soever we look, we see something new,
something significant.' (Daniel Defoe, *A Tour Through the Whole Island of Great
Britain*)

Our discussion of the manner in which curriculum development has been
viewed and undertaken by the Schools Council over the two decades of its
history has raised questions about the relationship of ideas and initiatives in
the curriculum to changing directions in the education system as a whole.
The Schools Council, in giving detailed attention to the processes of curriculum change across the whole curriculum, provided schools with
opportunities and access to resources, and offered guidance on how to
change and develop the curriculum at any age or stage of schooling. Thus,
definite if quite optional leads were provided and an emerging pattern of
school curriculum–national system relationships may be discerned in the
Council's working and discussion papers and research reports, as well as in
its individual projects. Some crucial issues were left unresolved, notably the
uses schools generally were expected to make of project outcomes and the
capability of the Council to effect the kinds of development it wished to
foster. Moreover, the pattern just referred to was a matter of suggestion and
inference rather than an explicit formulation of policy by the Council itself.
All of this began to change quite dramatically from the mid-70s onwards.

For many people, the ambiguities and incompleteness of the Council's
stance in the curriculum were quite satisfactory since an impression was
thereby given of openness and diversity in the curriculum which could
nourish teacher freedom. Enthusiastic and energetic work going on right
across the curriculum: what more was needed? For critics and sceptics

alike, something was lacking. From the early official criticisms of the Council, in the Yellow Book and elsewhere, there grew an unease in Westminster and Whitehall about what, precisely, the role of the Council was. Academic critics had been openly sceptical from the inception of the Council on the grounds either that it was ineffectual or that it had a potential for dominance and manipulation.

In the 1970s a new style of criticism emerged: often covert, potentially very dangerous for the Council. This, coupled with strong and frequently stated misgivings about the politics of decision making in Council committees, undoubtedly contributed to its ultimate demise. However, long before the closure of the Council was announced in 1982 by the Secretary of State for Education and Science, Sir Keith Joseph, a gathering momentum of national-level curriculum activities outside and independent of the Council was pointing very definitely towards what can be regarded as an alternative way of relating school curriculum construction to the national education system. To this change, I have applied the term 'national curriculum framework'. Because the creation and operation of that framework is now manifestly a major object of official educational policy, and because in all of its components there are assumptions about or declared roles for the school in the curriculum, we must attempt to analyse it, try to explain its origins and consider its purposes, uses and limitations. School-based curriculum development has now moved into an era when action at the school level can no longer proceed independently of national-level activities (as in the heyday of the Schools Council it might have done) but must be construed and carried out with reference to an emerging set of policies and programmes – some prescriptive and all directed towards effecting changes and responses in schools. Although they are, for reasons of convenience, classified together as a national curriculum framework, the changes and influences are a loose amalgam with elements of explicit educational policy, social and technological change, and school practice.

The term 'national curriculum framework,' already mentioned in Chapter 1, needs explaining before its relevance to school-based curriculum developments can be teased out. Briefly, as used here the term 'framework' refers to the attempts being made, mainly by DES officials and HMI and government ministers, to establish national goals or objectives, a broadly agreed common or required curriculum and a reformed pattern of assessment of students. The framework is thus a structure, with definable content; it needs also to be treated as a process, amalgamating political, bureaucratic and professional purposes.

Where there is considerable initiative and sustained activity, including changed patterns of funding at the level of national policy for the curriculum, as there has been in Britain since the mid-70s, all schools will, eventually, experience its effects. Some are better prepared for this and more able to redefine their own roles than others. Adjustments to these emerging curriculum policies and to changed practices within the school will become inevitable. Knowing what is happening nationally, appreciating the forces and reasons behind it, and making well thought out appraisals are all necessary for effective management of curriculum change in schools. My contention is that the management and organization of school-based curriculum developments needs to change to take these tasks in hand. Those in leadership and management position in schools need this understanding and adaptability, but so do classroom teachers if they are to play a full and responsible part in school curriculum decisions. We ought not to assume, however, that the role of the school is simply responsive and adaptive: it has creative and constructive curriculum tasks to undertake, perhaps greater now than ever before.

Moves towards a national curriculum framework

In Britain, the idea of a national framework for the curriculum was, until quite recently, unfamiliar – although it is not without precedents if we think back to an earlier period in the history of national education. The construction of a new framework, although relatively recent, has moved to the point where it would be unwise for any school engaged in curriculum review, evaluation and development to ignore it. LEA curriculum initiatives, for example, even where only of a limited review-for-accountability type, are increasingly affected by the curriculum strategies of central government, as Ron Letch shows in the *Readings*. All schools are under an obligation to review and evaluate their curricula. (DES 1981b, 1983a)

On the more positive side, of evaluation for development, the emerging national framework provides useful ideas and guides to action. This is true even where there are serious weaknesses and gaps in that framework. Vigorous curriculum initiatives at the local level can be a means of addressing these gaps and weaknesses, leading in turn to modifications in the national plans, principles and programmes. Before looking more closely at all of this, we have some preliminary questions to consider. What are these national-level moves towards a framework and why are they taking place? What has led to the idea of a 'national curriculum framework' in a system where so much emphasis in the past has been given to local decision making? Are the moves towards a greater central role in curriculum making justifiable? In seeking answers to these questions we will also be considering whether there is a fundamental inconsistency between the idea of the framework and school-based curriculum development.

Several short quotations from a little-known House of Commons report give us a clue to what is now emerging as one of the most remarkable and fiercely debated changes ever to have occurred in curriculum making in Britain. The erection, from apparently very unpromising materials, of a government-sponsored national curriculum framework is a phenomenon of very recent origin. The House of Commons report in question dates only from the mid-70s. It is the *Tenth Report from the Expenditure Committee*. The theme, in the passages I have selected, is control:

> It is a generally accepted wisdom of the British educational system that the DES does not control the curriculum. The Education Act, 1944, places curriculum control in the hands of local authorities and the governing bodies of the schools . . . One observer of the education scene, Mr Stuart Maclure, (editor of 'The Times Educational Supplement') stated that 'the location of responsibility for curriculum and content is obscure, and governed less by law than by custom and myth. It seems inevitable that there should be, at some time in the future, an increase in public participation in the management of the public curriculum' . . . The DES, itself, would like to see the ambiguities attaching to the Secretary of State's position in relation to the curriculum clarified . . . We think *he (Secretary of State) should be prepared strongly to encourage and participate in educational development without seeking to control it.* In this, HMI would have a key role to play . . . The Committee does not share the view that the curriculum is a 'secret garden' which none but the initiated may enter. (Expenditure Committee of the House of Commons 1976, p. 7)

Seldom can so few thoughts expressed and exchanged in a parliamentary committee have presaged such a comprehensive displacement of curriculum assumptions, policies and structures as we have witnessed in the period since the Expenditure Committee had its say. The whole report is a most useful document for understanding the contemporary history of British education, at the national level. Our interest lies in its assessment of changes that needed to be made in the exercise of responsibility and the mechanisms that were to promote them. From the Expenditure Committee's statement, we may note several interesting themes:

1. The belief, mythical or otherwise, that curriculum is a local matter for schools and LEAs is identified.

2. Winds of change are stirring: customary beliefs are seen to be under challenge.
3. Interventionism is proposed: the DES wants a clearer, more definite curriculum role for the Secretary of State (and itself) – change needs to be guided.
4. Resurgent roles are identified: HMI (after years of publishing practically nothing on the school curriculum) can find a way for the Secretary of State to intervene, exercising responsibility but without controlling the curriculum.

Several studies in the politics of education – itself a relatively new field in Britain – have pointed up and documented the changes foreshadowed by the Expenditure Committee's Report (Becher and Maclure 1978; Kogan 1978; Lawton 1980; Salter and Tapper 1981). Curriculum policy has been shown to be susceptible to Ministerial intervention; the older style of partnership, involving an alliance of LEAs, teachers' unions and the Department, has been broken (most decisively with the closure of the Schools Council); HMI have come to play a prominent and powerful role in curriculum review and analysis; and there has been a definite – although by no means decisive – shift in the locus of control from a large and varied group of institutions, including schools, to a relatively small number of central sites, conspicuously the DES itself.

This enhancement of central power and authority in the curriculum has attracted strong criticism. For reasons already given, I think the criticism of the *principle* is unsatisfactory. The exercise by Parliament, the Government and appropriate Departments of State of authority in relation to national policy towards education requires that major aspects of the curriculum be taken up. The argument that all children need access, opportunities, resources and provision in respect of fundamentally important areas of knowledge, skill and understanding certainly raises the question of the role of central government, both in policy and resource terms. How the principle is exercised is, of course, another matter and there is plenty of room for criticism here, as we shall see. Let us not overlook, however, the manner in which central decision making in one part of education already functions. This is the further education sector where, as Gerald Fowler points out, there is a well-established role for central government.

Fowler's argument is that the government does in fact influence the curriculum, that it could do so in a more satisfactory manner and that open acknowledgement of the issue, with attention to improving ways and means, would be preferable to the myth of nonintervention which he dubs 'English compromise or English hypocrisy'. He continues, 'If administered sympathetically, a system offering more guidance about the curriculum need not detract from the freedom that teachers possess. Nor need it foster an undesirable uniformity: on the contrary, it could help to promote experiments in new directions and lead to more diversity than at present' (Fowler 1975). The argument is strong in principle but events since those words were written have to be examined for an assessment of the practice.

The Expenditure Committee Report is but one of several places where the stirrings of a new curriculum interventionist strategy were first heard. We have already mentioned the Yellow Book, whose acid comments on the Schools Council foreshadowed changes in that area. In 1975, there was the OECD Examiners' Report which, in its criticism of bureaucratic secrecy, opened up the question of how the powers of the Department ought to be exercised, given its relatively restricted direct authority over large parts of the education system (OECD 1975). It has been over at least a decade and through a succession of events, only some of them adequately documented as yet, and including speeches and meetings, reports, a policy statement, circulars, conferences, legislation and parliamentary manoeuvres, that the national curriculum framework can be seen to have emerged (Callaghan 1976; DES 1976, 1977a, 1977b, 1977c, 1977d, 1977f, 1978b, 1979a, 1979c, 1980a, 1980b, 1980d, 1981a 1981b, 1982a, 1983a, 1983b; Expenditure Committee of the House of Commons 1976; Joseph 1984a; OECD 1975b; Skilbeck 1981, 1982a).

It may be many years before the scope and implications of the changes now in progress can be assessed. Already, in the quite early stages, the moves known to have been taken and several of the key statements have been widely discussed and strongly criticized, both for the content of some of the proposals and, more often, because they are looked upon as unwelcome intrusion by central government which is destroying the older ideal of partnership. We need to take these criticisms into account, but more to our purpose is a reflective analysis of what these moves do or might mean in establishing a new sense of the roles *schools* have to play. So far from these roles having been curtailed or undermined, they are more demanding and challenging than ever. We shall see, as we examine the changes under way, that they imply for all but the most active schools a considerable increase in the scope, and a sharpening of the focus, of curriculum review, evaluation and development and a wider involvement of students, parents and the public than is common at present. The jobs to be done are not different in kind from what many schools are already familiar with, but they are being presented systematically as interrelated duties and responsibilities and are expected, eventually, to involve all schools in the country, not the minority who have pioneered self-evaluation and curriculum development. While the jobs may not differ in form or content they have a new meaning, since the frame of reference is no longer the individual school or LEA but the educational system and its place in society: this is an important shift in ideological terms affecting how schools' tasks and roles are perceived and evaluated.

Let us now see what the framework comprises. To do so, we shall not use either the chronological style of a succession of events or the ideological perspective of power and control. Our approach to the framework is to see it heuristically, as a kind of map or chart of curriculum proposals, functions and suggestions, a guide to be used in action. By seeing it thus, and giving it a reference to action, we can get a better understanding of how the framework may be used, and what its possibilities – and limitations – are in school curriculum making. We will notice weaknesses and problems but again our interest in them here is mainly as a kind of unfinished business which requires further attention if schools are to assume the responsibilities expected of them. This is not the same as saying schools need extra resources – which undoubtedly many do – in order to undertake what the policy makers understand by curriculum review, evaluation and development. Criticisms are useful in showing where those policy makers themselves have yet to sort out problems which are a direct consequence of their new roles in curriculum.

Diagrammatically, the national curriculum framework may be represented as areas in and for which action of specified kinds is to be undertaken, nationally and locally. Some of this action, as indicated, has been taken, in other cases much remains to be done even to establish the framework as a workable set of constructs. Active involvement by schools in the developing framework is itself a way of ensuring that that action is undertaken and that the problems that are already apparent do receive further attention. In turn, schools would need to have confidence that the framework is coherent and rational in its signification of the curriculum tasks that it indicates. Some critics have doubted this but have not produced convincing rebuttals (White et al. 1981).

Tables 5.1 and 5.2 are intended to pin-point a range of actual or proposed changes together with roles that are being performed and might be strengthened in various ways. From the tables we get a sense of the scale and

Table 5.1

Systemwide developments	*Proposed or possible school-level responses*
1. A situation calling for change has been defined	1. Reviews and evaluations of existing practice are required
2. Educational aims have been proclaimed	2. Formulation of curriculum aims and objectives is suggested
3. Outlines of required learnings for all have been proposed	3. Modification of curriculum structure and content is proposed
4. Assessment of students is under review	4. Modification of assessment practices is under consideration
5. Resources are being shifted in accordance with priorities	5. Allocation of resources for curriculum development is needed, but complicated by cuts, amalgamations etc.

Table 5.2

Local education authority roles	*Teacher education and educational R and D roles*
1. Linking national policy and school action	1. Linking academics, researchers, developers, students with national, LEA and school change
2. Organizing reviews	2. Reviewing, developing, researching, according to government priorities and moves in the curriculum
3. Constructing or fostering curriculum policy statements	3. Independently reviewing and evaluating curriculum policies and practices
4. Allocating resources	4. Collaborating with schools and LEAs
5. Managing the system	5. Proposing possible future developments in curriculum

comprehensiveness of the national framework, even though only the main elements are represented, leaving a lot of detail to be filled in. What is immediately apparent is the scale of the transformations that are occurring or are proposed, bearing in mind that the framework envisages action by *all* LEAs and *all* schools. In all of this, we must not overlook, either, the related changes occurring outside education, as for example financial relations between central and local government, or the opposition to what is happening in education coming mainly from local government bodies and teachers' unions. The framework is an interrelated set of arenas for action, where conflict and confrontation sometimes seem more evident than agreed and cooperative decision making. We cannot go fully into this here and even in discussing the framework as envisaged by national-level policy makers, will have to select only a few themes from those identified in the diagrams as systemwide in their applications.

A systemwide view of the curriculum

The aspects of the emerging central or systemwide view which we shall consider are:

- the definition of a situation calling for change
- stated educational aims
- the kind of overall curriculum proposed for all school learners
- proposals and procedures for assessment of learning.

The use of resources, identified in Tables 5.1 and 5.2 as one of the key elements in national policy and planning in the curriculum, is beyond the scope of this volume. Although rightly seen within the profession and local government as one of the most contentious of all issues, resource allocation in relation to a general policy of curriculum review, evaluation and development has scarcely been examined. Given the political and fiscal problems of defining an adequate level of funding for education, there is nevertheless scope within education budgets nationally and locally to give far more attention to curriculum issues than has been the case. 'Curriculum-led' staffing policies are one example; authoritywide proposals for a 'curriculum guarantee' or 'entitlement curriculum', are another.

Let us start our discussion of how the framework is being assembled with how a 'situation calling for change' was defined. The situation to which the Department of Education and Science has addressed itself is a mixture of officially defined conditions, achievements and shortcomings in schools, professional, public and political comments on schooling and changes in the social and economic environments. Taking the observed school conditions first, as noted in Chapter 3 we have experienced several decades of accelerating, systemwide change. Whether day-to-day practice in schooling changed radically is much more debatable, as the HMI surveys of primary and secondary education indicated (DES 1978b, 1979b). But changes there have been and certainly the education profession talked change, partly, as we have seen, because of the great organizational upheavals of the

1960s and early 70s, following abandonment of the 11+ and the introduction of comprehensive secondary education. Expansion of student
populations, the erection of new and often innovative school buildings, the
climate of curriculum change of which the Schools Council was the chief
manifestation, the reports of the Central Advisory Council and the Bullock
and Cockcroft Committees on aspects of primary and secondary education,
and a rapid succession of changes in the content and organization of teacher
education all contributed to a widespread belief that the system was on the
move and making progress, despite the turbulence. However, a series of
official and semiofficial reports pin-pointed problems and affirmed needs.
In their 1977, and 1979 reviews and surveys of secondary schools, while
they generally commended the state of secondary education, HMI commented on the wide disparities in staffing ratios and levels of qualification
among teachers; they criticized imbalances, excessive complexities and
overspecialization in the operation of the options system; they likewise
criticized inadequate curriculum provision for children with learning
difficulties, the dominance of external exams in the curriculum and the
inadequacy of preparation for 'living and working in the adult world'. Other
criticisms, too, were made which challenged the hierarchical but individualistic nature of much school curriculum decision making. Altogether,
for secondary schools, HMI called for many quite substantial changes in
curriculum practice and policy. This was summed up in the suggestion that
the time had come for 'a new rationale for the secondary school curriculum',
a simpler structure based on a broad common programme for all students,
with 'an acceptable range of variation' in the subjects studied and in content
within those subjects.

Although there is very little evidence that in making their assessments
HMI and others were drawing on other countries' experience, there are
some interesting parallels between their 'definition of a situation to be
changed' and 'directions for change' and those in some of the countries
participating in the late 70s and 80s in the OECD reviews of basic education
policies and practices (OECD 1983). Many of the countries participating in
the OECD study had centralized education systems and there were broad
economic and social similarities among them. We need not be surprised,
therefore, at the convergence in some of their views. It is interesting that,
despite the system differences, HMI comments frequently coincided with
those of other OECD countries. Common to these and other studies is an
interest in more critical appraisals of the whole curriculum; encouragement
to schools to be more self-critical, to undertake or share in review,

evaluation and development; and a quest for curriculum bench-marks, whether in the form of agreed aims, criteria and values or commonly agreed areas and forms of learning. More specifically, the sense of the inadequacy of the secondary school curriculum to changing social circumstances, economic changes and the needs and interests of individuals and groups is all but universal. Thus, schools are called upon to overhaul, discard and renew subject matter and to practise a wider range of teaching procedures: in short, to be less academic in content, style and approach.

In Britain, action called for was national, but also local, in that HMI claimed that individual schools and LEAs, too, could achieve much by 'evaluating their own policies and practices, identifying priorities for future development and deciding where a start can be made' (DES 1979b, chapters 12 and 13). The situation was not one where nothing could be done locally until grand designs were drawn up centrally.

Turning to the official assessment of primary school curricula, an equally strong critique emerged from what seems, at first glance, to be an analysis that is generally supportive of the status quo. In that no fundamental structural changes were recommended the HMI Primary Survey (DES 1978b) did appear to leave things to a considerable extent as it found them. Maurice Holt laconically remarks, 'the survey gives a picture of primary schools as being worthy places, but perhaps rather dull' (Holt 1983b, p. 16).

Events since the publication of the Primary Survey suggest that it is not at this level that the national curriculum framework is generating most interest, activity – or criticism. Blenkin and Kelly, commenting on change in the primary curriculum throughout the 1960s and 70s, remarked that 'Primary teachers have not been expected until very recently to respond to the same dramatic administrative and political demands that have been made of their secondary colleagues'; and that 'it may be seen as fortunate that they were, for a large part of this period, left to develop in their usual evolutionary manner' (1981, p. 140). Elsewhere in their book these authors show how some important moves, nationally, did something to upset the even tenor of primary education, including the Plowden Report, NFER and APU testing programmes and some of the Schools Council projects, notably Aims of Primary Education, and the much publicized Bennett research study (Bennett 1976; Dawson 1984).

The Department's Primary Survey, despite its apparent even-handedness as between more traditional curriculum approaches to timetabled subject teaching and more progressive, integrated and interest-based approaches, did contribute quite firmly to the emerging view that clear aims and goals and definite learning attainments needed to be specified. This general tendency was reinforced in the subtle shift of emphasis away from the child as such, as found in the Plowden Report, and towards structures for the content and organization of the curriculum conceived as areas of experience, understandings, skills and values; the advantages for pupils of their teachers having specialized curriculum responsibilities and the problem of balancing this with the recommended model of class teaching; the need for maintaining a balanced curriculum in small schools (declining rolls) and the general problem of how to raise teacher expectations of the performance of children. Two additional points stand out:

1. the Primary Survey was carried out in parallel with NFER surveys of children's reading and mathematics performances and it incorporated those survey findings – it was using research as part of its own analytic framework;
2. the authors of the report called for what the Primary Chief Inspector, Norman Thomas, termed a 'consensus curriculum', which is perhaps a move towards a common and a planned curriculum going beyond what the individual school determines.

Thomas was at pains to point out, however, that any attempts to be more systematic in the planning of the curriculum would need to avoid children 'working through more series of exercises . . . On the contrary, what is advocated is that the necessary skills and ideas should be clearly identified and taught in a context that enables the children to see the point of learning them' (Thomas 1979). These innocuous remarks sounded like a cautious but definite edging away from one of the most powerful of all ideologies in the education of young children, that which sets 'the child' as a phenomenon around which the curriculum is constructed (Boas 1966; Gammage 1982, chapter 1; Kirby 1981, chapter 3). What was therefore coming under question, however indirectly, was that each school should evolve a curriculum through creative encounters between children and teachers, without seeming to succumb to systemwide curriculum planning and design with predefined objectives, courses of study and performance standards. These may have been no more than straws in the wind in the Primary Survey but when seen in the context of the official reports and statements of the period they are indicative of a new trend. Nothing resembling the systematic attempts made by John Dewey to reconcile child-centrism, social movements and subject content emerges from the Survey or any of the official statements on the curriculum during this period.

The Primary Survey did, nevertheless, suggest that the school's role in curriculum making would be important for future actions and it called for a whole-curriculum, not merely a subject-by-subject approach. Significantly, and for the first time for decades, specific and detailed attention was given to performance scores in the context of a generalized belief that 'things could be better'. In these ways, the Primary Survey, if less sharply and definitely than the Secondary reports, made its contribution to the emerging national curriculum framework. The primary curriculum, as a result, is now very firmly anchored, through declared and clear aims, well structured, defined areas and sequences of learning, and systemwide assessments of student performance. As a consequence, when HMI issued their general statement on the whole curriculum in *A View of the Curriculum* (DES 1979c) they proposed, for the primary (as well as the secondary) school:

1. common, or systemwide aims and purposes;
2. a broad curriculum defined by 'areas of experience' and picking up particular 'gaps' such as science;
3. greater attention to the needs of specified groups of children, notably the abler ones;
4. systematic attention to assessment.

Schooling under question

It is worth recalling that schooling in Britain was being widely criticized throughout the 1970s. Before proceeding to the statements about 'a situation to be changed' in two key DES 'framework' documents of the early 80s and the subsequent steps taken to implement them, we should briefly note the scope and scale of this criticism, paying attention to a couple of points that are directly relevant to our present theme. Prime Minister Callaghan's Ruskin College speech in 1976 was but one of several widely published criticisms (Becher and Maclure 1978; Kogan 1978). He charged schools with being out of touch with the 'reasonable' needs of society and called for higher standards in literacy and numeracy and in personal relations, for better school–industry links, a greater technological bias in science teaching and more encouragement to girls to study science subjects. He wanted schools to do more to allay public anxieties about teaching methods and content, and his speech presaged a national move towards a common core in the curriculum and common performance standards (Callaghan 1976).

Foreshadowed by the leaked Yellow Book and absorbed into the Great Debate which he launched, Callaghan's speech is easily passed over lightly. But, seen against events since, it can be appreciated now as another decisive turning-point in the emergence of the framework. A prime-ministerial speech on the curriculum is a rare event and the occasion was well used by officials to achieve both political backing for and public notice of the national strategy for change that was just beginning to come together. Another aspect of the speech is its capturing of the flavour and part of the substance of the spirited (and frequently biased) criticism of public education made in the late 60s and well into the 70s in the education *Black Papers* – one of whose principal authors, Rhodes Boyson, subsequently carried his attacks on school practice into Parliament and the Government. The *Black Papers*, very much in the style of and using several of the arguments advanced in American critiques of progressive education in the 1950s, alleged a decline in standards of student attainment, attributing this to child-centred methods in primary schooling and the introduction of comprehensive secondary schools and innovative curricula (*Black Papers* 1969–77). They attacked what they characterized as left ideological infiltration of schools and teacher education; and they called for firmer discipline, greater orthodoxy in the curriculum – as in more emphasis on teaching traditional subjects through didactic methods – and more stringent testing and examining not least in the primary school. They, too, like Prime Minister Callaghan, wanted schools to be more adaptive to social, technical and industrial needs and to be steered away from socially and culturally reconstructive values.

Thus there was, throughout the whole of the 1970s, a constant background buzz of well-orchestrated criticisms of education innovations, with wide press coverage and, it seems, growing public support. Politicians were sensitive to these criticisms and it is reasonable to assume that they were read in official quarters, as evidence that changes in style and direction of curriculum and assessment towards greater central control would, at the very least, not provoke a hostile public response. This has proved to be the case.

We have considered a selection of the surveys, reports and commentaries of the late 60s and 70s on primary and secondary school curricula which indicate an interpretation of events and trends in schooling and a consistent line of criticism. The criticism of schooling, the debates – and indeed the surveys – had about them a distinctive ideological colouring.

In the first place, many of the faults and weaknesses attributed to schools, especially by the critics, were shown through empirical investigations to hold true of only a relatively small number. Press publicity had dramatized and highlighted particular instances of difficulty which were not typical; the schools were much more stable and in a sense ordinary than their critics alleged; and the great bogey of 'declining standards' was revealed as a myth when it was eventually shown that there was no evidence of a worthwhile kind to sustain the alarmist allegations. The critics were not satisfied, however, and turned previous allegations of declining standards into new demands for 'higher standards', commensurate with increased rates of public spending on schooling.

In the second place, there was a convergent set of themes in the research analyses and surveys, with a discernible emphasis on the kinds of curriculum issues being publicly debated at the time. Consistent use was made by the critics of arguments which featured subject-centred learning and a greater concern for formality in planning and evaluating the curriculum, structuring and organizing learning and assessing students, than the informal and process approaches usually identified with progressivism in education. In other words, what was surveyed as 'curriculum' and recommended for 'curriculum change' was a mixture of fairly traditional ideas about curriculum as an assemblage of subject content under separate subject headings, and the planning and management of curriculum change conceived as a system of derivations – starting with affirmed national needs and proceeding to educational goals, curriculum objectives, classroom learnings and, ultimately, assessments of performance. These ideological preferences or predilections, however inchoate they remained in the documents and speeches, gave to the concept of a national curriculum framework a very distinctive tone and it is this more than anything else that has caused its critics to deplore its 'centralism' and 'managerialism' and 'retreat from progressive values and practices'. These criticisms are themselves partial but they have not been adequately met and are likely to continue as long as the more fundamental ideological and values issues are ignored in the official responses and proposals.

At the same time as the official surveys of schooling and the debates over curriculum standards and needs were occurring, Britain was receiving a great deal of internal attention and international comment on its economic performance. Industrial relations, manufacturing and exporting problems, declining terms of trade, rising inflation and general economic stagnation or worse resulted in a barrage of negative assessments and gloomy prognostications. The aftermath of the oil crisis, local government reorganization, the IMF salvage operation, adverse OECD commentaries, including the critical observations on the management of the national education system and the relationship of schooling to working life, strife in Northern Ireland, complicated manoeuvering on EEC membership – all contributed to a general sense of rapid, undigested change and unresolved, chronic problems, malaise and even crisis, in which political and administrative issues were never very far below the surface.

Relationships between these social, economic, political and administrative pressures on the one hand, and educational policies and practice on the other, are not easy to sort out. It may be an oversimplification to try to establish direct links. As we have seen, criticisms had been made of innovation in school curriculum before this great mass of social and economic issues surfaced in the early 70s. Thereafter, however, a direct coincidence between these events in the wider society and education was discernible. It was not long before education itself began to be singled out as a contributory factor in Britain's troubles. This criticism, never worked out in any depth and often quite incoherent, has been reiterated many times and is part of the explanation for the large-scale youth training programmes of the Manpower Services Commission. Largely the responsibility of the employment and industry sectors of government, not education, these programmes are avowedly an attempt to compensate for the alleged inadequacies of schooling.

Toward new school roles

What follows from all this dissent over education is a tendency for government priorities for the curriculum to be phrased in a language that is becoming increasingly congenial to those who wish to see education, and hence the curriculum, used in pursuit of goals of social utility and economic efficiency. The particular usages are often crass, but is the idea of relating a national curriculum framework to the wider concerns, aspirations, goals and needs of the society such a strange one? On the contrary, not to try to relate school curriculum to the culture and the society would be myopic and indeed quite unrealistic. The problem is that of working out the social role of the school in a situation of strong ideological conflict and competing bids for control of the curriculum. Is the curriculum, in social terms, intended to be reproductive and reflective of the status quo; is it to be a means of anticipating and preparing for an unknown and unknowable future; is it to be one of the means of reconstructing or developing society – and, if so, whose vision of the future is to prevail?

It is difficult if not impossible for central government and its agencies to address these awkward and rather abstract questions directly. The answers come out indirectly and gradually a pattern emerges from which we can draw inferences about how the role of the school in the curriculum is being perceived. Thus, by advocating such interventionist strategies as positive multicultural programmes and better provision in the education of girls, or universal science teaching in the primary school, governments in recent years have picked up problems in the larger society and tried to encourage schools to play a leadership role in solving or ameliorating them. Examples are given in the *Readings*, by Lesley Kant and Alma Craft. Greater emphasis also is being given to specific in-service programmes including management training for heads. All of this points towards a view of the school curriculum not merely as reflective or reproductive of some predefined social order (which it may be in practice) but as reconstructive in intent. This issue has been, unfortunately, obscured by both a lack of clarity and consistency in overall policies and a continuing struggle or debate, rather, over control, and by indecisiveness about the direction of change for the whole curriculum. While this debate may be inevitable at the national level, as schools and local education authorities become more extensively engaged in socially critical analyses of the curriculum the issue of reproduction versus reconstruction will undoubtedly emerge. The school's definition of the situation to be changed, to which we shall return in Chapter 8, will be vitally affected by its judgement of this issue. Clarity and consistency may prove just as troublesome for schools as for national policy makers (Kemmis et al. 1983).

We have seen that the 'secret garden' of the curriculum, once entered, ceases to be a sheltered enclave. It has already lost its professional mystique. Not only can schools and professional educationists no longer regard it as their exclusive preserve, they must be alert to the evolution and development of national policy if their own roles are to be intelligently and flexibly handled. Conversely, central government officials and ministers have taken on a task of defining and implementing major new curriculum policies without, it seems, all the authority that will be required to see them through and with very little resource flexibility. It is not surprising that the moves now under way should seem to fall well short of a decisive and clear-cut set of initiatives. We must bear in mind that what is determined as the national framework in the early 1980s is not something fixed and settled but will continue to evolve. Given the shared responsibility for education in Britain it is always likely to be of a broad general character. Schools and LEAs will therefore continue to have a major role in giving substance to national curriculum policies. This means, for school principals and those with overall curriculum responsibility in schools and LEAs, greater attention to, and attempts at forecasting, trends, and the building up of curricula that have a future reference. For this purpose, we must try to see the directions of policy, not merely its history and present state.

The national framework 1. A situation defined

Turning from criticisms of schooling and official responses by way of new school roles, to the *content* of the national framework, we have first to see how the DES, in the light of the foregoing, has itself construed the educational situation that needed changing. Two key documents are the 1980 consultative paper *A Framework for the School Curriculum*, and its 1981 successor *The School Curriculum* which was published as government policy and followed up in departmental circulars.

The consultative paper *A Framework for the School Curriculum* is flimsy and incomplete; it is not in the least surprising that it was heavily criticized by the education profession and is regarded within the Department itself as very inadequate. It gives only the sketchiest of rationales for change and quickly passes over school–wider-society relations as a basis for curriculum analysis, a topic of much concern earlier. Despite its flimsiness, *Framework* is a document of the utmost importance in the emerging national curriculum framework. *Framework* reaffirms the positions taken by the Department in its 1979 *Report on Circular 14/77 Review* (of local authority curriculum arrangements), that Ministers of Education have a responsibility under the Education Acts to ensure that schools are matching their work to national needs, that partnership is necessary to effect an 'agreed view' of the curriculum, that LEAs must 'exercise leadership and interpret national policies and objectives in the light of local needs and circumstances' and that in their direction and conduct of the curriculum within the school, governors, head teachers and staff must work together with the closest possible cooperation (DES 1980a, p. 1).

The consultative paper goes on to treat policies and decisions on the curriculum as decisive for the provision of building and equipment, staff, teaching and learning resources and such support items as teachers' centres and in-service training – all within 'resources available for public expenditure as a whole', a predictable, if circular, rider. Basically, the paper is attempting to use the curriculum as a focus for educational policy, so it is devoted mainly to a review of aims, an overall structure for the curriculum and the role of key subjects – which are identified as English, mathematics and science, modern languages, religious education, physical education and (in Wales) Welsh language.

These subject areas were picked up again in *The School Curriculum*, though without much more being added. What we can infer from their inclusion and treatment is that the official view of the curriculum is grounded in existing school subjects: they are the basic building blocks. On the other hand, the treatment of subject matter, the content of the blocks, was felt to require quite considerable changes. Without going into further detail, these changes were a mixture of the kinds of pedagogical reforms proposed in the surveys of HMI, and of the doctrine of social utility, in that the contents of subjects like mathematics and English were regarded as potentially valuable in children's *future* lives in a changing society. This theme had come out strongly in the Regional Conferences in England during February and March 1977, when the DES organized the 'Great Debate in Education' in the aftermath of Callaghan's speech, and it has recurred ever since (DES 1977f).

True to its own brand of utility, where schooling becomes the means of meeting projected future rather than felt present needs of individuals and of serving the labour market, the concluding section of the consultative paper *A Framework for the School Curriculum* claimed a place in the curriculum, for every student at some stage or another, for a whole string of subjects and topics under the broad heading of 'preparation for adult and working life'. The most important situational requirement to be met by school curricula, it would seem, was that they should be oriented towards the future with a clear bias towards future working life. 'The Secretaries of State consider that substantial attention should be given at the secondary stage to the relationship between school work and preparation for working life' (ibid. p. 8).

This doctrine of 'schooling for working life' has formed the basis of a very substantial set of changes in the education and training of adolescents and young adults which falls outside the scope of our discussion here. But mention must be made of the shortsightedness of this diagnosis, given the impending collapse of the youth labour market. Neither on educational grounds nor for reasons of social utility can it be regarded as a satisfactory foundation stone, even allowing for the possibility that a policy of training for all school leavers (16+) might alleviate the youth unemployment situation and hence be regarded as a rational policy. This, by the way, has not been demonstrated. Education must have a future reference, yet it must also draw upon the experiences of the past, its focus is the present life and felt needs and interests of the learner, and its concerns touch upon wide and varied aspects of human learning. The school curriculum would be unduly constricted if 'preparation for future work' or even 'preparation for future life' were to edge out these considerations.

I have criticized the preparation doctrine on the grounds that in its particular form of projecting working life and certain adult responsibilities it is too restrictive. Not only may the predictions about 'the future' prove false, the means chosen in light of them are likely to be too narrow. This difficulty might be lessened if we were to engage in comprehensive, not partisan, projections, speculations and forecasts – as proposed by Richard Slaughter in the *Readings*. Even so, the separation of the present lived experience of the child and youth from some hypothesized future state of society has always provoked educational disquiet: human action in the future is a progressive realization and fulfilment of present experience and activity, Dewey points out (Dewey 1916, chapter 8); the present experience cannot be sacrificed in the expectation that tasks done now will gain their rewards later, as Rousseau says (Rousseau 1911 translation, pp. 42–3). In adopting this explicit thesis of preparation, the Department has moved away from one of its own long-standing educational principles, reiterated – and with good reason – by innumerable inspectors and advisers. In the words of one of the nineteenth-century inspectors: 'The most important truth of educational reformers is this, that in discussing the subjects of instruction you must consider the child's present needs first of all, – its future and contingent occupation only in the second place. You must not set the end of the child's education entirely outside the daily life of the child' (Rooper 1907, p. 112).

This has been part of the creed of the liberal curriculum for centuries and acceptance of it entails neither a disregard of the future nor a neglect of structured knowledge. The best preparation for an uncertain future is a sound general education that engages the present interest of learners. There are many factors to be brought together in achieving this. The Department has failed on this most crucial point, to show the way towards a new educational relationship among these factors. As a consequence of adopting a restricted view of the role of education, focusing it too much on preparation to meet a particular set of future social requirements, the DES in *The School Curriculum* gave too much prominence to subjects and subject matter which, valuable in themselves, yield only part of a well-rounded education.

In subsequent chapters I suggest that considerations such as emotional and physical development, environmental and political education, education for leisure and experience of the arts must also be given attention. The DES has been too narrow in its assumption of 'a situation to be changed', hence its curriculum analysis is shallow.

Preoccupation with preparation for working life has proved to be a dubious practical principle in an era of large-scale youth unemployment. There could be no greater irrelevance in the secondary curriculum than the ordering of studies according to the single or dominant criterion of 'working life'. It is a cause for satisfaction that this criterion has not been the dominant motif throughout the whole range of reports and statements which provide the basis of the national curriculum framework: the 'preparation' thesis has been given greater prominence in certain parts of the rhetorical presentations than in the design as a whole.

Let us now turn to *The School Curriculum*. We have, in the opening paragraphs of this highly influential, if rather unpopular, policy paper the clearest possible assessment of the situation into which the national curriculum framework is to be set. The emphasis is once more upon education as preparation for adult life. Starting with a nod in the direction of 'the fundamental aim that education should serve the individual needs of every pupil and student', the Secretaries of State continue:

> Since school education prepares the child for adult life, the way in which the school helps him to develop his potential must also be related to his subsequent needs and responsibilities as an active member of our society. Parents, employers and the public rightly expect the school curriculum to pay proper regard to what the pupils will later want and be called upon to do. It helps neither the children, nor the nation, if the schools do not prepare them for the realities of the adult world.
>
> Indeed, the future of the children in the schools and of the country depends heavily on what the schools have been able to do for them. In an increasingly competitive world economy, and with the prospect of ever more rapid changes arising from technological developments, especially in computer science and information technology, the quality of school education will become even more important than it already is. (DES 1981a, p. 1)

The view of the world presented here is partial. For example, international cooperation, as Helen Connell argues in the *Readings*, must also have a place. Furthermore, the Secretary of State's thesis is that the school's task is preparation of the child for adult life, and yet this is to be reconciled with individual needs which may be very immediate and personal, where 'wants' rub shoulders with 'realities' and 'needs' with 'responsibilities'. There is much to puzzle over in these elliptic paragraphs and the document has been rightly criticized for its conceptual weaknesses as well as its ideological slant (White et al. 1981).

One of the most interesting criticisms of *The School Curriculum* came from the National Union of Teachers, who challenged the capability of Secretaries of State to determine national needs as a basis for the curriculum and rejected the effort to ground these proposed needs in a national consensus. What was needed, they said, was 'pluralistic decision making and resource allocation, not centralist solutions which may be irrelevant or inappropriate to local needs and circumstances' (National Union of Teachers 1981, p. 2). This criticism gets at the nub of the official position since the whole national curriculum framework exercise, in a democracy, depends upon consent, agreement or consensus over some fundamental goals. It would not be necessary to have achieved this consent in advance, but the framework should itself provide the means and point the way towards achieving it and this it has not done.

The explanation for the central weakness of *The School Curriculum* lies in the nature of the exercise itself which was not in fact a quest for universal assent to something being worked out in partnership and through dialogue, but a response at the official level to a particular, rather controversial and unavoidably political critique of the disjunction between school curriculum and trends in social and economic affairs. This contrasts with the more familiar professional and theoretical curriculum analyses which take as their starting point structural analyses of culture and society and the reconstructive and critical roles of schools (Lawton 1983; Reynolds and Skilbeck 1976), or the identification of fundamental transforming forces like science and democracy and their impact on everyday life (Dewey 1916), or a developmental view of the child and his needs in a particular historical setting (Rousseau 1911), or indeed the areas of experience approach adopted in *A View of the Curriculum* by HMI (DES 1979c). We should not, of course, look to a brief policy outline to provide us with analyses of a kind appropriate to sociological or philosophical treatises on education. *The School Curriculum* is a policy statement, not an educational theory. For this very reason, it cannot stand alone as a guide to national curriculum policy. It is too sketchy, for one thing; it is also, as we have seen, questionable in many of its assumptions about the functions of schooling and the bases of curriculum action in schools. For purposes of school curriculum making much more than this kind of paper is needed. While we must bear in mind the inevitable partialities and limitations of any government policy paper on the curriculum, when we try to work through the implications of that policy in so far as they relate to school practice, we run into difficulty. The policy paper is not in itself a basis for action or a clear guide to practice; rather, it is a declaration of intent and can serve as a means of legitimating subsequent action (as in the case of the circulars requiring schools to review their curricula and define their aims).

We have seen how, over several years and through a vigorous and sustained programme of reviews, reports, conferences, surveys, studies and policy statements, governments in Britain have come to a set of conclusions about a national curriculum situation in need of change. My remarks on these developments have been necessarily selective: much has been omitted and the picture is in reality more complex than how it is presented here. A retrospective overview of the kind we have been engaging in can confer order, sequence and interrelationships on viewpoints and events that, as they evolved, followed rather separate and different courses. Another point to keep in mind is that the period we have been considering has witnessed quite dramatic changes in the fortunes of governments and political parties. These have certainly lent a colouring to events, even when they have not basically altered their direction. And, finally, let us not forget that the situation for change as defined officially is not necessarily the situation as perceived by different nonofficial groups in the community, nor by local government nor by the teaching profession at large.

The old consensus has dissolved or been fractured and the historic concept of partnership has given way to a more confrontationist style of relationship. The 'official' definition of a national curriculum scene and the consequent calls made for changing it must therefore be kept in perspective – they can be regarded as but one of the factors in the total situation, to which schools need to attend in their own policy planning. This does not mean, as is often assumed, that official policies on the curriculum can be safely ignored in practice. On the contrary the DES is one part of our educational system which is manifestly expanding, growing in power and influence and able to generate and focus a great amount of curriculum activity. We cannot respond merely by criticizing the trend, observing limitations in the analysis and hoping that the fuss will die down.

The School Curriculum may be, as its critics have argued, a thoroughly confused document. This has not prevented officials from using it as the bench-mark in a series of moves directly involving LEAs and schools in curriculum review, evaluation, and development. The circulars of 1981 and 1983 calling upon schools and LEAs to review and evaluate, define aims, and begin to adjust their curricula in the ways outlined in *The School Curriculum* are but part of the follow-through which may be expected in the years ahead to lead to a very different style of curriculum making in schools from what we have known in the past. Similarly, the responses to all of this by some LEAs, such as the Borough of Croydon (Croydon Education Committee 1984), is to assume an authoritywide role in the curriculum which will, if successful, put schools into a quite different set of relationships with local councillors and officials, governing bodies, parents and community groups. Likewise, the effects of the 1980 Education Act, requiring LEAs to provide for parents information on school curricula, discipline, examination results and so forth will result in a shift in curriculum power relations.

The national framework 2. Educational aims and objectives

So much for a situation of change; what of the aims and objectives for the curriculum which have been proposed? A search through the official literature would give us a large and perhaps unwieldy set of aims if only because much of the discussion, especially by HMI, has inferred or implied aims that have been taken for granted or only partially spelt out. Aims are not only explicitly stated; they are also implicit in curriculum proposals, in our ways of addressing curriculum issues and exchanging views about them, and, most of all, they are emergent in our actions in designing, developing and implementing curricula. So, weight has to be given to aims as an outgrowth of activity, as Dewey said, as distinct from statements for, about and outside the activity itself (Dewey 1916, chapter 8). There are immanent aims within the national curriculum framework which will become clear only as the processes of constructing and acting upon it continue in the years ahead.

The separation of aims and objectives, conceived as ends, from curriculum design and programmes, conceived as means, is unwise if not positively dangerous. Yet there has been a growing interest in formal statements of aims and objectives as part of the curriculum process. They help in indicating intentions, pointing towards action to be taken and inviting dialogue about the nature and purpose of the curriculum. Cynics may say that all of this is purely symbolic or ritualistic: aims and objectives, once stated, are immediately forgotten except when a question is asked, or are conveniently rephrased when unexpected results occur:

We've all heard about clarifying our objectives over and over again. But what happens? You set up a course. You write down an ambitious list of objectives. The course is a great success but when you come to apply the tests you find it hasn't attained the objectives. So what do you do? You change the objectives. (Maclure 1968, p. 46)

The reference is to course objectives and the speaker, an American partici-pant at an international curriculum conference, had in mind the objectives model of course planning which we discuss in Chapter 8. But when the aims are stated more globally, other kinds of criticism are made: the aims are at such a level of generality or ambiguity as to be of no practical utility or they deflect attention from the matter of procedures: *how* we implement aims being held to be the crucial point (Peters 1959).

Do we therefore need aims and objectives? Is the whole enterprise of outlining aims within the national curriculum framework mistaken? Not at all; there are uses, for aims statements, either as a critical device, wherein they may be applied evaluatively or questioningly to actual programmes or performances, or as directions or guidelines for the preparation of cur-riculum designs and programmes. The problem with aims is not their formation as such but an unwillingness to phrase them so as to relate them systematically to action – a process which can be supportive of the action by structuring it. In practice, this means getting greater clarity and coherence into the statement of aims, expressing them operationally or with reference to procedures and taking them seriously in action. Thus, a well-constructed set of aims should be part of every school's curriculum plan.

Within the national curriculum framework, there are explicitly stated aims which schools can use in constructing their aims. In *The School Curriculum*, they are presented as an outcome of earlier work, as a system-wide guide to action, 'as a checklist against which local authorities and schools can test their curricular policies and their application to individual schools' and as a starting point for individual authorities and schools in drawing up their own aims statements (DES 1981a, pp. 3–4).

This seems a reasonable approach for school-based curriculum develop-ment just because it is treating the aims themselves as provisional and inviting schools and LEAs to take the kind of action through which the aims themselves can be critically reflected upon, developed and, in the course of time, restated. The aims listed in *The School Curriculum* (ibid. p. 3) are:

(i)   to help pupils to develop lively, enquiring minds, the ability to question and argue rationally and to apply themselves to tasks, and physical skills;

(ii) to help pupils to acquire knowledge and skills relevant to adult life

and employment in a fast-changing world;
(iii)   to help pupils use language and number effectively;
(iv)   to instil respect for religious and moral values, and tolerance of other races, religions, and ways of life;
(v)   to help pupils understand the world in which they live, and the inter-dependence of individuals, groups and nations;
(vi)   to help pupils to appreciate human achievements and aspirations.

The list has been criticized, for example by John White who argues that it is incoherent, lacks priority and leaves open the question as to what kind of educated person is presupposed by these rather general expressions (White et al. 1981, pp. 10–14). It is, however, wrong to look upon policy statements as if they were educational treatises. They often make points of a rhetorical kind, use language which refers to a current political position, and have to try to reconcile or hold together in a single document diverse and perhaps conflicting views on matters of current concern. This does not condone confusion or incoherence but it does mean that we need not be unduly concerned about some roughness at the edges. After all, the aims are approximate and schools are expected to get to work on them. The aims may be inadequate, but are they educationally objectionable? It is not at all clear that there is, as alleged, a narrow or repressive vision of life and development behind the aims. Despite the rhetorical emphasis given elsewhere in the document to preparation for adult (working) life, the aims as stated here do not have that kind of bias and could be more readily criticized for their individualistic assumptions and for insufficient attention to communal values and a common or shared way of life. It is precisely this bias which David Hargreaves has drawn attention to in his critique of comprehensive schooling (Hargreaves 1982, chapter 4).

Let us compare the DES aims with those proposed in one of the most persuasive of educational reports in recent years, that of the Warnock Committee, on special educational needs. The aims of education are said to be:

> first, to enlarge a child's knowledge, experience and imaginative understanding, and thus his awareness of moral values and capacity for enjoyment; and secondly, to enable him to enter the world after formal education is over as an active participant in society and a responsible contributor to it, capable of achieving as much independence as possible. (DES 1978a, p. 5)

These aims are more felicitously stated than those in *The School Curriculum* and they draw attention to important educational considerations that the Department's own document neglects, such as children's experience, imagination and enjoyment, and their capacity for independence. None of these can be supposed to be specific to the handicapped children and young people who were the subject of the Warnock Report. They are concerns that ought to feature in all general statements of educational aims. However, allowing for the slightly different focus of the Warnock aims, they have much in common with those outlined in *The School Curriculum*. Together, they give an account of expectations of education in which, despite the rather cramped and narrow utilitarian character of some of the earlier official statements on the curriculum, there is a very marked emphasis on a broad, liberal education for all with a rather modest role for 'preparation' for adult working life. After all the soul-searching about the state of the nation, the quality of schooling, the shortcomings of pedagogical innovations and the country's need for skilled labour, the aims sound very much like what thoughtful and imaginative teachers would hope for from all of their students, whatever the state of the economy! As so often happens in curriculum documents, the stated aims do not have any clear and firm relationship to the analysis made of the situation to which they are intended to apply. We shall see that this is true also of the proposed curriculum content. In the case of *The School Curriculum*, the rhetoric of the aims is preferable to the social and educational diagnosis.

Before moving from the government's statement of aims let us recall its status. It is, first, part of an official policy document; second, it is a statement that the Secretaries of State have *offered* to schools and LEAs for use in drawing up their own aims statements; third, it is *commended* as a checklist, whereby schools and LEAs can evaluate their own policies and practice. The aims might be seen, therefore, as a springboard for further action, notably by schools. They could also be reflected back into the DES itself, as a contribution to evaluating the direction, consistency and adequacy of its own curriculum enterprises, in whatever shape and form. As far as the curriculum is concerned, the translation of aims into proposals for curriculum content and classroom procedures has been disappointing in its lack of imagination or even knowledge of what many schools are already doing to reform the curriculum.

The national framework   3. Required learnings for all

The third strand in the national curriculum framework comprises the outlines of a required – or perhaps a recommended – curriculum for all students. At present, the government lacks the necessary authority to require of all schools and LEAs that they should construct and implement curricula to conform to this outline, although, in the circulars requiring schools and LEAs to review their curriculum, it 'expects' them to take cognizance of the curriculum outlined in *The School Curriculum*. A further influence is being exerted through the very active and increasingly interventionist style being adopted throughout the Department: by officials, HMI, Ministers and Secretary of State – and as reflected in commissioned research and development and training programmes including the inservice education of teachers.

What kind of curriculum, then, are schools expected to provide? In very general terms, a curriculum is called for which is coherent, balanced, suited to the needs of pupils, and focused on essentials (DES 1981a, p. 4).

In the context of the curriculum work undertaken by HMI and officials over the previous seven or eight years, each of these rather vague terms can be explicated:

– *coherence* refers *inter alia* to the need for explicit relationships to be drawn between as well as within subjects, to the need for definite statements of aims and clear patterns in primary school topics and themes, and to continuity and reinforcement in learning;
– *balance* is a signal of the absence from or weakness in many schools of whole areas of study (e.g. science or music in primary schools, practical experience, technology and school–work relations in secondary schools) and of the randomness or excessive specialization resulting from the options system in many secondary schools;
– *suited to student needs* refers to the poor adjustment of many school courses to children with learning difficulties and the failure to stretch and extend bright children; and
– *focused on essentials* is an indirect criticism of the additive process whereby new subjects and topics are introduced, due to outside pressure or student and teacher interest, without due thought to the overall curriculum; it is also, and very significantly, a reminder that the Department does believe in a required core of subjects for all students.

These considerations of balance, coherence and so forth take us only so far, even when referenced to the whole corpus of official literature on the curriculum post-1976. There is still an assumption, but not a clarification, of a 'proper' range and sequence of studies. Behind *The School Curriculum* is an unresolved debate. There are those who would like a curriculum comprising, for all students and in orderly sequence, consistent programmes of study in the HMI eight areas of experience (see the section, 'Curriculum as a structure of forms and fields of knowledge', in Chapter 2). Behind the 'areas of experience' approach lies a belief in an agreed or comprehensive order of knowledge and understanding for all students in school. On the other hand, the curriculum in practice is often a diverse mixture of subjects, themes, topics whose variability in practice reflects diverse local situations and needs. In secondary schools, this is focused through subjects and teachers have usually been trained as subject specialists, though less now than in the past. Should the curriculum achieve a general consistency throughout the nation or retain its variability?

The authors of *The School Curriculum* try to cut through these difficulties – by *commending* the areas of experience approach and a skills-based analysis of the curriculum whilst themselves *talking* in subjects! (ibid. p. 6). In addition, out of a concern for what I have called 'curriculum dimensions' in the *Readings* (Section 2), they refer to social trends and values which need to be attended to, adding various 'constituents' of the curriculum, such as moral and health education, which are to be distributed among subjects. The result is, unfortunately, a rather confused mélange lacking some of the very qualities of coherence, balance, priority and, above all, clear relationship to aims that are enjoined on schools in their curriculum making. This mixture of subjects, themes, concerns and so forth comprises, for the secondary school, English, mathematics, science and modern languages and the legal requirement of religious education. To this list of definitely required subjects, occupying a 'key position', is added a less clearly defined set of 'important' or 'specially important' subjects: the uses and applications of computers; craft, design and technology; and such assorted items directly geared to preparation for working life as careers education, school–industry link activities, practical work and economics. For the primary school, there is a very sketchy list including English and mathematics, elements of history, geography, internationalism, aesthetic studies, physical education. Topic work is singled out as needing special attention, as is science.

In both primary and secondary schools, emphasis is expected to be given to multiculturalism, practical work, technology and the need for special attention to the education of girls. All in all, the curriculum proposals, whether viewed as a map or chart of areas of experience, as types of academic content, as an analysis of concepts, skills and values, or as a set of overarching themes, is irresolute and unfinished not to say thoroughly muddled.

Several of these weaknesses were picked up in the Second Report from the House of Commons Education, Science and Arts Committee, and the Government, in its response to that Report, was stung into a defence of its conservative allegiance to the traditional subject-based secondary curriculum: 'subject titles are used in the document [*The School Curriculum*] because secondary school timetables are almost always devised in subject terms, because they are readily recognized by parents and employers and because most secondary school teachers are trained in subjects' (Secretary of State for Education and Science 1982, p. 3). The response went on to explain that absence of detailed discussion of the arts and humanities in *The School Curriculum* did not imply indifference. Altogether, this was a disturbing response in that none of the arguments given inspire confidence that the Department had thought seriously about the design of curricula for the future – despite the extent and depth of criticism and dissatisfaction with current practice: much of it by HMI themselves.

The most serious deficiency of the national framework is indeed precisely in those areas where clarity and precision are most needed: the structure, general content and organization of the curriculum perceived as a relationship between the experiences and needs of students and the range of learnings for which the school is to take the central responsibility in pursuing generally agreed educational aims. Nor is there any indication, in what has followed *The School Curriculum*, that this weakness is being addressed. It might have been expected that the new agency, the School Curriculum Development Committee (SCDC), would take on this problem but the Secretary of State has intimated that this is not his wish (Joseph 1984b). This means, as things stand, that if the SCDC does not take on the job, either a new agency must be created for national curriculum policy planning or the Department itself will have to continue the task. This would be the worst option for reasons that are perhaps now clear. What is required is a more impartial, skilful, judicious and comprehensive analysis of the existing curriculum, in its socio-cultural setting, than the DES has undertaken or could handle. The one-sided and very skimpy analysis of what we have called 'a situation to change' left the policy makers with no real guidance for curriculum action. The proposed aims are an acceptable starting point, which could be strengthened, mainly by schools and LEAs themselves reviewing their aims and constructing curriculum objectives. The outline of content for the curriculum, as proposed by the DES, is quite inadequate even for the situation it defined and its own aims, and shows poor understanding of school practice or of the need to draw student experience into curriculum proposals.

As we shall see in subsequent chapters, there are ways out of this confusion whereby schools and LEAs can make their own situational analyses, and a restructured general framework for the curriculum, at the national level, can serve as an effective guide to and resource for local curriculum review, evaluation and development.

Since the publication of *The School Curriculum*, no general statement on the whole curriculum has been issued by the DES, but very shortly after its publication the Schools Council issued another kind of document *The Practical Curriculum*, which is relevant to the national curriculum framework because of the processes of review, evaluation and development that it recommended all schools should undertake in their own curriculum work (Schools Council 1981).

In the Department's contribution to the formation of a national curriculum policy, we can detect a direction for policy and practice, structured by critiques of practice, an affirmation of national need, a set of broad aims and the fragmentary analyses of areas and themes for the curriculum. In *The School Curriculum* and even more so in the follow-up circulars, we may observe a press towards school and LEA self-evaluation and development, which is likely to result in a more self-critical, evaluative and developmental approach to the school curriculum than was achieved through the Council's team-based projects of the 1960s and 70s. These are strengths to be set alongside the problems and shortcomings we have identified.

The national framework   4. Assessment

Finally in this chapter, we shall look briefly at what is still a very confused, uncertain and volatile part of the national curriculum framework: proposals and procedures for the assessment of learning. There is no need for us to dwell on the existing assessment arrangements, which, at the secondary level, have been frequently written about in respect both of the organization and administration of examinations and the more recent attempts to introduce school assessment profiles, records of achievement and so forth (Balogh 1982; Broadfoot 1979; DES 1980c, 1982a; Goacher 1983; Mortimore and Mortimore 1984). Both in the companion volume of *Readings* on school-based curriculum development and in the author's book of readings on evaluation (Skilbeck 1984c), the issue of relating assessment to the curriculum is critically examined. All of this is highly topical because the attention of DES and Examination Boards collectively has been turned, at long last, to the ramshackle structure for secondary school examinations and their manifest weaknesses and injustices.

It is difficult, at this stage, to see just where the future patterns of assessment will lie if indeed they are likely to change much, given the uncertainties regarding such key items as school assessment roles in the new 16+, the likely school response to new examinations at 17+, the possible take-up by schools and LEAs of local assessment including records of achievement or profiles of performance, and research and development work in graded tests, to say nothing of how, in practice, the national criteria for 16+ examinations will affect the curriculum. These are all secondary and further education issues. With the abolition of the 11+, primary schools have had the opportunity to experiment and innovate with assessment. There is little evidence of their having done so.

It is a depressing thought that in proposal after proposal the Schools Council's efforts to reform the examination and assessment system were defeated either by direct resistance or a studied indifference. We have no assurance at all that the numerous official and examination-board-sponsored initiatives to restructure will result in significant reform. Schools and LEAs are therefore likely to encounter continuing frustration in their own attempts to rethink assessing and examining. Is it, then, no more than an unstable, unclear picture that we are presented with and, if so, how can schools play a constructive role in the assessment phase of curriculum development? There are indeed tasks and potential opportunities for schools, but the greatest need is for a structural reform of the whole examination system. The national pattern, for the present, incorporates three distinct kinds of assessment:

1. Systemwide surveys of student performance in the subject areas of mathematics, science and language (English and foreign) at ages 11, 13 and 15. These are discussed by Jean Dawson, Caroline Gipps, Wynn Harlen and Maurice Holt in the author's book of readings on evaluation (Skilbeck 1984c). The surveys are likely to be continued, on a five-year cycle, until such time as their quite considerable demands on a limited research and development budget in the DES can no longer be justified, a time which some commentators feel is already past. They are already, in being put onto a five-year cycle, less frequent than in the first stage. Their function is to provide an overall profile of children's performances and they will assist in establishing trends, indicating areas of the country where, perhaps, additional resources are required, and in pin-pointing

particular kinds of difficulty children have in learning. They will not be so useful at either the individual school or LEA level, although it is quite possible that parallel local surveys will be set up, which will not be restricted to the APU light sampling and matrix sampling techniques whereby individual student and school performance could not be identified and minimum disruption to teaching occurred.

2. The second level or type of assessment is that rendered by the external examination system which is sufficiently well known and debated to require little further comment here. The assessment phase of the curriculum development cycle, at the school level, cannot be adequately carried out through reliance on external examinations, even in the upper secondary school and even if, nationally, the new, and still partial and divisive 16+ examination were to be replaced by a unified system open in practice to practically all students completing five years of secondary education. It is obviously not a relevant consideration in the assessment of children in the primary school and it is a general weakness in the national curriculum framework, that so little attention has been given to the question of the nature and place of student assessment in the curriculum. Nevertheless, external examinations are not only dominant over the other kinds of assessment but growing (Hammersley and Hargreaves 1983, section 3).

3. The third level or type of assessment consists in school or local authority policies and procedures for assessing student learnings by means of course work assessments, records and profiles. As already noted, within the national curriculum framework ideas and proposals for assessment are scanty. Recourse was taken, in *The School Curriculum*, to a declared need 'for further research and development work' (to be undertaken by the Schools Council whose abolition the Secretary of State announced, a year later). This work is proceeding but the history of reform in England in examination and assessment has been dismal. Despite the successful operation, in many countries, of internal school assessment, externally validated, the ideas has met stiff opposition in Britain. Practical schemes have been proposed and some are in operation, on a limited scale (Mortimore and Mortimore 1984, chapters 4–6). It is interesting to note that, in his response to the Second Report from the Education, Science and Arts Committee, the Secretary of State declared his support for a record of achievement for *all* school leavers (Secretary of State 1982). At the time of writing this commitment is far from realization in practice. The stumbling block is the lack of any national validating body, com-

bined with that kind of resistance within the education service as well as in society at large to radical examination reform experienced by the Schools Council in its successive and largely abortive efforts to get examination reform going.

Is within-school assessment, then, a lost cause? So far from this being the case, it is already the standard practice throughout the whole of primary school and well into the secondary school. Much more can be done to reform assessment procedures and it is within the competence of the school, or rather of schools cooperatively and with outside support, to do so (Burgess and Adams 1980). The manner in which external examinations have been allowed to dominate assessment in the later years of secondary schooling with a spill-over effect throughout a large part of the curriculum lower down is the most serious problem of all. Unless they are reformed in a quite radical fashion, they will remain the chief problem for curriculum planners, designers and developers seeking to implement the broader aims and more positive structures which are emerging in the national curriculum framework.

Summary

The displacement of the Schools Council's open style of national curriculum development by a more directional approach under the sponsorship of the DES is the most important of recent developments in England and Wales in curriculum policy and organization. Curriculum plans and designs to meet these changes are still at a very early stage of development. Through a recent and rapid succession of reviews, reports, investigative committees, policy papers and circulars, the first steps towards a new national curriculum framework have been taken. By virtue of this movement, the educational system of England and Wales is being brought closer in style of curriculum decision making to many other national systems where central ministries and their committees determine the curriculum in association with local authorities, schools and other branches of the education profession.

An official definition of 'a situation for change' has been made in Britain, taking into account many of the well-publicized criticisms of schooling, perceived social, technological and economic changes and a general climate of opinion about school–society relations. From this definition, inferences have been drawn about changes that are required in school curricula.

The proposals for the curriculum are very loosely related to formulated aims which, paradoxically perhaps, have a strong individualistic flavour. The aims are generally more open and educationally acceptable than are the proposals for the content and organization of the school curriculum. Continuing ambivalence over the extent and nature of desirable changes in subject matter in both primary and secondary education characterizes the national curriculum framework. The ambiguities notwithstanding, there is a discernible bias towards an outdated, subject-centred approach combined with uneven efforts to achieve 'balance', 'coherence', 'relevance' and 'practicality' through various additional studies, thematic emphases and other enlargements of the orthodox curriculum. A pervasive theme is that the curriculum should show greater sensitivity towards economic and technological changes, hence an emphasis on preparation for adult life and socially useful knowledge and skills. There is confusion as well as ambiguity in the official understanding of what should be taught in schools, and a corresponding need for a more articulate curriculum analysis than has thus far emerged. In the matter of assessment, the national curriculum framework is weakened by a combination of long-standing resistance to examination reform and vacillation over new forms of assessment for use within and by schools.

The conclusion is that a shift of profound importance is occurring, but that the official moves towards a national curriculum framework are as yet an insufficient as well as a contestable guide to school action. In order to strengthen and sustain the call to schools to review and evaluate their curricula, define their aims and make changes in their practice consistent with the changing needs of students and society, the national curriculum framework itself requires a great deal more development.

CHAPTER 6

POSSIBILITIES AND PROBLEMS
IN CORE CURRICULUM

'Our garden wasn't enough to hold all kinds of plants.'
(Erasmus, *The Godly Feast*)

Who should make the strategic decisions, and the scope and nature of the whole curriculum are the two recurring issues in the debates about the school curriculum which have accompanied the piecing together of the national curriculum framework. The very idea of a framework constructed outside schools and LEAs at the national level and very largely through the agency of department officials and HMI has given offence. Despite the cogency of the argument for some broad national guidelines, the framework has been construed as a retrograde step, which seems to strike at the heart of a belief about professionalism.

In this professional orientation, the school appears as the place where curriculum decisions ought to be made and teachers and associated professionals as those who should make them, drawing upon their knowledge of the individuals and groups of students in their care. The style may itself have some mythological elements since there are readily acknowledged influences and even constraints on school curriculum making which ensure that, at the very least, decision making can never be an independent or isolated affair.

We cannot be sure, either, that teachers really want to exercise the freedom that is often claimed for them. The acceptance, by secondary schools, of academic subjects and externally devised examination syllabuses, and of published reading and number schemes by primary schools, suggests that schools readily identify with preexisting curriculum structures: perhaps the ones they are familiar with. A little reflection shows that there is no necessary contradiction between school freedom and the acceptance of external structures or even constraints. What is important is the nature of those structures and constraints. Professional autonomy is a principle of action wherein the knowledge, understanding and values of the teacher are given full play, not a sphere or arena shielded from other influences and forces wherein the teacher can exercise unchecked control. According to the well-known distinction, the teacher may be *in* authority, by virtue of enjoying a status and occupying a role which are duly constituted and recognized; the teacher may also be *an* authority, by virtue of knowledge, skill, experience and aptitude for teaching. In curriculum decision making, however, at the school level, teachers, whether singly or collectively, are not alone in being either *in* or *an* authority. Authority, with respect to the curriculum, must acknowledge distinctive professional roles, yet it cannot justifiably be exercised by any one group independently of others who have a legitimate interest. This point applies as much to relations between office holders within schools, including principals and deputies, in their relationships with teaching staff, as it does to relations between teachers, students, parents and others outside the school.

Claims to power and influence over the curriculum are not the exclusive prerogative of any one group or office holder. We have to identify those who have some measure of legitimate authority whether legal, moral, institutional or traditional. If we are to avoid authoritarianism or anarchy, there must be a meshing of their interests, a reconciliation of roles, a quest for consensus over what is legitimate authority and how control is to be shared and distributed. Difficult though this is, it is preferable to crude power ploys. To bring it about, we need improved knowledge of just how the curriculum is influenced and affected by wider social forces, as well as better arrangements than exist at present for shared decision making both outside and within schools and clearer allocations of roles and responsibilities. The efforts discussed in the previous chapter to construct a national curriculum framework, criticized as unilateral and intrusive, in another light can be seen as a valuable way of raising these issues for discussion and resolution, albeit within new sorts of arrangements having about them an unfamiliar ring which some find unpleasant.

What is true of the control of the curriculum applies with no less force to the closely related, and equally vexed, issue of whether there ought to be a national core or common curriculum and, if so, what it should consist of – and who should determine it if it is thought to be desirable. In this and the following chapter, the case for core curriculum will be put, observations made about its general character, and the question taken up of the roles that schools need to take in curriculum decision making. We shall also discuss some of the criticisms of core curriculum in so far as they seem to challenge either its general form and character or its usefulness in school-level curriculum making. If it can be shown that there are ways of drawing up an educationally sound, potentially acceptable and practically useful national core curriculum, one of the weaknesses in the national curriculum framework that we identified in the previous chapter will have been at least partially overcome: a satisfactory core curriculum could help to fill the lacuna of *The School Curriculum* arising from the hesitancy, confusions and ambiguities about a recommended curriculum. But first, it is necessary to clear away some confusions about core curriculum, starting with the assertion that by its nature 'core' must refer to detailed central prescription of the curriculum. This is one concept of core, but by no means the only one.

Central prescription

Confusions about core curriculum arose in England in the 1970s through the Great Debate and have lingered on to cloud the issue of whole curriculum planning. Core curriculum then, in British educational parlance, as in some other countries at about the same time, was equated by many people with a set of required subjects, or subject matter, embodied in a centrally imposed syllabus of basic information and skills to be taught to all students. On this account, the core at its simplest would be reduced to compulsory, prescribed courses in English, mathematics, science, religious education and some vague assemblage of history, geography, and civic and moral studies. Physical education, when remembered, would also be tacked on. Externally devised tests of performance would be administered at three or four age points during primary and secondary schooling. In practice, this could mean a central ministry or department of education determining, for all schools, and within the compulsory subjects, the main topics to be taught, and authorizing text and other materials for use in classrooms.

Despite the qualms of many of the critics, this is not, in fact, the direction that policy since the mid-70s has taken in Britain. In the early days of the Great Debate there was fear that it might. Reference back to the papers originating that debate is helpful. The DES, in *Educating Our Children* (1977f), introduced studied qualifications into its declared interest in a prescribed core:

A common core most often suggests an irreducible minimum essential to the education of all children, with room for variation beyond and around it. In the context of common primary and secondary education for all, even the essential minimum is likely to prove substantial. Some people use the term 'common core' to cover a small number of what they see as priority areas, for example, English and mathematics; others go further and mean a basic minimum of information and skills to be acquired by all pupils, by a certain age, if possible, within these priority areas. Those areas are usually identified for convenience as 'subjects' – English, mathematics, science for example. It is unlikely, however, that a common core, or even a common curriculum, described solely by reference to subject names, will advance us sufficiently far in the analysis of needs . . . common labels on the timetable do not necessarily amount to a common curriculum. (ibid p. 4).

Educating Our Children was carefully taking the temperature of educational opinion with its guarded suggestions about 'uses' and 'possibilities'. Negative responses and a disappointing set of regional conferences resulted in a dampening down of the whole issue with no real progress towards defining an acceptable and useful core. As we saw in the preceding chapter, the rather unsatisfactory outcome in *The School Curriculum* shows just how little by way of curriculum planning and design was achieved. There have been similar results in other parts of the world, where at about the same time, forthright bids were made by State officials or politicians to introduce a centrally controlled core (British Columbia 1976a, 1976b; Education Department of Victoria, Australia 1980a, 1980b; Hersom 1978; Hunt and Lacy 1979; Skilbeck 1982a; Turner 1981).

With these various forays by national and state ministries in mind, we can give one meaning to the term core curriculum: *that part of the whole curriculum of schools which is prescribed by central government in accordance with declared needs and priorities, structured by objectives, divided into subjects or subject areas, supported by approved texts, assessed in an approved manner.* This is an 'ideal type' in the sense that the definition encompasses a related set of intentions to act or influence decisions; only some parts of the action may be accomplished. A curriculum of this type would be 'core' in several senses:

1. it is a part but not the whole of the curriculum;
2. it is that part of the whole curriculum which specifies subject matter that all students are required to study;
3. the core content will be spelt out in guidelines, syllabuses and approved teaching materials;
4. it follows that all schools must systematically provide opportunity for core studies;

5. the provision of opportunity and student response will be tested through a systemwide type of assessment.

Since it is compulsory for schools to provide and students to study the core, it is also a common curriculum, although we must be careful to note that it is not the whole of the curriculum that is common to all students – there are options and elective areas with freedom to specialize.

Taking the definition a little further we may see just how powerful is the role of the determining body – in this case, central government and its agencies – and how important it would be, if this approach were to be pursued rigorously, to ensure that the core curriculum met fundamental educational criteria. To *require* certain kinds of study of every child, to *oblige* every school to meet these requirements, means having powerful and well-reasoned justifications. This is where aims of education, criteria and principles of procedure come in. Are the aims authentic, educationally sound and likely to be generally accepted?

Statements of educational aims are usually very general. Behind them are assumptions and values, perhaps principles of procedure and criteria which are largely unexamined, or part of the shared way of life of a society, or they may represent the interests and viewpoints of powerful minorities who command office or influence action without themselves being representative of society as a whole. Is the core being used to insert or impose a sectional interest, a political bias, a doctrinal position that has not been openly debated? Are these subject learnings, including the prescribed materials, consonant with universally, or even just professionally agreed learnings? Is too much emphasis given to traditionalist views, held by government, officials and advisers, about what it is good for the nation to learn, know and be able to do? Is it clear that the core curriculum will enable all individuals, as they grow and develop, to gain the knowledge, skills values and freedom of mind to make wise choices of their own? How appropriate is the core to an open, democratic, multicultural, pluralist society? These and like questions must not be obscured by the machinery of government or practical exigencies.

Whilst government may *claim* the right to educate the children of the nation as it chooses, this right is not and cannot be absolute. Are there not also the rights of parents and of the children themselves? How do these enter into the equation? And is education not itself a process, a cultural form which has emerged through practical experiences; are there not educationally significant theories about human development which have evolved over many generations? These are all valid claims and they are not capable of being reduced to a series of political and bureaucratic policy moves. There are also practical, as well as ethical and conceptual, problems since the actual mechanics of reaching conclusions about just what is to be required, nationwide, provide plenty of scope for poor communication, misunderstanding, exclusion of interested parties and so forth.

These are but some of the questions that would have to be resolutely addressed if we were to take seriously the claim that we should accept a centrally imposed core. And even if they were taken up, we may be reasonably confident that suspicion would remain, agreements not be reached and damaging losses sustained to hard-won freedom for society at large as well as the education profession. For a country such as Britain, it is by no means clear that there would be substantial benefits to offset these losses. We may recall that the HMI Reports are generally favourable, even rather complacent in many of their assessments of the basic curriculum structures in British education, and the reforms that they suggest are, on the whole, intended to make those structures work better, not to bring about a greater concentration of power in a single government department. There seems to be no good reason for taking any further this unequivocal concentration of decision making over the core curriculum within central government. Looking ahead, it is preferable to strengthen the capability of local structures both in and out of schools, to enhance teachers' professionalism, and instead of detailed centralized syllabus making and approvals, to treat the political and bureaucratic centre as itself part of the support and guidance system with, granted, a specific role as defined in legislation and by virtue of the special place of parliament in national life. Such a role would be quite consistent with another concept of core curriculum which we shall discuss shortly.

Turning the matter around, the nature of an imposed core curriculum, spelt out in some detail and accompanied by required text and other teaching and learning materials, and set against some device for assessing performance, carries with it a kind of guarantee: a minimum curriculum resource and opportunity which the system is guaranteeing to provide. In practice we could expect a considerable gap between the written requirement and what schools actually do, a gap which reflects resource problems, the need for professional development and the practicalities of everyday life. It is a gap that could very easily be ignored by governments not wanting to be reminded of *their* obligations. This is where the role of a well-staffed, independent inspectorate can be quite crucial and it is interesting to observe how, in contemporary Britain, even without the kind of core curriculum we have been considering, the inspectorate have been consistently, if somewhat obliquely, commenting on the gap between the government's statements about the effects of education spending cuts and conditions in some LEAs and schools (HMI 1984).

A nationally prescribed core curriculum with its implicit guarantees would sharpen this kind of reporting considerably as the implicit is made explicit and evidence about provision is assessed. It is a question whether, under these circumstances, the traditional independence and integrity of the inspectorate, a great asset in the British education system and one which has had to be fought for, could be maintained. Inspection, too, would have to become more inquisitorial: are the teachers delivering the goods and what, precisely, are children learning? We have had experience of this in the past, under the nineteenth-century 'payment-by-results' system in the Elementary Code (Gordon and Lawton 1978).

Matthew Arnold's notable attacks on an education system dominated by 'machinery', by the urge to manage and control the detail to the neglect of the ideas, and Edmond Holmes's charge that the Code resulted in a degradation of human personality and loss of freedom were, in their time, notable examples of leading members of the national inspectorate (both were HMIs) sounding timely warnings (Arnold 1960; Holmes 1911). As Holmes put it:

> For a third of a century 'My Lords' [Education Department] required their inspectors to examine every child in every elementary school in England on a syllabus which was binding on all schools alike. In doing this, they put a bit into the mouth of the teacher and drove him, at their pleasure, in this direction and that. And what they did to him they compelled him to do to the child. (Holmes 1911, p. 7)

For Arnold, the weaknesses of the Code, the butt of his criticisms in Reports to the Committee of the Privy Council, were but a particular instance of a failing he found to be general in English education, the urge to control: 'to model education on sound ideas is of more importance than to have the management of it in one's own hands ever so fully' (Arnold 1960, p. 209).

There would be, therefore, as well as the issues in educational theory, problems and pitfalls in the implementation of a centrally determined, required set of minimum learnings for all students in schools. Even if we could be assured of its educational desirability, it would be imperative to consider its ramifications in practice before proceeding any further along that line.

School prescription

So much for core by central diktat, an idea which is uncongenial in a society with long liberal traditions and where culture is pluralistic, and unnecessary given the overall quality and strengths of the education profession. As a matter of practice it would be politically dangerous as well as administratively unmanageable. Further moves along these lines may of course be essayed in the future by incautious or adventurous politicians and administrators, impatient with the somewhat untidy processes of review, evaluation and development of their curricula that schools engage in. Some LEAs may be tempted, similarly, to lay down a core of basic subjects, providing little room for interpretation and development by schools and demanding detailed assessment and evaluation procedures for accountability purposes. Despite the vigorous rebuttals of such moves, from the education profession itself during the course of the Great Debate that followed delivery of Callaghan's Ruskin College speech, it cannot be assumed that the momentum has petered out. Teachers must first have sounder alternatives to offer.

Is a school-determined core curriculum, made by the individual school independently of all others, a satisfactory alternative to a centrally determined core? When asked to explain what they mean by 'core curriculum', teachers in Australia and England have referred to *those subjects, topics or themes which are required learnings for all students within a given school*. It is in this sense that we talk of the school's required or compulsory curriculum and usually it is identified on the timetable as 'lessons' or 'periods' and as the syllabuses studied therein (Fifield 1981; Reid, M.I. 1978–9).

Many schools seem to be quite satisfied with the idea of core curriculum, provided it is taken to refer to what *they* decide shall be compulsory learning. Core is acceptable in principle if not always as it appears in practice, because it is the outcome of professional judgement exercised within the school – even though that judgement may be no more than what the principal of a primary school is prepared to authorize, or heads of subject departments or faculties embody in their course outlines or syllabuses. These judgements are seen to be professionally valid, whether or not the individual class teacher shares in the decisions, being made by authority figures within the school who belong to the same community as the class teacher in a way that outside administrators and officials do not.

The issue here is thus partly one of the locus of control, but not entirely so. The staff on the spot, it is said, have the kind of knowledge and understanding that is most relevant to curriculum decisions. If it is justifiable for *anyone* to make a compulsory curriculum, it is reasonable for *them* to require of all the students in their charge certain kinds of study, on the grounds that they know them and understand their circumstances and environment. They can, in any case, make more realistic assessments than any central authority of what, in practice, can be provided by way of a guaranteed minimum: what the schools find it difficult or impossible to teach is not included in the core and this helps to explain why there's variability in core curriculum in practice. All primary schools might perhaps agree that music should be available for everyone, but there are insufficient teachers able to meet the demand so it is not included; craft design and technology may be good for all secondary age students but schools may lack workshops or specialist teachers, so it is passed over.

It is also said, quite reasonably, that there are important group and community differences within our society which must be acknowledged and respected in schooling. Leaving decisions about the core curriculum to each school could be a way of making all schools more responsive to these differences, capable of building in learning required (and elective and optional studies as well) that suits the distinctive characteristics of the particular population on which the school draws. Obviously applicable in communities where there are marked ethnic differences, this argument could apply as well in single-sex schools or schools trying to build up strong community links or relationships with particular kinds of industrial or commercial bodies.

These are persuasive arguments but are they entirely convincing? What is gained in realism, flexibility, freedom and initiative for individual schools can very easily be a loss to the system as a whole as custom, expediency and a kind of complacency about what can or ought to be done spread. Fixed views about what this particular community needs, or what can be provided, readily develop. It may be an *object* of policy for all schools to reach the standard of professional responsibility and capability where whatever they determine as the core curriculum will suffice for the nation as a whole. It can scarcely be accepted that this is a currently workable principle when, for a variety of reasons and by no means all of them of their own making, many schools cannot fulfil the obligations entailed by the principle. Having the curriculum determined according to local characteristics can also be stultifying and parochial when citizenship of the world is becoming as great a need as national citizenship and community identity.

A number of objections to school autonomy in curriculum making were entered at the time of the Great Debate. Even though most observers of the Debate, including some of its senior sponsors in the DES, now feel that it was of limited value, it did at least focus issues which are of continuing significance as the national curriculum framework comes to be erected. From a review of these issues we shall see that it is by no means easy to determine the 'correct' focus of decision making with respect to the core.

A fairly obvious if not altogether convincing argument in the Great Debate was population mobility: disadvantage would arise for students, as a result of internal migration, if schools did not have a broadly similar curriculum. This argument has not been substantiated by research and could be a reason for schools to attain a certain quality of education and a readiness to adapt and adjust to meet diverse needs of students rather than for them to provide a superficially identical curriculum. Transition problems as between primary and secondary schools, some of them a consequence of the diversity of primary schools and the lack of continuity between curricula in the primary and secondary sectors, were also noted at this time. But would it not be an unnecessarily drastic move to try to resolve them by taking basic curricular responsibility away from the schools? Might it not be easier and more constructive simply to find ways of improving communication and to build up staff interchanges among the schools? These arguments, deriving from the Great Debate, are not, therefore, particularly plausible reasons for rejecting school definitions of a core curriculum as against national ones.

Another argument, carrying rather more conviction, is that inequalities and disparities of provision and opportunity in the educational system already apparent, need to be remedied. A start could be made by setting minimum standards including an adequate core curriculum. This argument is the same as the guarantee we have already discussed: unless there is some agency outside and beyond the school indicating a desirable minimum standard, of some sort, we cannot be sure that all children in schools will have access to whatever is determined as a minimum provision of learning. But, as in the guarantee case, while we may feel that the decision should not be entirely that of the school, we cannot be confident that some offer of a guarantee from outside will always mean much in practice.

From this brief review of some of the arguments that have been advanced against the idea that schools should plan and design their own core curricula according to local needs and circumstances, it appears that the issue is still unresolved. Schools, it might seem, could do just as good a job as any other body or group in determining the core. In practice, however, we have to acknowledge that not all schools do produce an adequate curriculum. We have seen in previous chapters how their efforts were criticized and why the moves towards a national curriculum framework were made. My argument is that, while it is necessary that schools play a major part in curriculum planning, design and development, their role is not sufficient to meet all the requirements. As a rider to this, I would argue that, in determining their curricula, schools inevitably draw heavily upon outside resources and are subject to external pressures and constraints. A resource – which need not be a constraint – would be a well thought out general design for the curriculum including a core curriculum. We shall discuss this argument shortly.

If we are looking outside as well as inside the school for a policy for the curriculum, might that not be provided by the LEA? Public schools are established in order to ensure, as far as possible, that there is a general standard of educational provision and performance throughout the society. They are provided by the community to meet community needs and, in the British system, one of the most important bodies representing the community is the borough, metropolitan or county council, with its Education Committee. An obvious principle might be that the providing community should make the basic, strategic decisions (which would include a general outline of the curriculum). In reaching them, it would use its representative agencies, its councils and committees and they would take expert advice including that of teachers. Such an arrangement would, however, mean that the nature and limits of curriculum decisions as between the community and its representative agencies (central and local government, voluntary bodies) and the teachers and schools would need to be determined. This is precisely what is at issue in Britain in the 1980s.

To substitute an LEA-determined core for one determined by central government or by the individual school would not overcome the kinds of problems about control, autonomy and freedom we have been considering. There is something of a move in this direction, towards LEA whole-curriculum policies as LEA assessment schemes spread, and proposals are advanced for 'curriculum led staffing' (difficult to sustain in the face of increasing expenditure cuts) and of course there has always been a tendency for influential and charismatic education officers and advisers to encourage in their schools curriculum practices which become ipso facto part of the core curriculum. We generally applaud these when they produce what seem to us a desirable kind of education, as for example the spread of the arts in the West Riding primary schools under Director of Education Alec Clegg or the activity-based teaching in the Oxfordshire primary schools of the 1950s and 60s.

Equally, however, we may regret it when an authority, perhaps for reasons of cost or because of a strongly held opinion in the education committee, declines to provide facilities for all children to study science or do craft work. It is doubtful whether the LEA is an appropriate body to take the major decisions about the curriculum, including core curriculum, but even if we were to accept the case in its entirety, would it follow that there ought to be some 100 schemes for core curriculum throughout Britain, each determined at LEA level and each, presumably, somewhat different from the others? Putting the matter in this way brings out an absurdity, since to anchor curriculum decisions in what are essentially administrative and political units – units, moreover, which are in a state of flux and about whose long-term future we can be by no means certain, would be to reduce the curriculum to an artefact of administration and government. There are no better reasons for doing this through LEAs than through the DES.

All things considered, the school, a pedagogical unit first and foremost, is more fitted to take responsibility for core curriculum than the local education authority. For the authority there is a crucial role in serving as the forum for curriculum policy discussions – whether initiated by schools, advisers or officers – on the one hand and, on the other, in translating into resource, management, financial and local political terms the national policy on the curriculum. Then it becomes part of the apparatus linking schools, central government and local community and its position vis-à-vis core curriculum is that of middleman not legislator. This is a role which many LEAs may be satisfied to play, once there is some further sorting out of national curriculum framework problems and an overall improvement in local–central government relations.

Thus far, we have considered two widely used definitions of core curriculum, which share a concern for decision making but locate decisions respectively in national ministries or local units (usually schools, sometimes local authorities). We have seen that the idea of core as a detailed prescription by a central authority would be unsatisfactory in Britain, whatever may be its advantages elsewhere. To transfer a determining power in the school curriculum to the DES would not seem to have anything very much to offer our society and its educational service that cannot be provided in other, less contentious ways. The alternative, of each school determining its own core curriculum, has also been criticized and, even in the variant form that some find attractive – of LEA-defined cores – leaves much to be desired.

In making this assessment, we have thus far avoided discussing the actual content of the core curriculum. But we have noted that, especially in secondary education, the content of the curriculum provided by most of our schools is in some respects inadequate on both social and individual grounds. What the teachers have in fact ultimately constructed – accepting that their constructions are constrained in many ways – are curricula which have met with well-merited criticism not only from HMI but also from those educators who are dissatisfied with the achievements of schools in meeting social goals and the expressed needs of students and parents (Hargreaves, D.H. 1982; Raven 1980, 1982).

We are thus faced by two, closely related problems: first, how is responsibility for determining and providing core curriculum to be shared among the several major interest groups and, second, what are the kinds of curriculum issues to which attention needs to be given in planning and designing core curriculum, within as well as outside schools? In this chapter, our concern is mainly with the first of these questions. The second is taken up in the next chapter.

Reaching agreement

There is a third way of thinking about core curriculum which may help us to resolve some of the questions we have been posing. We are looking for a means to satisfy at least some of the aspirations of those who would like greater homogeneity and more central guidance, and a way of addressing the central problems of what we ought to teach and what children ought to learn to meet both social and individual needs. We need also to preserve essential school autonomy and, in generating important new tasks for schools and local authorities, to ensure that they are realistic. Let us start this ambitious quest with a third definition of core: *core curriculum is that part of the whole curriculum which in broad outline is common to all schools and students, is defined in partnership by both central and local bodies, and is interpreted by schools.*

This, the third definition and approach to core curriculum that we have identified, can point us towards the national curriculum framework and to the goals, values and processes of school-based curriculum development. Can it do so without leading us into contradiction and confusion? I believe these can be avoided and to help in the task I shall draw upon studies and projects in which I have participated over several years, including those in the Australian Curriculum Development Centre, and also draw upon a long, and too little used, theoretical literature. Our discussion must take us towards the content of core curriculum which, in the British debates of recent years, has received much less attention than it deserves.

Let us start by looking more closely at the definition that has been proposed. First, it refers, like the others we have discussed, to a part, not the whole of the curriculum. It is assumed that there are other parts of the curriculum, possibly quite substantial, which are a matter of individual choice, whether by schools, local authorities, parents or students – although the practical exercise of choice by the last of those depends a great deal on what each of the others does and says. Curriculum planning, design and development cannot, of course, be confined to the core, however large or small it may be, but must address the whole curriculum, including relationships between the core and the remainder of the curriculum. For our present purposes, we may accept this principle but postpone discussion of its implications.

It is important to emphasize that both within the core and as between the core and the optional and elective parts of the curriculum there are major decisions for the school to make. Thus, in this third approach to core curriculum, reference is made to a curriculum being common *in broad outline* to all schools. This means that there is an agreed plan for the curriculum for all schools with scope for development, diversity and variation within the plan. It will be recalled that, in *The School Curriculum*, the Department's attempt to sketch out a curriculum common in broad outline to all schools, it was made perfectly clear, as also it has been in the follow-up circulars and was in the Inspectorate's *A View of the Curriculum*, that it was only a broad outline being proposed for adoption by all schools. The third and first meanings of core have this much at least in common.

A curriculum plan, however, requires more than a statement that all schools should have some parts of their curriculum in common. Let us take the case of the HMI areas of experience. It is unclear whether it is intended that *all* students will study all subjects or areas of experience throughout the whole period of schooling. Every school, in planning its own curriculum, has to decide whether what is to be studied is required of all, or some students, throughout the whole of their schooling or only during part of it and of course detailed decisions are needed about sequences and levels of study. We do not know what the intention of the proponents of the national curriculum framework are in relation to many of these practical issues. Perhaps it does not matter? From a planning perspective it certainly does.

When it was suggested, in *The School Curriculum*, that science be studied by all, was this intended to mean, by all students consistently and continually throughout the whole of primary or secondary schooling? Or was it expected that, following the American unit system, at some stage in their schooling all students would 'take' a unit (or more) of science, the timing and content of that course to be left to local option? Since these are rather important practical questions, it may seem surprising that, as yet, within the official national curriculum framework they and many others of a like kind have not been answered. Is it assumed, then, that whatever answer the schools give, will be adequate? Clearly not, for there is throughout the official literature on the curriculum an assumption, sometimes made explicit, that there will be certain standards achieved and there are the regulating concepts, which we have discussed already (p. 135) or breadth, balance, coherence, sequence and so forth. These are not specified, however, in planning terms. While the official statements point in the direction of a broad, common core of studies they leave a great deal unsaid about what it is to comprise. In the next chapter I shall seek to reach some conclusions on these points, by adopting the position that a core curriculum plan for schools should specify a range of studies, chosen by schools from broadly agreed areas of experience, and that they should be sequenced throughout the whole of schooling.

Continuing with our preliminary analysis of this third meaning of core curriculum, we come to the phrase 'defined in partnership by both central and local authorities'. This is just what has been lacking thus far in the official moves to define a core curriculum: they are presented and perceived as a central determination within government and the DES. Partnership is not easy to achieve, and some say it is inconceivable that we should be able to agree on a broad common core curriculum for all (Crittenden 1982; Harris 1977). But an agreement reached in partnership does not presuppose some prior consensus or understanding throughout the nation as to what the core is to comprise; instead, it refers to ways and means of striving towards these agreements. An agency like the Schools Council might have provided these means but this was never set as a goal by or for the Council. Had it been in any formal way, perhaps it would have been resisted just because of the assumption, throughout almost the entire history of the Council, that it was the schools' and LEAs' business to fix on overall design of the curriculum – the Council was there to assist with materials and other resources for use in particular subject areas.

Since the Schools Council did not, or could not, serve as the means whereby a national agreement on core curriculum might be hammered out, when the time came for statements to be made on the subject, they emerged from official sources, provoking, as we have seen, fierce resistance. With the closure of the Council, its replacement by two separate bodies for curriculum and examinations with more limited briefs than even the Council had, the government's refusal (since 1966) to call together the Central Advisory Council, and with no national education council or committee or body of comparable stature, there are no formal means available for starting the difficult and long drawn out negotiations that would be required for central and local authorities, the profession and representative public interests to agree on a broad outline core curriculum. Central government has moved in to fill a vacuum which is partly of its own making. It is difficult to see how local education authorities, let alone the major professional and other interests that ought to be involved, could independently act to establish the kind of forum and its supporting services that would be necessary. The education profession should continue to press for the setting up of a *national education council or commission*. Failing this, through its own membership it could move towards voluntary structures which would provide opportunity for discussion and debate on these matters. The alternative, of growing central government power in the curriculum, is not an attractive one.

Unless we are able to move towards a structure for curriculum decision making at the national level which commands general assent, any attempted 'definitions reached in partnership' are likely to be of that unsatisfactory kind where the initiatives for curriculum policy proposals, including those for a core curriculum, will come from the DES or its sponsored programmes and agencies with reactions of varying degrees of support, indifference and resistance from 'the field'. This situation can be summed up, in the familiar language of change strategy, as a power-coercive strategy with some overtones of the rational-empirical (Bennis, Benne and Chin 1976). An approach of this kind may have short-term success but, apart from the objections one might raise to it as an antieducational form of direction, it is likely to fail in the longer run because of both the ideological resistance it generates and the severe difficulties of diffusion and implementation (OECD/CERI 1973, chapters II, VIII, IX; OECD/CERI 1982, 1983).

What has emerged, then, from this discussion of the third way of thinking about core curriculum is that, on the one hand, to clarify some general set of common learnings for all students is a considerable undertaking to which the national curriculum framework has contributed relatively little and, on the other hand, that at present we lack effective ways of reaching agreement about them through some kind of partnership. This leaves us in the situation of a) schools defining their own core curriculum but b) DES trying to gain support for its views against strong opposition. The proposed 'third way' in core curriculum is suffering from severe practical disabilities!

I have suggested that the way out of this difficulty is for a new rapprochement to be sought, at the national level, to ensure that further moves towards the development of a national curriculum framework will proceed through a partnership instead of an attempted imposition, or one-sided drive from government and officials. The difficulties associated with achieving that partnership are very real and they have to be addressed; but further discussion of them lies outside the scope of this book. It is assumed, however, that we are not witnessing the collapse of shared decision taking but only a setback to it. In the years ahead, renewed efforts will be needed to strengthen national curriculum policy making by restoring a collaborative approach – if not the old partnership exemplified by the Schools Council, then a new alignment of representative professional and public interests.

Regardless of the success the advocates of partnership have, there can be no doubt that schools will increasingly face the challenge to give flesh to policies, guidelines and other external representations of what is needed in the curriculum. In discussing our third meaning of core curriculum, we have focused equally on the sharing of decision making – partnership – and the need for schools to be able to read, critically and creatively, the messages of the core proposals. For these 'readings' to be successful, several conditions have to be satisfied. For example, schools cannot adequately interpret a general scheme for core curriculum if they are not aware of it, familiar with its requirements and able to respond positively. A further point is that interpretations are both individual and collective acts. The school is a collective, but one in which there are varied and unequal roles with considerable ambivalence, at present, in relations between professionals and nonprofessionals. Thus, interpretation entails constructive and creative acts: interpreting a broad core curriculum proposed with a view to translating it into action and, in the process, modifying and adapting it to local circumstances – this indeed is very largely what school-based curriculum is about. Communication and the need to clarify curriculum roles and responsibilities of different people in the school itself require further explanation.

First, schools cannot interpret curriculum policies, whether emanating from the DES or LEAs, nor can they make sense of the debates about whole, core, and common curriculum unless they are actually familiar with the material. Although perfectly obvious, the matter was not given proper attention when the large-scale project movement was in full swing. Many teachers simply did not know what was going on. There is a communication problem to be addressed, which cannot be solved by the common practice of issuing a copy of whatever is being proposed to every school, or by the newsletters, workshops and so forth that are our normal modes of information dissemination. When surveyed in the aftermath of such communications, schools and teachers have frequently shown obliviousness of the proposals. A communication system that assumes active response is doomed to failure where there is not some basis for a shared culture, a common wish to join in the message system and opportunity for a two-way flow. As Raymond Williams says, the mistake is to suppose primacy of some reality with the communications about it only a secondary affair (Williams 1968, p. 19).

The issue, therefore, in respect of core curriculum as with other kinds of curriculum proposals, is how far the aspirations, values and assumptions behind the change are shared and whether the construction of the new curriculum is to be genuinely a joint undertaking. Schools cannot interpret what they do not value, appreciate and know, or have not seen, read or heard about – or have encountered and perhaps forgotten about.

There is an immense gap between the school environment and the culture of the national bureaucratic and political centre with its apparatus of policy planning, general curriculum proposals, guidelines manufacture, and national-level decision making in committees and departmental offices. Improved technical means of communication are useful of course, and will doubtless be further apparent through advances in information technology. The school itself has a role in improving communications and to perform it adequately needs to review its own procedures for receiving, filing, classifying and accessing as well as acting on these external messages. Curriculum proposals and ideas are all too likely to be found in filing cabinets or on shelves along with the numerous other messages schools receive from public and private sources. Where a government or LEA can deploy a power-coercive strategy – as for example the requirement, laid down in circulars, that schools respond to *The School Curriculum*, or an LEA's insistence that standardized testing of pupils be carried out – there will be a response of sorts. Such a strategy is inappropriate when, as in the third meaning of core curriculum, a voluntary agreement is sought. The onus then falls on schools to show that they have the capability and are willing themselves to respond, as it does on central bodies to build a common interest with schools.

Curriculum planning and organization, at the school level, cannot proceed rationally if there are not adequate procedures within the school itself, for receiving and responding to significant developments outside the school. When such response does not occur there is likely to be further erosion of school autonomy and greater recourse by public authorities to coercive strategies.

A second issue arising from the expectation that schools have a role in interpreting proposals for the core curriculum takes us back to the definition of the school itself. We have shown that it is not satisfactorily defined as either the hierarchy of senior staff or even the teaching force as a whole. An assumption of the core curriculum movement is that the school, in its planning, will take a whole curriculum approach. But the school is often, in practice, a loose collection of individual teachers, groups or departments. Not only this, the school embraces parents' and community interests as well as students'. The suggestion that the core curriculum, conceived as a broad, national outline, is to be interpreted by schools reminds us that individual teachers in schools often make their own individual interpretations of such proposals. That this is not sufficient for purposes of school-based curriculum development, in the context of core curriculum, needs to be underlined. The point can be brought out by considering what is involved in personal reflections on teaching. It is through the teaching that curriculum guidelines have much of their effect.

Analysis of one's own teaching usually shows how that teaching might have been different; knowledge of what other teachers do, of research, of educational theories, can all suggest options and alternatives. What one does is itself a result of knowledge and experience including an understanding of the goals and direction of externally devised courses and curricula. These processes, at the purely individual level, are well captured in an Australian book which makes an imaginative reconstruction of the situations of teaching (Dow 1982).

There is perhaps nothing very remarkable about the numerous interpretations individual teachers have to make – of guidelines; syllabuses which have to be read and worked out in terms of classroom events; school and LEA policies which likewise have to be thought about for their particular relevance and applications; and so forth. But these are, as described, purely individual acts. They can also seem mundane, routine, mechanical responses to clear-cut stimuli. As we have seen, however, curriculum proposals, plans, designs are seldom clear-cut, and nor are the situations of teaching simple, unitary events in which all meaning and significance lie on a thin surface. The act of interpretation, in curriculum analysis, as in teaching, is complex, personal, judgemental, inferential. Interpreting entails reaching into a situation or a plan or programme proposal, grasping for and constructing meanings. The quest is for declared intentions, hints and suggestions, possibilities and particular uses of language and modes of behaviour. All of this, whether the subject matter be a living classroom situation or a document, will be apprehended and assessed through experience. In the act of teaching, interpretations of student responses, learnings and needs may be individual and private, or shared and reflectively analysed in group settings. In considering what is involved in 'interpreting a broad outline common core curriculum', however defined, we are envisaging activities that include but go beyond the personal and private responses of the individual classroom teacher. Looking back at the third definition of core curriculum (at the beginning of this section) we see that it is the school, *a community or a corporate entity*, that does the interpreting, not the isolated, individual teacher. Throughout the whole recent history of curriculum studies, the emergence of the Schools Council, the discussion of school-based curriculum development, the arguments about where authority for curriculum decisions properly resides, there has been a persistent tendency to blur lines and to confuse 'school' and 'teacher'. It is easy to assume that 'interpretation by schools' means 'interpretation by teachers'. Even this, as we have just seen, leaves unanswered the question as to whether this is to be the individual teacher or teachers collectively.

Decisions about core curriculum must be collective to the extent that there are vertical and horizontal relationships in teaching and learning that cannot be left to chance: learnings have to be sequenced and they ought to be related to one another across subjects. In the all-age, one-teacher school we can perhaps leave all this to the individual. In all other situations there will have to be a measure of collaboration in decision making.

Apart from the difference in roles between class teachers and principals, deputies, curriculum directors, faculty and subject heads, year teachers with posts of responsibility, careers teachers and so forth, there are the 'clients', who may be thought of as parents, community and students. They are, as we have seen, an integral part of the school. From one perspective, therefore, the students are scarcely clients at all but full partners and participants. Yet another interpretation of 'the school' is that of a small-scale, public institution, run by a board of governors to whom the teachers, through the principal, are responsible, as the staff of the enterprise for which the governors are responsible to the LEA. Who, then, does the interpreting of whatever proposals for core curriculum emanate from outside the school?

How we define 'school' thus proves to be no less important for thinking about the practicalities of curriculum decision making than how we think globally about structure and content of the core. My argument in this book has been that the school should see itself as both a community and an organization where there is genuine participation by all the named parties in crucial decisions, with the practices of decision making regulated according to such criteria, for students, as age and maturity and, for parents, as the distinction between responsibility for teaching and responsibility for general school policy. However, the participatory style is demanding and requires systematic, highly efficient organization and management. Thus the school should aim so to gear its own structure that participation becomes a reality not a mere slogan. To say that the core curriculum is to be interpreted by the school consequently requires us to look into these matters of structure and organization. In the context of the national curriculum framework, we need to say a little more, here, about how decision making in the school is changing.

Circular 6/81, the first of the circulars by which the government set about implementing the policy set forth in *The School Curriculum*, is addressed to local education authorities and the governors of aided secondary schools; the Secretary of State requested the LEAs 'to draw it to the attention of the governing bodies of their other maintained schools (including special) schools'. This, it might be thought, is a pure formality – the governors will follow the time-honoured practice of referring it to the principal and his staff as their business, curriculum. However, the Circular goes on:

> He [Secretary of State] believes that governing bodies have a valuable role to play in this field in bringing together the views of teachers, parents and the local community. He recognises also the central role of head teachers and their staffs in shaping the curriculum of individual schools. He considers that all these partners should work towards the common end of securing a planned and coherent curriculum within the schools, taking account of national and local considerations and the needs of individual pupils . . . The Secretary of State looks to governors to encourage their schools, within the resources available, to develop their curricula . . .

The Circular continues its reference to governors by involving them in the writing of curriculum aims, in pupil assessment and in evaluation of the curriculum, asking 'that these matters be pursued, in close collaboration with the head teachers and other staff of schools' (DES 1981b).

Why, one wonders, is there such emphasis on partnership within the school when, nationally, probably the greatest setback education in Britain has suffered in recent years is the negation of partnership and shared decision making through unilateral decision making by central government and a deliberate choice of confrontation in preference to a collaboration of equals. This principle in the Circular could as well be addressed to Westminster and Whitehall as to schools! It is, nonetheless, a welcome move for schools since it is an attempt to bring out a sense of community responsibility and to give at least one dimension of school democracy the recognition and encouragement it needs. It is the governors who are seen as bringing into play the views of parents and the local community and it is the governors who are to be held accountable, together with the principal and staff, for the educational quality of the school. That this Circular is not an isolated phenomenon is evident if we recall the emphasis given to parents' rights in the 1980 Education Act, and the increasing official interest in the role of governors in school management of which the Taylor Report is one manifestation (DES 1977e). It is consequently no longer credible to take a restricted professional position on the subject of 'school interpretation' of curriculum guidelines including core curriculum proposals, although, as Joan Salis, a member of the Taylor Committee remarks, implementation of parental roles will not be easy. She sees the Taylor recommendations as a spur towards making schools more accountable to their communities, by giving parents an equal status with other parties on the governing board; but: 'It is difficult to see how such a body can work if it is excluded, as many teachers' organizations would advocate, from a share in curriculum decisions' (Salis 1979).

We may expect, in the years ahead, increasing efforts at both local and central levels to strengthen the roles of governors, parents and community groups. Teachers and principals will continue to have a crucial but not an exclusive part to play in relating school policies and practices to these external policies and movements. The linkage and hence the decisions will have to provide full and active roles, on an equal footing, for parents and community. Part of the responsibility of the profession will be to ensure that these partners are well informed on professional matters and understand the practical implications of their interpretations for the daily life of the school; part of the professional's art will be to find ways of ensuring that fundamental curriculum issues are not lost to sight in the inevitable debates over 'standards', 'tests', 'resources', 'discipline'. For their part, community and parent groups will provide knowledge and support which many schools lack. Difficulties there will be but they are not a reason for teachers to resist the widening of decision making.

Why core curriculum?

Our discussion thus far in this chapter has been structured by three competing definitions of core curriculum. Behind the definitions there are considerable differences about the nature of decision making, control, authority and responsibility in the school curriculum. To maintain a healthy balance between local initiatives, freedom and responsibility and the legitimate and powerful forces in our society that are leading to concentrations of power nationally, we need to explore the meaning of school-based curriculum development in a context both of these wider forces and of national policies. To particularize, we need ways of relating national-level moves towards core curriculum with the curriculum responsibilities and prerogatives of the school. Of the three meanings of core, conceived as a set of requisite learnings for all students – central dominance, school autonomy and a participatory agreement – only the third sets out to overcome or to harmonize the apparently contradictory tendencies. We have not avoided the problems but have suggested ways of addressing them which call for school action. However, the puzzles and complexities, to say nothing of the risks of the core curriculum movement, have led some critics to reject the whole enterprise, as undesirable, or unnecessary, or unworkable.

In concluding this chapter, we shall review the arguments that may be advanced for core curriculum, placing against them the most powerful objections that have been made to it. Only by clearing our minds on this issue can we move with any confidence towards reconciliation of the role of the school in curriculum development with that of external authorities.

We have seen that, regardless of the arguments about whether we should or should not have a core curriculum, in our second meaning of that term practically all schools do have a core curriculum of one kind or another. It is in principle arguable whether they should impose a compulsory curriculum, but in the end this argument comes down to whether or not there should be compulsory schooling. Merely by being at school, the student is subjected to a curriculum which in its most rudimentary sense is a requirement and has some elements in common with every other student's curriculum. Although he denied any compulsion in learning, A.S. Neill, often regarded as the most forthright advocate of freedom in schools (conceived both as absence of constraint and freedom to choose), established at Summerhill a regimen which undoubtedly included a common, social, moral, interpersonal-relationships curriculum. Thus when Neill said 'learning' was not compulsory, or that he had no faith in 'lessons', what he really meant was that attendance or participation in lessons was voluntary and that the life experience of the school itself was the crucial thing. This was his curriculum – although it was not a term he used much (Neill 1960, pp. 23–28).

It is to the deschoolers that we would need to turn for avoidance of any kind of core curriculum at all. While they oppose compulsory schooling they are usually enthusiastic about education and support increased opportunities for education on a communitywide basis. This simply moves the argument a stage further: what is the citizen or member of society obliged to know and to do for basic survival and social participation, and to what sources of information and knowledge should access be provided? Thus, Ivan Illich's repudiation of schooling entails affirmation of another kind of 'life curriculum' – in his case, a cultural revolution which provides access to all the forms of awareness, tools, techniques, skills and levels of understanding (Illich 1971, chapters 8 and 9).

At this juncture, we find that the position adopted by Illich and other deschoolers is very similar to Rousseau's: alongside a rejection of contemporary social institutions is a deep yearning to define the conditions and relationships that are the basis and foundation of a good life for all. That is just the aspiration of the advocates of the core curriculum and the argument comes down to whether or not the school is capable of fulfilling it, for all students. It is a proper question to ask but the answer is best given by the schools themselves and in their own actions. Once we admit the principle of universal schooling, however, including compulsory attendance and participation, it seems impossible to resist the suggestion that there will be a core curriculum, however minimal, at the level of the school itself.

We have already discussed advantages and disadvantages of leaving to the individual school the sole right to determine this core curriculum and our conclusion was that this was neither desirable nor feasible. In practice, it does not happen, whatever the mythology. We have also touched upon some of the criticisms of what it is that schools require students to study (postponing fuller consideration to the next chapter). Similarly, we considered the alternative practice, that core curriculum is ultimately a matter for the State, through its national department, Secretary of State and Members of Parliament, to determine, perhaps with advice and assistance from various consultative and advisory bodies. We concluded that this, too, is neither a desirable nor a feasible approach in contemporary Britain, noting that the strong and recurrent emphasis on partnership, the roles of local education authorities, local communities, parents and schools suggests that an extension of central control, were it to be sought by government, would be an unsatisfactory solution to the core problem. Finally, we considered a broader, more open concept of core curriculum, where partnership is a central feature and the curriculum is presented as an outline to be interpreted and worked through in depth by schools. Our conclusion was that this might be a way ahead, at least as a policy goal, and that, even if not fully worked out and officially supported, it is consistent with the national curriculum framework and highly relevant to school practice. In the next chapter we shall see how far the rather inadequate set of core learnings already proposed by the DES might be substantially improved. But this could be a wasted exercise if there are indeed, as some of the critics claim, fundamental flaws in the whole notion of a broadly defined, generally acceptable core of studies for all students.

There seem to be four major lines of criticism:

1. Core is impossible or virtually so because we cannot reach agreement over educational aims or on what are 'essential' learnings for everyone.
2. Core is an imposition inconsistent with the diverse values and cultures of the open or pluralistic society.
3. Core, to be generally acceptable, can only be defined in the loosest, open, most general ways, hence core theory is superficial or trivial.
4. Core is too vague and remote from schools to be of practical use.

How relevant and valid are these criticisms? In some respects they are irrelevant, since the problem we are now facing is how to modify, strengthen and otherwise improve what has already been outlined within the national curriculum framework as a kind of core. The word may not be used much, but the concept is there and if we keep an eye on the policy moves, research and development programmes and other activities of the Department of Education and Science, we can observe consistent, steady support for it.

This is a practical point and it certainly affects schools facing the requirement to respond to already stated aims by developing their own and using them as a way to review, evaluate and develop their curricula. It seems rather pointless to suggest that aims, and other parts of the national framework, are 'impossible'. They may be unsatisfactory, because poorly worked out, contradictory or implausible. These would be reasons for undertaking further work on them, not for abandoning the enterprise altogether. Our concern just at the moment, however, is not with the criticism of the national framework but with objections to what I have termed the third way in core curriculum analysis. Let us see, then, how far these objections are likely to prove crucial and therefore to what extent they bring into question the whole concept of an agreed, collaborative style of national core cur-riculum planning, design and development.

Taking the first of these criticisms, so far from aims being impossible to formulate in an agreed way, we already have a statement of aims to which, in as much as they have been advanced in a government policy paper in a democratically elected Parliament, we have a kind of agreement, or at any rate assent. But it is undoubtedly a weak agreement: the aims have not been debated in Parliament, they have been criticized widely, and the govern-ment has resisted the idea of establishing the kind of representative national education council which might, with a high degree of legitimacy, adopt a list of general educational aims. We do not then have agreed aims in any strong sense. But we can easily exaggerate the difficulty of getting them, just as we can overestimate the problem of agreed 'essential' learnings for everyone. There will always be, in an open society, a body of critical opinion which ensures that no general propositions about what the society should set as its aims and goals will command universal assent. What is important here is genuine discussion, debate, free and full dialogue, the opportunity for the aims to become an object of public concern and interest, recognition that the aims will be to a degree speculative, tentative, open for review and revision, and an explicit quest for consensus. These are surely fundamental considerations for a democracy; the defining of aims and essential learnings could perhaps best be seen as an objective, something which it is a responsi-bility of all citizens and not only governments and departments to work towards. Aims are not given, not promulgated from on high and handed down, but nor is the need for them to be established or worked towards through participation, debate and dialogue a reason to regard the quest as hopelessly utopian. One of the achievements of a sound education system will be equipping people to exercise democratic responsibility and that includes concern for shared social purposes. We should not start with the assumption that this is impossible.

The second objection made to core curriculum as we have proposed it is that core is inconsistent with the diverse values and cultures of an open society. It seems to suggest that there is something about pluralistic society, or our society in its particular phase of political evolution, which would make it either a practical impossibility or an undesirable venture to try to introduce a common core of learnings for everyone. It is true, our values and our culture are diverse: pluralism is in part a product of the movements and mixing of people. The different ways of life of ethnic cultures, religions, social classes and the other subcultures and groups which make up modern society cannot be swept aside in some monolithic structures wherein a homogeneous, uniform 'superculture' is imposed on everyone. Warnings are rightly given about cultural displacement as an object or at least an outcome of educational policy: meritocratic educational policies which encouraged bright children to reject their cultural origins and take up middle class values; insensitive attempts to eradicate dialects and even languages by school language policies are but two examples.

The plurality of values and cultures is often presented in terms of ethnic minorities, as in the multicultural movement discussed by Alma Craft in the *Readings*. In postwar English education, the issue has revolved more around class than race or ethnicity with, first, the case for equality of opportunity, then the theory of cultural deficiency and, more recently, the claim that particular youth groups reject school culture as a positive act, a creative response to a situation which is not of their choosing. Some writers in this tradition have decided that an overtly political response is required; at times they would seem to join with Illich in supposing that serious reform of the school, including a reconstructed common core curriculum, is not worth attempting. One recent study in the genre which makes this kind of analysis but still finds a place for school reform is more successful in identifying the problem of cultural diversity and associated political issues than in reaching any conclusions about what is supposed to be done by way of curriculum renewal (Centre for Contemporary Cultural Studies Education Group 1981).

Cultural differences and social inequalities must be faced, not avoided, in curriculum planning. In some cases they will fundamentally affect decisions. Granted there are good reasons for the maintenance or enlargement of diversity, yet, as far as education is concerned, we can equally well make out a case for some common learning experiences – in part, just because of the differences and diversity. All individuals, regardless of language and culture, can claim a right to those relationships, situations, areas of experience from which they can gain the powers and qualities by which we define human life. These include imaginative experience, moral sentiments and insights, communication with our fellows, the means of gaining and testing knowledge, and a basic understanding of the social, cultural and physical environments in which we live. When we look at these matters more concretely, we observe that, in any given society, there is a structure of concepts or organizing ideas, institutions, values and beliefs which inform the whole life of that society. Embodied in political and legal institutions, social groupings, common ways of organizing relationships among people, codes of conduct, manners and so on, these phenomena must also enter into our curriculum plan. There is also a great number of variants which may in some instances coalesce in a whole subculture: a thriving ethnic community, a religious sect or whatever. Children can live in this subculture and at the same time participate fully in the wider culture. But children are also part of a world society and need some understanding of what this is and of their relationship with it. These needs are discussed by Helen Connell, Alma Craft and others in the *Readings*; they do not lead us to the conclusion that the diverse cultures and ways of life associated with them stand in the way of a common culture.

In short, the reality of diversity in values and subcultures is not in itself a reason for denying common, indeed universal, items with which to structure the core curriculum. These universal items give us our common humanity and remind us of universal needs and of the concept of universal human rights, including our right of access to a world heritage, not only a localized culture. They need not be at all inconsistent with the maintenance of a lively diversity and variety in society which can be reflected in the curriculum in many ways, including optional studies – for example of ethnic languages or varied religions, or the interests and ways of life of particular subcultures or groups in society.

The third objection is that core, to be generally acceptable, can only be defined in the loosest, open and most general ways. This renders it superficial or trivial. Some of the attempts to present core as basic learnings are open to this objection but, curiously, they were criticized less for this than because they project what was taken to be a narrow, restrictive view of learning and the school's responsibility. That is, they were assumed to be something quite definite and by no means trivial. Even a very minimal statement of core, in affirming an educational value and a point of view about action, can provoke opposition.

It is more often the manner of the proposal than the matter of it that is at fault. But supposing we grant this, are we not still left with something that is too general, hence superficial and trivial? The answer to this question must come from an examination of actual core proposals and even then it is perhaps more to the point to examine the setting of the proposals, the action they generate and the way in which core programmes evolve and change over time. In other words, it is the process of trying to design and implement curricula throughout a school system (or a single school for that matter) that is important, not the single document proposing a framework of studies. Guideline statements can be very concrete whilst retaining a desirable openness and flexibility, if they are seen as a factor in a dynamic process of planning, design and development. What people are being asked to commit themselves to, therefore, is not a manifesto which they are expected to endorse, but a project – a procedure of curriculum making for which the policy or planning document provides some direction and can serve as a checkpoint. Whether core, defined in an open and general way, is or is not superficial and trivial will depend on whether or not it is cast into an active mode. That is, the curriculum design and development tasks embodied in particular core proposals are more telling than general statements about areas and types of learning.

The fourth objection is closely related to the third: that core is too vague and remote from schools to be of practical use. This criticism has been made of the whole curriculum programme outlined in *The School Curriculum*. It has not, in its orientation to curriculum practice, succeeded in identifying actions and roles for participants; instead it has seemed to present a summation of conclusions and decisions, the residue as it were of the Great Debate and the flurry of official documents following it. But this may be an overhasty reaction. *The School Curriculum* has been followed by the Circulars which certainly are producing curriculum activity.

I have already tried to show how the programmes of action envisaged by *The School Curriculum* might be strengthened, but whilst its recommendations regarding core curriculum might be made more effective and could certainly be given a practical emphasis as far as schools are concerned, the kind of core that might emerge would still in all likelihood be educationally unsatisfactory. Thus, there are ways in which core can be made of practical use – by pinpointing specific roles and tasks for schools, illustrating general proposals through exemplary courses or materials, showing how implementation of core could relate to the day-to-day running of the school – but unless the core proposals are themselves educationally sound they may very well prove to be undesirable over time, however immediately practical they may be made to seem.

Can we then, produce programmes for core curriculum that are able to withstand these and other objections and difficulties? Are there versions of core curriculum which we can use as frameworks and guidelines in school curriculum making and for which we might feel there is a sound educational justification? In attempting answers to these questions we must be ready to satisfy the needs and demands of school curriculum making, which are varied and cannot all be met by a neat set of educational principles and criteria or an imposing curriculum framework designed and engineered at head office.

Summary

The prevalence of whole curriculum policy statements, guidelines and other kinds of directives to schools to plan and develop their curriculum along certain lines is a relatively recent revival in Britain but is familiar in most other countries. In an educational system where schools have become accustomed to wide latitude in curriculum making, even in the face of such pressures as examination requirements and community assumptions about basic learnings, these directives mark the beginnings of a new era of school–community–authority relations. Schools increasingly will need to focus on whole curriculum issues and to draw up plans and programmes for the curriculum which show a responsiveness to the recent changes in national curriculum policy. In making their responses, schools must re-think the concept of core curriculum in order to plan their own strategies. The thread running through the national curriculum initiatives of recent years is that core curricula need redefining in accordance with the national curriculum framework. This work is still at an early stage and schools should press for participation.

Core curriculum has three distinctly different meanings which have become obscured in the course of the Great Debate and its aftermath. They need to be unravelled:

1. Core curriculum is a set of required subjects or subject matter embodied in a centrally imposed syllabus of basic information and skills to be taught to all students. The DES does not formally subscribe to this approach but its actions at times have veered towards it.
2. Core curriculum is a set of required subjects or subject matter deter-mined by a school and embodied in required courses and activities for all students. This is how schools commonly define 'their' core curriculum.
3. Core curriculum is a broad outline statement of required learnings for all students defined in partnership by both central and local bodies and interpreted by schools. This is an attempt to accept central guidance

but ensure a collaborative and participatory approach with substantial school roles.

In each of these approaches to core, a distinction is made between whole and common curriculum: all admit elective and optional studies and freely chosen activities in addition to required learnings. A principal difference lies in the locus of decision making and control. Differences also appear when the ideas and practice of core curricula built upon each definition are examined. While there are difficulties in all of these approaches to core curriculum, I suggest the third one is the direction we should follow.

The core curriculum enterprise has been criticized for weaknesses ranging from the difficulty of achieving consensus to the remoteness of the debate from school practice. These criticisms point toward further refinements that are needed in curriculum constructs as well as in planning, design and development but they are not decisive. There are good reasons for schools to accept a wider frame of reference in curriculum making than their own immediate environment. A national approach to core curriculum, including well-planned programmes and designs, could have advantages for schools. Collaboration in this approach is preferable by far to the imposition of a narrow set of 'basics', which will diminish education and produce resistance.

CHAPTER 7

DESIGNING THE CORE CURRICULUM

'A schoolmaster may discover by trial a better way of teaching a subject than the way he began with, but it will not so readily occur to him to doubt the expediency of teaching a particular subject at all.'
(W.C. Seeley, *Liberal Education in Universities*)

In the two preceding chapters, we have examined changes in national curriculum policies and the emergence of a view about core curriculum, as a requirement for all schools and students in them. These, together, constitute a significant new, or revitalized, dimension of curriculum planning not only in Britain but in several other countries. In discussing core curriculum, we approached it first as a set of central curriculum prescriptions which, while not built into educational legislation (as religion is in the 1944 Education Act) is proffered in the strongest form of advocacy short of legal requirement. This centrally determined core cannot be a satisfactory basis for national policy or an adequate guideline for schools and should be abandoned. Second, we examined the argument that core curriculum may be left entirely to individual schools or perhaps local education authorities to determine. Our conclusion here was that this cannot be regarded as satisfactory either, even though, in any kind of determination of the core curriculum, schools and local authorities must play a major role. Third, we proposed core curriculum as a general set of curriculum guidelines, agreed by interested parties and implemented, with a considerable measure of freedom and initiative, by schools. Despite objections to the very notion of core, our conclusion was that this is an approach worth pursuing. Our aim, therefore, in this chapter is to look more closely at what the core should comprise, and we shall examine a major national project in core curriculum analysis and design undertaken in Australia, to illustrate several outstanding issues in the school's role in core curriculum planning and design.

This project is useful for us because it was carried out primarily as an effort to define and clarify issues about core curriculum in an educational situation where decision making is shared by schools and state Departments of Education. The Federal Government's powers are limited, although they have been widened through large-scale funding programmes (Smart 1978). A national approach in circumstances where the agency undertaking it, namely the national Curriculum Development Centre, had no control over schools and no administrative authority for an educational system necessarily involved consideration of shared roles and responsibilities for action. The Australian project was, moreover, planned as part of a longer-term programme intended to foster an interest in national curriculum questions and the relationships between school decision making and state and national policies towards education. The Curriculum Development Centre, like the Schools Council, was a representative body independent of government (in the sense that its policies and programmes were of its own making – they did not derive from government decisions). The Centre's authority in curriculum planning and design was therefore a function of its own financial resources and their applications, its professional capability and expertise and its overall standing in Australian education. Its core curriculum programme could be in no sense prescriptive or directive, but took the form of proposals for consideration and suggestions for action with invitation to various educational and community groups both to participate in Centre-sponsored activities and to initiate their own. The Centre's core curriculum programme was explicitly linked with its support for school-based curriculum development and presented to the community at large in this way, both through projects, workshops, conferences etc. and in a series of publications (Curriculum Development Centre *School Based Curriculum Development Series* 1981).

An Australian project

The Curriculum Development Centre (CDC) produced its planning and design proposals for core curriculum in a series of empirical and conceptual studies of the curriculum and through a number of national research and development projects begun in the mid-70s. The Centre's proposals have been widely discussed and debated (Apple 1982b; Crittenden 1982; Holt 1983b; Tripp and Watt 1984; Skilbeck 1982a and 1983b). As a result, we can make some comparisons with the British work on core curriculum and begin to draw conclusions about strategies including the implications of core or common curriculum proposals for school-based curriculum development. Discussion of the Australian programme, as we should expect, has highlighted some of the difficulties yet to be resolved in the concept of core as well as practical issues. The focus of the core debate in Australia has shifted from the federal to the state sphere, where education is the direct responsibility of state departments. In one state, Victoria, attention was initially concentrated on the state's own attempt to impose a narrowly defined core on all schools, and to introduce statewide performance tests. Following a change of government the issues have been widened out to take in the kinds of concerns which we have been addressing in this book (Ashenden et al. 1984).

By contrast with the British initiative, the Australian core curriculum programme, from its inception, was formally and explicitly linked with studies and projects in school-based curriculum development. This was done for two reasons: first, in order to reduce the risk of these potentially opposed approaches being pursued without constant reference to each other; second, the core project was aimed to help meet the criticism that too much in-school planning, designing and implementing change was rather piecemeal and lacked any point of reference in a general or comprehensive view of a curriculum of general education for all. This underlines a long-term need in curriculum planning which was seen to be relatively uncontroversial. However, early responses to the Australian proposals suggested that the potential conflict between advocates of core and those supporting school initiatives in curriculum construction had not been avoided.

It is still widely and I think erroneously believed that there must be an opposition between a national or systemwide approach to core and school-based curriculum development. By the inclusion in this book of extended discussion of core, I hope to go some way towards mending the breach: core is not a displacement of or substitute for the school's role in curriculum development, but a way of articulating it, and of building connections with the goals of general education and the emerging national curriculum framework. Thus a well planned and designed core curriculum, put together through a participatory process, can serve as a contribution by the educational system to the school's work in curriculum development. It must be broad and open, and not be a mandatory set of procedures and techniques for constructing the curriculum or an aggregation of details, topics, themes and syllabus outlines. Most important, it must not be put forward in such a way that nationwide testing is its natural corollary. To do so would be to destroy schools' confidence and to ensure that the tests themselves would become the curriculum. It is interesting to note that some of the critics of the core proposals made in Britain at the time of the Great Debate found in the emerging APU a preferable alternative: tests could provide the framework and schools could design curricula freely (Judge 1976; Wrigley 1978, 1980). In fact the APU has not served this purpose and is not a curriculum model at all. To have made it so would have ensured a reversion to teaching for the test (Gipps and Goldstein 1983).

The CDC project was quite definitely not aimed at producing a syllabus: the Centre was not able nor did it express a wish to exercise any kind of control over schools; and the central document *A Core Curriculum for Australian Schools* was published and distributed as a policy discussion paper. It was seen as one step towards the generation of a consensus over values, aims and structure for the nation's schools. The Centre also opposed proposals in Australia to set up some kind of equivalent to APU on the grounds that this could have a narrowing effect on the curriculum without raising standards. (CDC 1981).

It is one of the hazards of issuing any kind of policy paper or general set of propositions on the curriculum that the qualifications and reservations of the writers get brushed aside as readers try to see what they are 'really getting at'! The CDC document was no exception and for some it seemed like a polite and disarming method of strengthening the hold of State authority over the curriculum. Thus, there were in Australia similar concerns to those voiced by teachers' associations in Britain. If *any* national authority or department launches itself into the curriculum arena with proposals for core curriculum, the spectre of State dominance appears (Apple 1982b; Tripp 1981).

On the other hand, the CDC proposals for core curriculum have been criticized both for their looseness and breadth: by seeking to define the core broadly, drawing from a wide array of human knowledge and experience, and by keeping the discussion of these areas at a high level of generality, the Centre was giving schools too little direction or support (Buxton 1983; Crittenden 1982, pp. 72–73). The basic problem with the Australian programme is its incompleteness: responses to the document *A Core Curriculum for Australian Schools* have pointed to structural weaknesses, and lacunae in the argument which require further attention. They have not shown that its further development would be undesirable (Crittenden 1982, chapter 6). Some of this more detailed work is proceeding at state level, through state curriculum departments supported by reports and studies (Keeves 1983; Skilbeck 1982a; Tasmania Department of Education 1978). While it is undoubtedly the case that more analytical work on core as an *intellectual* project is required, it is even more necessary that research, development, planning, design and implementation projects be undertaken with active and widespread school participation: the structure of core curriculum will never be satisfactorily elucidated by conceptual and critical means alone.

Dimensions of core curriculum

Core curriculum needs to be conceptualized, planned, designed and executed in three distinct but related dimensions (as set out in Table 7.1). The separation of areas of knowledge and experience from learning processes and the environments of learning is necessary for purposes of discussion. Thus far, most of the debate has centred around the case for (or against) core, power and control, and, to a lesser degree, the subject matter to be included in the core. Too little notice has been taken of the second and third dimensions.

Table 7.1 Dimensions of core curriculum

1. Areas of knowledge and experience
2. Learning processes
3. Learning environments

Nine areas of knowledge and experience were nominated in the Australian CDC proposal. It is from these nine areas, by careful selection, sequencing and interrelating, that the content of the core curriculum is to be drawn. The areas of knowledge and experience are outlined in Table 7.2. On pages 193–196, we give a résumé of the contents of each of these nine areas. Some general points need to be made first.

Some but not all of the nine areas bear a recognizable resemblance to school subjects. But they are not in any sense a list of subjects, nor are they distinguished, as are Hirst's forms of knowledge, by unique logical structures. Instead, they are intended to serve as a chart of the major domains through which human experience and understanding has been organized and represented. Arts and crafts, for example, are to be thought of not as a set of syllabuses in different arts and crafts but as areas of

Table 7.2   Areas of knowledge and experience to be drawn upon in constructing the core: *a task for schools*

Arts and crafts
Environmental studies
Mathematical skills and reasoning and their applications
Social, cultural and civic studies
Health education
Scientific and technological ways of learning and their social applications
Communication
Moral reasoning and action, values and belief systems
Work, leisure and lifestyle

---

structured, organized and universal human activity, with a long, varied and rich history all over the world. It is the carefully structured study of the *activity*, including its values, concepts, methodologies and institutions, using selected examples – and with substantial opportunity for practical experience which involves students rather than treating them as spectators – that is the aim in the core. Moreover, the core is a chart, so relationships among and between the areas need to be suggested. Bearing in mind that the core is only a part of the total curriculum – not more than half and perhaps rather less – opportunities for specialized learning in particular arts and crafts (and in all other areas) must be provided for, over and above core learnings, in the optional or elective part of the curriculum. Any statement *about* an area of knowledge and experience that appears in the kind of national guidelines we have in mind will of necessity be global and general – a guide for the well-educated professional teacher upon whose success in designing appropriate programmes and courses of study and implementing them depends the success of the whole scheme. The question that must always be put in relation to the core areas is *which* activities, skills, learnings can we justify as essential learnings for everyone? By applying this test consistently – and courageously – we will find that an actual curriculum design, proposed by a school and drawing from the areas of experience, has itself effected the necessary selections. Applying this criterion becomes the means of eliminating a good deal of rather idiosyncratic, repetitive and unimportant subject matter from the curriculum.

But how do we determine what is essential? And could – or should – this be the same for everyone? Only by seeking agreements over aims, common understandings of how they are to be realized, including the relationship of means to ends, and an acceptance of values, principles of action and criteria for assessment, can we hope to reach corporate and agreed conclusions about what is 'essential'. It has been claimed that all this is impossible, yet these are neither more nor less than the crucial processes of planning and designing curricula, showing how learnings interrelate logically and psychologically. They should be carried out in several ways: within schools in relation to particular students, collaboratively and nationally for a whole education system. In the first instance, the discourse will be specific and concrete, in the second, general and universal. There are no standard moves to be taken, no ready-made solutions, whether intellectual or practical, to be applied. The core curriculum does indeed have to be constructed, in detail, in order for us to know what we mean by 'essential'. It may be, as Crittenden says in his critique of the Australian core curriculum proposal, that 'social cohesion' and 'respect for diversity' can be our guides but when it comes to determining what is to be taught they, too, suffer from the very vagueness and lack of sharp definition for which he criticizes the core proposals (Crittenden 1982, pp. 88–89).

What curriculum planners and designers must do is propose their structures and designs for essential learning for action and be ready to enter the debate that will ensue. There are, however, principles that will help. 'Essential' refers, *first*, to learnings deemed necessary to give students initial awareness of and access to the principal modes and forms of human experience as in the arts, working life, scientific thinking and so on; *second*, to learnings deemed to be necessary for participation in a democratic society (social responsibilities and obligations); *third*, to learnings deemed necessary for individuals to define, determine and take control of their lives (self-actualization); *fourth*, to learnings which facilitate choice and freedom in work and leisure; and, *fifth*, to learnings which provide the concepts, skills, techniques and strategies necessary for learning itself to become self-perpetuating. The application of these principles scarcely yields us either a subject-centred curriculum for secondary schools or a basic skills programme for primary schools. Instead, they provide us with a means to reflect critically upon traditionalist assumptions about what every student should learn, know and be able to do, and a way of examining the proposed nine areas of knowledge and experience.

The answer to our second question, as to whether in defining essential learnings we are prescribing the same curriculum for everyone, is that every individual student will have a curriculum that is in some vital ways unique, and everyone will have a curriculum which has some elements in common with all others. The purposes of the core programme are satisfied only when all students are working consistently in all of the defined core areas, and in ways that respect their individuality and personality. The practical implications of this require detailed treatment but they need not raise any difficulties of principle; instead they take us directly into questions of school and classroom organization.

Perhaps one further point needs to be made about the essentiality of core learnings. Although in our discussions we have concentrated on curriculum proposals and activities of the past decade, core curriculum has been part of educational theory for much longer than that. Most work on it has been done in the United States by individual theorists (Smith, Stanley and Shores 1957, chapters 14 and 15) and national committees (Cremin 1971; Kliebard 1979), but American thinking in turn has been heavily influenced by Herbart's theories through which the ideas of 'correlation', 'concentration' and 'organizing centres' have come into the curriculum field. We cannot go into this line of development here, except to mention Herbart's concern that moral education should be central, and his attempt to show how the mind assimilates, organizes and reconstructs ideas by building them into what he called 'apperceptive masses' or what might now be called schemata (Adams 1899, chapter 3; de Garmo 1895, part 1: chapter IV, part 2: chapter VII, part 3: chapter 11). Herbart thus defined two key issues which have been

Table 7.3   Programme designs to meet 'the common needs of youth'

1. logically organized subjects or fields of knowledge each of which is taught independently
2. logically organized subjects or fields of knowledge some or all of which are correlated
3. broad problems, units of work, or unifying theories which are chosen because they afford the means of teaching effectively the basic content of certain subjects or fields of knowledge (which retain their separate identity)
4. subjects or fields of knowledge which are unified or fused, usually by one subject or field serving as the unifying centre
5. broad, preplanned problem areas, from which are selected learning experiences according to defined psychological and societal needs and problems and interests of students
6. broad units of work or activities planned by the teacher according to needs perceived by the group

Source: Alberty 1953

worked upon by successive generations of educators in developing ideas about core curricula: the need to determine a core of values and the principle that the right kind of curriculum is one which facilitates in individual students the progressive organization and reorganization of thought.

The principle of unity and wholeness in knowledge and experience is an enduring theme in core curriculum. This is shown in several of the programme designs described by Harold Alberty, who was prominent in American curriculum theory after the Second World War (Table 7.3).

Requirements for a core curriculum

From a school curriculum perspective, several conditions need to be satisfied by proposals for a core curriculum: the core must be, and be recognized as, a sound means of achieving the educational aims of the school; the areas need to be comprehensive enough for *all* students to find them rewarding; they need to be the sources of learnings of which, with good and adequate reason, it can be said 'these are basic and essential' not merely 'useful' or 'interesting'; they need to be close enough to school practice – including existing subject groupings – not to seem impossibly idealistic to teachers in the actual conditions of schooling; and they need to be of a kind where public concerns about and expectations for the curriculum can be readily identified, and be shown to be met. Schools and education authorities outside the school need to be satisfied that there is sufficient rigour and clarity in the formulation of the areas to support curriculum planning and design that will be robust and effective in practice.

The requirement that core curriculum be 'practical' is as much a matter of the amount and quality of curriculum development work that has been done, or is under way, as of abstract argument about the structure, origins and authenticity of the areas. The point of core curriculum proposals is to encourage and support good curriculum work in schools, for the benefit of student learning and development. Their purpose is not political legitimation or school accountability, nor are they epistemological exercises. By focusing on power and control, critics of core have failed to address the important curriculum question of what schools ought to do (Apple 1982b; Tripp and Watt 1984).

Inevitably, core curriculum planning documents give only an indication of content and methods of teaching. They need to be augmented. It is one of the contributions of national curriculum agencies, including the Schools

Council and the Curriculum Development Centre, to have embarked upon subject or area-specific curriculum development projects which have added substantially to our knowledge and understanding of curriculum possibilities in all nine core areas. The outcomes of such projects may be used by schools in their curriculum review, evaluation and development including core curriculum planning. The work of HMI in partnership with English LEAs has been of great value in demonstrating that what they call the 'entitlement' curriculum (a core based on their eight areas of experience) is feasible in schools (DES 1983b).

As for the CDC's nine areas (Table 7.2) we may see at a glance that they are capable of accommodating the narrow and popular version of core, as comprising 'basics' in tool subjects like language and mathematics. But the areas go well beyond this since they are a representation of a theory of general education not a list of rudimentary skills. There are similarities between the nine areas of core curriculum in our analysis, the HMI areas of experience and Hirst's forms of knowledge. With respect to the latter, the CDC core accepts the need to differentiate knowledge structures for analytical purposes but does not insist on their distinctiveness being brought out in the organization of the curriculum. Referring to the Alberty programme designs (Table 7.3), we can locate the CDC model: a mixture of 3 and 5. On the other hand, the CDC proposal does not have quite the timelessness of the HMI 'areas': it is an attempt to get at ways or forms of life, in the contemporary world, drawing the subject curriculum in as a major resource. The nine core areas embody forms of knowledge, cultural systems and major problems or issues of contemporary life and experience. They are built upon claims about a shared culture, a democratic way of life and human self-actualization: an educational world view which in its theoretical underpinnings owes much to Ernst Cassirer and philosophical anthropology, John Dewey, Karl Mannheim and the social reconstructionists and the perspectives and values of the progressive education movement (Cassirer 1944; Dewey 1916, 1920, 1938; Connell 1980, chapters 3, 5 and 10; Mannheim 1951). The theory of core curriculum, and in particular the development of the 'areas' idea, needs further development and is open to a number of criticisms. In making this observation, I am mindful that precisely the same comment can be made about any of the structuring elements in curriculum – including the established school subjects.

Turning to the connections between the core areas and trends and movements in contemporary life, we have, first, a question about how *any* curriculum establishes its relevance to 'life'. How 'relevant' are examination syllabuses, sports, papercraft, reading for pleasure, geometry, French literature, work experience and so forth? For a curriculum to be 'relevant' it is neither necessary nor sufficient that it be drawn wholly from contemporary sources, and be of obvious practical use or interest. Relevance does not consist of an immediate and direct engagement with a miscellany of everyday events, as for example a curriculum constructed around the daily round of TV and newspaper snippets.

Relevance in education is established, first of all, by the material or task in question being related in some fashion to the basic structures of thought and action in culture and society. These are the sources of human development which provide the elements and strategies of the curriculum. Secondly, however, these relationships must be concretely experienced and appreciatively understood by the student. It's all very well for the teacher to see the relevance of science or history or of a particular proof, experiment or exercise but if the student doesn't, an important condition of relevance has not been satisfied. Third, the relevance of learning has to be established by relating it explicitly to the purposes and aims of the curriculum. Thus, particular items in the curriculum are relevant because they are the means whereby these aims and purposes are economically achieved. These aims and purposes must embody rational standards, principles, values which are capable of being justified and of attracting assent and support in the community. Fourth, the relevance of the curriculum must be grasped and apprehended as a whole – it must seem to students, teachers and communities to be authentic, real, vivid, vital and living in both social and personal terms. This is a difficult condition to satisfy, calling as it does for a sensitivity of curriculum planners and designers to the social and cultural worlds and close working relations between the school, the community and society. It is the very condition that many school curricula in Britain have been failing to satisfy.

Demonstrating the relevance of the areas of experience requires that we work through the above criteria, and that would be a lengthy affair. To take an example, if the core of the curriculum did not succeed in interesting students in work and working life, equipping them with understanding of the nature of work and its value in society and for personal fulfilment and enabling them to have direct access to recognizable work experience, it could be criticized for lack of relevance. In planning and designing curriculum we need to apply the same kind of analysis to the place and role of science, language and other core areas.

The core areas are *sources* from which schools are to construct core curriculum and since we have in mind all the years of schooling from five (or below) to sixteen, a heavy onus is placed on schools to structure, detail and organize learning programmes which are comprehensive in respect of the areas, sequential and interrelated. The core must be presented and perceived as a foundation, a common set of learnings, and as having some unity and coherence as a whole. Thus a school curriculum designed and planned in accordance with the core model would be inadequate if it were to totally omit or truncate an area or form. They are intended to provide a continuity of experience throughout the whole of schooling, not snippets or an assemblage of isolated 'units of study'. Construction of the core curriculum provides wide scope for school choice – except that no area may be omitted altogether and all must be presented systematically in long sequences over many years.

We have noted that the core areas are not distinct, epistemological categories, each differentiated according to unique concepts, logical structure of propositions and criteria for truth. This in no way weakens the areas for pedagogical purposes. On the contrary, there is no reason to suppose that subject matter is better organized for school curriculum use around distinct 'disciplines' than around a map of areas of experience. Learning experiences within and across the areas can incorporate, where it seems appropriate, discipline-structured study.

The arguments for the separate disciplines are themselves implausible: school subjects are not analogous to forms of knowledge, as Hirst himself says; but nor is a 'discipline' simply a logical structure: it has a history, is a social phenomenon, has institutional dimensions and, as practised, is more like a community or a culture than an abstract intellectual system (King and Brownell 1966). Since there is a widespread presumption, especially in secondary education, of a natural order or hierarchy in the curriculum, with certain 'disciplines' or distinct subjects (the 'hard' academic subjects) at the pinnacle and others trailing behind (the applied, the integrated, the 'fields' rather than the 'forms' and so forth) these points have important practical consequences and merit exploring in the context of the areas of knowledge and understanding.

It is worth noting that one of the most powerful of the attempts to invest the disciplines with a distinctive logic, that of Paul Hirst, has been effectively challenged and the criteria for differentiating the forms do not seem to yield sufficiently definite results. In any case, when Hirst responded to these criticisms in his essay, 'The forms of knowledge revisited', he reminded readers of his original argument, that an analysis of forms of knowledge is not the same as a curriculum design. Nothing, he said, would necessarily follow for the organization or even the content of the curriculum from a demonstration that there are x or y forms of knowledge and that each has its own distinctive concepts, logical structure and truth test (Hirst 1974a, chapter 6). To some readers this will seem a slightly disingenuous response, given Hirst's own interest, over the years, in curriculum analysis and his frequent use, in that work, of his own forms of knowledge. It does indeed seem to have been a central concern in his ideas about curriculum planning. It would be interesting to know what kinds of connections he would now like to see made between the forms of knowledge and curriculum designs for general education. In his original 'forms of knowledge' essay, 'Liberal Education and the nature of knowledge', Hirst proposed a knowledge-based general education (Hirst 1965). The forms were presented in this context. It seems that one of his concerns has been to ensure that when questions of teaching are raised, the logical form of the subject and its relations with forms of knowledge should be paramount. This is also true of his views on integration which derive from the same insistence that the logical priority of the distinctive form itself brings into question any kind of integration that does not formally acknowledge this. But if we accept Hirst's other proposition, that curriculum planning and design and the forms of knowledge theses really *are* quite distinct, then we can quite consistently prepare curriculum plans and designs on other bases than the forms of knowledge, while yet drawing them in as and when that kind of schematization seems helpful. That is what has been done in the CDC nine core areas approach.

We may therefore take from the analysis of forms of knowledge one of the central ideas. What Hirst proposes as criteria for *differentiating* the forms provides us with an instrument for the selection of knowledge items in the curriculum and assists us in interrelating or integrating subject matter which is commonly identified with discrete subjects. To these criteria (tests of knowledge) we need to add three other considerations about areas of experience which are germane in curriculum planning:

1. areas of experience are socially organized and differentiated by the groups and organizations through which they are sustained;
2. areas of experience have characteristic activities, products and outcomes in human affairs;
3. areas of experience are extended, enlarged and reproduced in society through social and individual action.

In structuring the nine areas of experience, for purposes of curriculum planning, we may therefore find it helpful to pose the following questions, to which, in the processes of curriculum construction, answers would be sought:

1. How is this area of experience socially organized through institutions and groups?
2. What are its characteristic activities, products and outcomes?
3. How is it sustained, extended or developed in society: how does it reproduce and reconstruct itself?
4. What are its distinctive concepts or key organizing ideas?
5. How are these concepts and ideas related into patterns or theories?
6. What are the characteristic procedures and methodologies for validating or evaluating the claims made and actions taken in this area?
7. What values or principles of action does this area embody or express?

Answering these questions is part of what is required for school planning of the 'core curriculum'. However, what has been outlined here is not a task that schools need or can undertake unaided. More curriculum development work through strategic, interrelated projects is required to take this kind of analysis further and to assist school decision making. Thus, we come back again to the core curriculum problem in the school, where the task is twofold:

1. to find a satisfactory way of defining basic and essential learnings for all;
2. to organize those learnings heuristically, in order to use them both in curriculum design and in teaching in schools, with all the forces and pressures that operate there.

On this latter point, for example, we need to recognize that most teachers in secondary schools are trained as subject specialists and that at all levels of schooling the predominant organizer of the curriculum is the subject. Thus we must so designate areas of knowledge and experience that subject-minded teachers can understand, appreciate and relate to them. At the same time, we are aiming to present the areas as a map of the culture, a means whereby students are systematically introduced to cultural processes, ideas and trends in the contemporary world. To construct such a map would seem to be a rather more difficult and puzzling task than defining distinct forms of knowledge! Why not accept that the school curriculum is a rough kind of amalgam of subjects – some quite ancient, others more recent graftings – and topics, themes and other items which have come together historically and in an unplanned and perhaps largely unconscious fashion? After all, no map or set of coherent structures that would be both widely acceptable and of practical utility for curriculum making seems to have been produced. Those who see merit in the areas of experience/culture mapping approach must anticipate considerable difficulty in the enterprise.

Our answers to these questions are threefold. First, the school curriculum, with its loose collections of subjects, its themes and topics and centres of interest, as it has evolved and for reasons already discussed, cannot be regarded as adequate, either in content or form, for meeting evident needs or for the future of our society. Second, the aims we have set and the roles we have accepted for schools call for a global, unitary approach to the curriculum, such that it becomes the primary means of the educative growth and development of persons. Third, the concept of culture as a mediating factor, despite its difficulties in use, best conveys the relationships we are seeking between the formation of the individual and the institutions, norms, intellectual, artistic and other resources of society. Three of the contributors to the *Readings*, Denis Lawton, Richard Slaughter and James Hemming, elaborate all of this, from their own individual standpoints.

Cultural mapping

One function of the Australian Curriculum Development Centre programme for core curriculum has been to stimulate discussion and debate of the questions we addressed above, within the framework suggested for the overall content and structure of the curriculum. Another of the Centre's aims has been to encourage curriculum review, evaluation and development in the school setting: that is, practical work on the core. The CDC's is only one of several such proposals which have, in recent years, drawn upon the concepts and strategies of cultural analysis. In Chapter 2 we introduced some of them, including Denis Lawton's proposals for planning curricula through application of a model comprising eight cultural systems. Lawton's purpose was both to contribute to the general curriculum debate and to suggest guidelines for school curriculum development. We can usefully look more closely at Lawton's ideas, which he summarizes in the *Readings*, in the light of the CDC proposals.

Lawton accepts the anthropological contention that the function of schooling is to transmit the way of life, or culture of a given society. In complex societies, formal education is entrusted with this responsibility which it must exercise by selecting from the culture the most important aspects, those moreover which are open to rational inquiry and justification. But how is this selection to be made, and by whom? Lawton, like the CDC, suggests that schools, not government offices, are the places to do the job and that the method to be used is cultural analysis, notably that form which endeavours to interpret the culture as a whole, using a selection approach, viz both measuring quantities and interpreting qualities. There are, according to Lawton, four kinds of questions for culture analysts engaged in curriculum construction to ask:

1. What kind of society already exists?
2. In what ways is it developing?
3. How do its members appear to want it to develop?
4. What kinds of values and principles will be involved in deciding how its members want the society to develop and the educational means to be used in achieving that development?

These are the questions proposed; they can be applied to eight systems or *invariants*, every one of which is to be found in human society (see the section, 'Curriculum as a chart or map of the culture', in Chapter 2).

Having identified and briefly described the systems, Lawton then moves on to stage 2, *cultural variables*, and applies his analysis to one society, contemporary England. He thus shows how schools might proceed in curriculum planning, by making a selection from the culture. Schools are expected to apply culture analysis on the model outlined, and focusing on their own society, here, now and as it may be anticipated in future.

Similarities (and differences) between the 'culture systems' and the 'areas of experience' are immediately apparent. Lawton's analysis in some formal respects resembles Hirst's approach more closely than that of the CDC since it is an attempt on purely systematic grounds to achieve completeness of structure: any society, all societies can be represented through the system (as any/all knowledge can be represented through the logic of the forms). The areas of experience are rather more eclectic than this, with perhaps a stronger historical slant and closer connections with school subject organization. On the other hand, Lawton's cultural orientation is quite similar to the CDC's – although not on the matter of 'culture transmission', a popular metaphor which seems to me to play down both the interactive nature of student–teacher relationships and the critical and constructive roles of schools whereby culture is not so much 'transmitted' as mediated and in some crucial ways 'reconstructed' (Skilbeck 1975, 1982b).

There are other differences in the positions we have been discussing, which are not crucial to the argument. Despite the limitations in all of these attempts to devise the core through a mapping of the culture, and to structure curriculum according to general principles of knowledge and understanding, we are justified in thinking that there is no need for our national curriculum policies to continue as if we lacked coherent planning procedures and designs for core curriculum. Since these designs are both basic and open and will require substantial planning, analytical and development work by schools, they are entirely consistent with school-based curriculum development. It seems, then, that with some further work, the missing curriculum centre of the Department's *The School Curriculum* could be provided. Whether or not that happens at the policy level, the several general formulations of core, common or basic curriculum that we have been examining can usefully contribute to school-level, whole-curriculum review and evaluation, and planning and design, by providing directions and criteria for mapping areas of knowledge, understanding, experience and culture.

Cultural analysis – including the attempt to map out areas of experience as the building blocks for curriculum design – is admittedly difficult for schools, many of which are not staffed or organized to cope. The difficulties can be exaggerated, however, and there is one aspect of cultural mapping we touched upon in Chapter 2 (see the section: 'Curriculum as a chart or map of the culture'). This is the pedagogical activity of mapping which could at one and the same time make the whole process much more manageable in schools than it might appear from these rather daunting lists and frameworks, and meet criticisms that have been levelled at the whole enterprise.

Let us consider the roles of teachers and learners in 'mapping the culture'. There is some risk of cultural analysis as a key procedure in core curriculum planning being reduced to a high-powered framework building – impressive but perhaps rather superficial and certainly inconclusive – together with a kind of survey method, in the classroom, of studying contemporary life and packaged courses in each of the domains. A school might just as easily make this mistake as any national curriculum agency. But suppose we take another tack and treat cultural mapping as in the main an orientation towards *study* as much as towards curriculum *planning*.

Is it not our goal, in designing the curriculum, to foster the process of studying subject matter as if it were capable of being organized and inter-related through areas of experience into a personal map of the culture? Students need to develop and use schemata and general strategies for learning. The idea of core curriculum is not to produce a vast and indigestible map of discrete materials to be transmitted for study, but to help students integrate knowledge and experience, to find ways of interrelating and organizing what they know, think, feel and value, and to find meaning, relevance, clarity and value in an otherwise confused and often remote world. For us to achieve or even to move towards this we have to be sure that students engage with 'the map', that it becomes a tool, a resource, not just another collection of items, put together by someone else, and imposed upon them.

Developing the areas of experience

The integration of learning by the student must be informed by principles and concepts and it must have specific and concrete materials to work on: mathematical processes require the analysis of mathematical problems using both concepts and particular examples; moral reasoning must incorporate substantive moral issues and draw on individual cases; they must not be muddied and confused in a general mélange. That is why we have syllabuses and course materials which specify particularities and sequences as well as principles and generalizations. Similarly, to claim of a core curriculum that it will enable students to 'map the culture' obliges us to produce appropriate designs, not only of the type proposed by Lawton or the CDC, but of greater detail and specificity.

We need not be unduly concerned if these designs are at first tentative approximations: the best way to strengthen them is to work them up through curriculum development projects, small as well as large scale, and to use them, in the school itself, to keep them under review and to refine them by critical reflection, discussion and further experience. Only in this way can we get beyond abstract analysis of new kinds of core curricula on the one hand, and, on the other, the continued dominance of schooling by either divided, outdated, academically derived subjects and the examination syllabuses in which they are enshrined, or a miscellany of poorly structured theme and topic work, leading nowhere in particular.

For schools to proceed thus still requires that the areas of experience be given more substance than any list of titles or naming of areas can provide. There are several ways of doing this. Detailed objectives need to be set. But this is surely the responsibility of the school itself, since objectives are a link between broader aims and areas of experience, school realities and students' needs. Also, simply setting objectives is not good enough: they have to be critically assessed and tied in with just the kind of general analysis of ways of rethinking what schools teach that the areas of experience approach is seeking: the content of objectives has to come from somewhere.

Another possibility for exploring the content of core curriculum, now being actively pursued in England and Wales, is that national committees might define 'criteria' for subjects. This would not suffice for core curriculum planning and design. It would have the double disadvantage of tying the whole analysis into a large assortment of separate subjects – and examination subjects at that – and leaving the impression that our focus is the upper years of secondary schooling. A core curriculum analysis has to be equally relevant at all ages and stages of schooling. It requires close collaboration between primary and secondary schools with agreements over sequences and continuities as well as scope of learning. The 'national criteria' have their uses, perhaps more in curriculum review and evaluation than in the construction of external examinations, but they are not suitable for our purposes.

Could we not perhaps seek from subject associations and other specialist groups short statements on how they see their specialities contributing to a broadly defined core curriculum? This would be useful and is already a major source of ideas for teaching. However, not all subject associations are productive in this way and they, too, tend towards the secondary sector. Even after consulting them we should still need an outline of what the curriculum designers understand by 'areas of experience'. What about national curriculum development projects? Whilst some of the project teams conceived it as their task to develop short general statements on the form and structure of subjects or areas of experience, others did not and it was never seen as a systematic enterprise by the Schools Council or anyone else, to bring project teams together for this purpose. Retrospective analysis of projects in an endeavour to reconstruct such a set of general statements would be a massive undertaking, beyond the capability of any school and of dubious value, given the age and variability of the projects.

It seems useful, nonetheless, to have short, discursive summaries or overviews of each of the areas. These can serve as markers for discussion and planning and for in-school design and development groups, and as checklists against which to review programmes and courses. Schools can, of course, produce their own statements, and have done so in experimental projects organized by HMI and LEAs (DES 1983b). Our argument has been that we need national statements as well, otherwise the concept of core curriculum reduces itself once more to what any school determines as its own. Seldom are schools able to draw upon the support of well-resourced projects for this purpose.

What might be meant by the nine areas of experience for one country was outlined in the CDC policy paper. We include these short statements to indicate a direction for planning, not because the individual statements are believed to be entirely satisfactory just as they stand. Every school, in preparing its prospectus and in drawing up rationales for the way subject matter is organized for teaching and learning is faced with the problem of determining a form and a suitable level of generality for such broad outlines. The CDC had just this problem and addressed it by inviting area specialists and working groups to outline the direction they would like the respective areas to take:

Areas of knowledge and experience

Arts and Crafts
Arts and crafts cover a wide and diverse area including literature, music, visual arts, drama, wood, metal and plastic crafts, and many others. Whilst in some respects it is not satisfactory to group these together, in the school setting they have many features in common, especially in regard to the techniques and tools used and the approaches adopted towards the shaping and manipulation of materials. The neglect of particular art forms, divided opinions about the need for general aesthetic education as distinct from expression through the arts, and the uneven approach to basic craft teaching in many schools, suggest the need for a comprehensive review of these areas of the curriculum. We have yet to define essential elements of experience, understanding, appreciation and skill, and to select a manageable array of learnings for schools. Until this is done and strong rationales produced, there will be a tendency on the one hand to multiply options and on the other to treat the arts as dispensable in schooling when other pressures obtrude. In fact, they represent major, fundamental forms of human expression, understanding, appreciation and communication. Given the range and diversity of arts and crafts, further studies are needed on the selection, organization and direction of a sequential core programme through all the years of schooling.

Environmental Studies
The central purpose of environmental studies within the core is awareness and understanding of both the physical and man-made environments and sensitivity to the forces that sustain or may destroy them. This requires both systematic knowledge drawn from such disciplines as biology, geography, landscape architecture, economics, etc., and a readiness by schools to participate in environmental maintenance projects which give students practical experience in the field. As in other areas of the core, there is an emphasis on social action – environmental studies represents a blend of theory and practice

which may be organized in many different ways. Within the core, what is important is not the particular kind of organization, but the environmentalist approach or perspective. This is an amalgam of types of knowledge and understanding, and a disposition to sustain and protect the environment.

Mathematical Skills and Reasoning and their Applications
In addition to an understanding of basic number processes and their application in individual and social life, the main role of mathematics within the core is as a form of symbolizing and quantifying. Mathematics contributes a view of the world, not merely practical skills, and this view needs to be fostered through problem-solving approaches, a wide range of applications and the training of reasoning. Applied mathematics relates to several other subject areas, for example, sciences, social sciences and some aspects of craft and technology. The relevance of mathematics to contemporary life has become increasingly apparent through calculators, computers and other technical applications, of which students need at least a general understanding.

Social, Cultural and Civic Studies
The focus of social, cultural and civic studies is the understanding of what is required for effective participation in social life, including the major political, social and cultural institutions and processes of Australia as a democratic and economically advanced society. These studies include consideration of the place and significance of belief and value systems (religion, ideology) in our society. They have dimensions which are both historical (social/political/economic history) and contemporary (social issues and trends, the law, consumerism, social values, etc.). They may be taught separately as 'social sciences' (including history, economics, etc.) and 'cultural studies' (including religion and values education), or in an integrated fashion. The scope of these studies should include the diverse sub-cultures and common cultures within Australia (including ethnic and Aboriginal sub-cultures), and in other societies, and the ideal of an international or world order. Opportunity should be provided for students to appraise and assess the evolution, present status of and trends in the social and civic order and to undertake practical action projects. As prospective citizens, students have a part to play in deciding the future of their country and of the international order. For these studies to have practical relevance they must relate to the present life experiences and interests of the students.

Health Education
Growing public concern over health standards of Australians, reflecting the economic and psychic costs of ill-health, and the introduction of extensive and costly community health programmes, suggest a need for sustained effort in school education. Health education has an immediate value to and impact on students which are available to few other areas of the curriculum.

The core curriculum needs to give scope to physical, emotional, mental and community health studies, and to provide opportunity for practical applications. 'Health', in becoming a school subject, may run the risk of being perceived as yet another body of knowledge to be known about rather than directly experienced. The health area needs to be approached through a wide range of studies ranging from the sciences of human biology and nutrition to programmes of sport and physical recreation, general health care and relaxation. As with arts and crafts, there is need for an overall review of the area, to produce a well-organized practical framework for teaching and to gain acceptance of the need for all students to become involved in self-help education programmes.

Scientific and Technological Ways of Knowing and their Social Applications

Science and technology are fundamental forms of human thought and powerful applications of organized problem-solving to practical situations in the everyday life of individuals, for whole societies and for the world order. They exemplify not only rational but also intuitive, imaginative and creative powers of the highest order. They are decisive forces in the transformation of social and economic life, belief systems and working life. Their study in the core requires an emphasis on forms of knowledge, synthesis, interpretation and extrapolation of data, problem-solving, decision-making, theory-practice relations and social action. They are a means of interpreting and modifying the environment. Thus, scientific and technological studies need to pay attention to social issues, inter-relationships amongst science, technology and social trends and needs, and the historical conditions giving rise to scientific and technical change. Although choice of material for learning may vary widely, science and technology in the core should provide opportunity for a common set of skills, understandings and dispositions – scientific and technical thinking and their applications.

Communication

Communication includes both verbal and non-verbal modes and relates equally to knowledge and feeling – and these frequently interact, as for example in face-to-face conversation. We must select for the core, those which are basic and essential. Language studies are an indispensable tool in many areas of learning and are intimately related to student thinking and expression. They include listening, speaking, reading and writing, which should be kept in balance throughout the school years. Non-verbal communication is equally a fundamental part of social life. Visual learning directs students towards an understanding and appraisal of the mass-media and visual competence is necessary in many school subjects. Body communication, apart from its significance in everyday life, has a central place in several of the arts. Should the core include languages other than English? Despite the persuasive arguments advanced for foreign and 'ethnic' languages, it would be difficult at present to justify these as part of a practical core for all students. What is indisputably essential is that all Australians should become competent users of the English language. How far the core should and could extend to include any language other than English is a question over which educators are divided and the Centre would wish to have more discussion – and evidence – on this point.

Moral Reasoning and Action, Value and Belief Systems
The development of morality and the capacity to discriminate amongst values and beliefs is both a crucial part of the overall development of the rounded person and a civic necessity. Transformation of moral action from the level of habitual and routine behaviour in childhood to a mature stage of critical analysis and reflective action requires a systematic, continuing approach throughout the years of schooling. Values education relates to many aspects of life in addition to moral behaviour, but has close affinities with it. Whilst the teaching of morality and values, as such, readily lends itself to abuse through indoctrination, its neglect in the curriculum may be regarded as a serious deficiency in many schools. The teaching of morality and values need, and perhaps ought, not to depend on a separate course, but may be incorporated in other areas – for example social, cultural and civic studies or the arts – and within established subjects and in a wide range of school relationships between students and teachers. Whilst the teaching of religious belief and practice cannot claim a place in a core, teaching *about* religion may be regarded as essential for all students in developing their understanding of the world in which they live.

Work, Leisure and Lifestyle
The notion of educating for present and future life is of central importance in schooling. Whilst all other core areas should contribute to this, there remain a number of aspects of universal human experience which may not be touched upon at all unless some additional, umbrella-like area is included in the core curriculum. There is much debate about the extent to which schools as distinct from other social agencies or indeed individuals themselves should shoulder responsibility for 'education for life'. The case is complex, and cannot be argued here. The Centre accepts that for many different reasons schools ought to incorporate into the core curriculum a progressive intro- duction to the working environment, to developing and changing human relationships, to leisure-time interests and pursuits, and to such universal requirements of our culture as the ability to drive a car, plan a budget, keep records, purchase goods wisely, and organize a household. Entire curricula have been built around such a 'life preparation' notion but the weakness of this approach has been shown to be a neglect of the fundamental forms of human knowledge and experience, and of the skills required to participate in them. It seems preferable, therefore, to build a life preparation element into the core, to plan it around a selection of requirements of everyday life, and teach it at the levels of knowledge, understanding and reflective practice rather than low- level skills and techniques. (Curriculum Development Centre 1981)

These nine areas were proposed by the CDC as a starting point for discussion, in anticipation of continuing and collaborative refinement. This explains the language used in describing the areas, and the frequency of suggestions that the contents and the relationships among them need exploration. It is unfortunate that the core curriculum debate has turned so much towards issues of control and decision making, with relatively little attention being given to what is to be taught and how schools can themselves contribute to core curriculum planning. Consequently, not enough thought is being given to curriculum content and to the ways of organizing and representing that content in practice. In this situation it falls to the schools to ensure that, in their own designs for the curriculum, the rationale for a comprehensive and unified set of required learnings is adequately developed, and to authorities outside the schools to balance their preoccupation with power by giving attention to what ought to be included in the core curriculum.

Learning processes and environments

We have focused our discussion of the CDC proposals for core curriculum on the nine areas of knowledge and experience, giving emphasis both to their content and to the question of how to establish interactive procedures whereby schools and external authorities cooperatively and constructively evolve an agreed core. In all of this we must keep in view the three-dimensional nature of Table 7.1. The core model incorporates three dimensions, not just one: learning processes; learning environments; areas of knowledge and experience. Several decades of research on learning and the immense and creative achievements in designing and constructing new kinds of school buildings and the enlargement of the very idea of 'learning environment' to take in out-of-school as well as classroom learning, have still not yielded 'process' and 'environment' models of learning comparable with our models for structuring subjects, forms of knowledge, areas of experience and culture systems. Curriculum theory and planning still favour learning content over learning process and learning situation. There is much talk about 'learning process' in preference to 'learning product' but the few attempts that have been made to construct general learning process theories, or theories of pedagogy or instruction specifically applicable to school curriculum, have run into difficulties. One of the best known of them is Jerome Bruner's 'instructional theory' (Bruner 1966).

Bruner's interest in the structure of a discipline as a key concept in curriculum planning was discussed in Chapter 2. By an instructional theory, what he meant was something which explains and helps guide growth and development ('Growth is characterized by increasing independence of response from the immediate nature of the stimulus', ibid. p. 5). As noted in Chapter 2 (in the section: 'Curriculum as a structure of forms and fields of knowledge'), an instructional theory draws upon psychological accounts of development and also upon knowledge structures, linking them in curriculum plans and designs.

Useful as such specifications are in helping us to think about sequences of learning, motivation in learning and teaching, and knowledge structures, they don't satisfy either the theoretician looking for something more scientific (Travers 1966, 1977) or the philosopher who is wary of schemes which skirt around the distinctions between logical and psychological structures (Hamlyn 1967; Hirst 1974b). These criticisms show the need for greater rigour in the specifying of learning processes and closer attention to distinctive types and patterns of learning in different curricular areas. Research and theory building is needed, but so also are the continued efforts by schools to answer curriculum questions:

1. Which learnings are we seeking?
2. How can we foster and encourage them?
3. How far can we assess them?
4. Are there research findings, theories and experience to draw upon in designing learning?

As for learning processes, pedagogical attention in the main has been given to (1) unitary approaches, as in general problem-solving methods; (2) programmed learning systems; (3) an assortment of innovations such as project work, inquiry methods, group discussion and so on; (4) traditional methods of instruction, communication and classroom organization.

We have mentioned Bruner's attempt to produce a more coherent theory. Other efforts have been made to produce comprehensive learning process models for curriculum planning, notably the Bloom/Krathwohl taxonomy of objectives, comprising learnings classified as a hierarchy of tasks of ascending intellectual difficulty or complexity (Bloom 1956; Krathwohl 1964). It is important to realize, however, that the intention in producing these handbooks was not to outline a theory of instruction or learning but to assist designers of tests of student performance to construct items that sampled the full spectrum of learning, from factual recall to synthesizing and critiquing theories or applying principles and judgement in action. Their authors wanted to improve the quality of tests by showing how learning is manifested in 'high-order' intellectual and moral activities, and to improve school and college courses by encouraging curriculum designers and teachers to use a full repertory of objectives to foster these learnings and to be more precise in defining their objectives.

The Bloom/Krathwohl taxonomy was presented first and most persuasively in the 'cognitive domain', then, with more difficulty, in the 'affective domain'; a 'psycho-motor' domain was envisaged but never completed. But incompleteness was not perhaps the main problem: the taxonomies were criticized, for example for postulating that learning is general, not content-specific, and that it can be adequately stated in terms of discrete items of behaviour (Hirst 1974a, chapter 2).

An interesting development of the taxonomies, meeting some of the criticism directed at them, is SOLO (Structure of Observed Learning Outcomes), an instrument for analysing student learning devised by two Australian educationists, John Biggs and Kevin Collis (1982). Recognizing the gulf between the abstract, psychological language of the taxonomies and secondary teachers' almost instinctive preference for the language of school subjects, Biggs and Collis designed SOLO for use retrospectively (and not only in test design) in assessing the quality of learning outcomes in the conventional subjects of the secondary school. Despite its acknowledged limitations (applying to reception learning where the concepts, facts, skills are known and specified in curriculum and instructional designs), SOLO is a promising development. It could be usefully extended and applied to the proposed 'areas of experience' as a way of giving greater precision and detail.

So much for some of the efforts being made to bring out the structure of learning through the analysis of objectives and outcomes of learning. There is, for the school curriculum maker, a more immediate task in respect of learning processes. Research evidence, and HMI primary and secondary surveys, highlights the one-sidedness of popular teaching styles: a preponderance of teacher talk and didactic instruction, an excess of desk-bound learning, and insufficient stimulus and support for either slow learners or very bright children. The problems of low achievers, discussed by Coralyn Williams in the *Readings*, are compounded by unimaginative and unfocused teaching. There are great difficulties for teachers, especially in areas of social breakdown, where resources are inadequate and where leadership is unenterprising or worse. However, the purpose of the kinds of criticisms we have mentioned is to suggest to teachers that insufficient use is being made of varied, motivating and effective procedures of teaching to facilitate learning. Psychological theories and taxonomies are not necessary to make the point, since there is plenty of experience in many schools of a wide repertory of learning processes which are more motivating, responsive to individual styles and rates of learning, better related to out-of-school life and more efficient in enabling students to complete tasks. Again, there are many examples, in the teaching of adolescents and young adults, of the use of such learning procedures as small group discussions, joint project planning and implementation, workshop and field projects, and involvement of students in goal setting and the design of their own study programmes. Finally, the long history of activity (discovery and inquiry) methods in the education of young children where encouragement is given to practical and concrete learning tasks directly related to children's own perceptions, values and experience, provides us with a rich resource of ideas and methods.

We are not, as a consequence, lacking in a wide and varied range of well-tried methods for use in school learning. To the items already identified, we could, through a systematic review of curriculum development projects in major subject areas, very readily add many more suggestions, relating to individual areas, topics and themes of study. Language work involving oracy and auracy, the use of graphic display and communication in science, craft, design and technology and of kinaesthetic learnings in drama and movement are but examples of a very ample collection drawn from two decades of research and development and documented in numerous project reports, not least those of the Schools Council.

Why, then, with this wealth of experience and ideas relating specifically to learning processes is so much of the discussion of curriculum and its implementation in schools directed by the assumption that the learnings are best presented as items of content to be mastered through teacher presentation and student assimilation using a limited repertory of learning procedures? No doubt the explanation is complex but part of it is perhaps to be found in the curriculum models themselves, where the curriculum is presented as content to be transmitted. Almost unconsciously, as in the writings of Benjamin Bloom on mastery learning, this idea comes through in the assumption that curriculum design necessarily specifies a fixed set of learnings to be mastered: the emphasis goes towards their content, student aptitude, and measured learning outcomes (Bloom 1971). Mention may be made in passing that it was Bloom, among others, who provided a powerful justification for one of the arguments for core curriculum, namely that a common core of learnings can be realistically set as a target for all students: the mastery concept treats aptitude for learning, not as a function of innate ability or upbringing but of the time required to complete a learning task: given enough time, the argument runs, all students can reach defined 'mastery' levels. The practical implications (and the evidence) for this claim are debatable matters and we cannot go into them here.

We have spent some time on the need to give more emphasis in curriculum planning and design to defining learning process objectives and outcomes. There is also, in the core model, the *learning environment* dimension. Historically speaking, one learning environment has dominated all others in public schooling: the isolated classroom. 'Isolated' because the classroom, with the door closed, is the individual teacher's most controllable space, the arena in which teaching and learning most typically occur at the discretion of that individual teacher. Probably the chief reason for the prevalence of didacticism in education is that the classroom is still the primary environment and traditionally the classroom is the place students have come to, and been grouped in, for instruction. The classroom as a didactic unit is also the most economic environment we have (at least if we ignore the greater economies now possible through the means of radio and television instruction). Curriculum planning often makes no mention of the need to draw upon the full range of learning environments and resources now available, including out-of-school environments. A moment's thought shows how diverse our actual learning environments are: the library, the workshop, the laboratory, the gymnasium, the playing field and the school hall. The classroom itself may be structured, and commonly is, in the primary sector, into large and small group learning spaces, quiet and noisy areas and so forth. Out-of-school, we have field study centres, the neighbourhood, places of special interest for visits, places of work, other regions and countries and so on. From even this brief listing, we may see that, as with learning processes, we already have a very large and varied repertoire of environments at our disposal, and others potentially so, if we would but use them, of which the classroom, organized as an instructional unit, is only one.

The planning and design of the core curriculum provides an opportunity to draw upon the full range of environments, locating particular learning processes within areas of experience and relating them to specific environments. The structuring of the learning environment must be given more prominence in curriculum development. This is both a conceptual and an organizational task, calling for a high degree of cooperative planning which, like all planning must be related to available or procurable resources. One of the consequences of engaging in this kind of planning, already familiar to many schools although not so frequently on a whole-school/core-curriculum-for-all basis, is that, thereby, a well-reasoned educational claim can be made on resources. This takes us beyond curriculum-led staffing to curriculum planning and design as a major criterion for resource allocation.

Summary

We have suggested, in this chapter, that the movement towards a core curriculum for all schools, still very much in its early stages, poses significant challenges to schools. Although these have been most often presented – and resisted – as a step towards central dominance, with the risk of an officially prescribed curriculum, closer inspection shows that another set of difficulties arises when core curriculum is examined as a distinctively educational enterprise. The authority and power relationships between the school as a decision-making body and central policy makers and curriculum planners and developers is one issue. For students, teachers and schools, for parents and communities, issues of structure and content in the curriculum are more crucial. Planning the curriculum to ensure a common set of learnings – a core – for all students while at the same time providing ample opportunity for choice and specialization outside the core cannot proceed unless we have a sound understanding of what a core curriculum is.

Different theories about the selection and organization of curriculum content and processes focus on selection from or maps of the culture, forms of knowledge and logical and psychological structures in learning. Core curriculum plans and designs can draw upon these but are more often based on assumptions about basic skills and essential subjects. The idea of 'essential learnings' raises questions about the kind of society we want and the images of human fulfilment that we entertain. 'Relevance' in learning likewise cannot be divorced from considerations of the aims and purposes of education. The Australian Curriculum Development Centre's core curriculum project was undertaken to stimulate educationists to rethink the core curriculum and to assist schools in curriculum review, evaluation and development. The three dimensions for planning design and development of the core curriculum as outlined in this project are:

    areas of knowledge and experience
    learning processes
    learning environments

Specifying a core curriculum along each of these dimensions requires the drawing together of information, ideas, and experience from a wide variety of sources. The school ultimately must determine the core curriculum but in doing so should avail itself of this source material. More detailed planning and designing are needed nationally, as are curriculum development projects to build upon the very sketchy outlines and proposals thus far produced. The attempts now being made to reconceptualize core curriculum, to free it of its 'back-to-basics' and 'control' associations and to demonstrate its relevance, raise some of the most difficult problems in the field of curriculum studies. It is necessary to continue this development work, both within and outside schools, if progress is to be made in school curriculum reform.

CHAPTER 8

OBJECTIVES IN CURRICULUM DEVELOPMENT

'They moved out of books, out of the schoolroom and university into the broader scenes of daily life.' (William Golding, *Rites of Passage*)

The starting point in our discussion of school-based curriculum development was ideas about change, development, the role and task of the school and changing concepts of the curriculum. Because none of these can be understood apart from the social and cultural environments and the educational purposes, intentions, plans and policies that characterize those environments, we moved on to a consideration of several of the most decisive changes in the national education system of one country, Britain, in so far as these pose challenges or set tasks for school-level curriculum innovation. Our conclusion was that a series of rapid and far-reaching changes has occurred which obliges us to rethink traditional views about both the content of the curriculum and our procedures for planning, developing and evaluating curricula.

Appropriate contexts for understanding school-level action in the curriculum are not only those of the immediate world of the school itself, its local community and the organizations and groups with which it chooses to identify. These contexts now extend to the national education system, and to the forces that operate in and upon education at that level. They are political, economic, technological as often as they are educational in inspiration. They find expression not only in the formation of education policy but in the public media and in the frequent encounters between the representatives of the various sectors of the modern society.

We adopted the convenient phrase, a *national curriculum framework*, applying it to the structures now emerging for the articulation of school curriculum policy, the transmission of those policies, and the numerous practical initiatives designed to give shape and substance to these policies. In our review of this movement, we noticed its principal features, including the official attempts to define aims and affirm needs and the very strong drive towards a countrywide programme of school and LEA curriculum reviews. A significant weakness of the framework was found to be its loose and inconclusive analysis of priorities for the curriculum and its perhaps unintended effect of underwriting an ill-defined assemblage of subjects and themes as the basis for school curriculum planning. Despite the very considerable problems associated with the concept of a generally agreed core curriculum grounded in a theory of universal, general democratic education, our discussion of this wider context of curriculum innovation concluded with recommendations for the continuance of attempts to achieve a common core curriculum for all students.

Problem solving and rational planning

Throughout our whole analysis, school-initiated activities, the roles of schools and challenges to them have been a recurring theme. The argument has been that schools in the future must go beyond incremental problem solving, small-scale action research and adjustments to outside pressures in their curriculum policies. They will need to plan and restructure:

1. to organize themselves and become equipped to gather and examine information about educational system changes and the social environment generally;
2. to play major constructive and creative, and not merely adaptive or reflexive, roles in whole curriculum review, evaluation and development, placing these processes within a planning framework and generating robust curriculum designs;
3. to find practical and economic ways to share curriculum responsibilities among their own constituent members (parents, local communities, students, teachers, ancillary staff) and with LEAs and national-level agencies; and
4. to enhance their capability in communications and improve their image in a society which no longer accepts that curriculum is exclusively a school affair or that schools can don a protective mantle against the winds of change.

These changes are proposed on the assumptions that (a) schools are, on the whole, not yet designed, resourced and managed as powerful centres for curriculum construction, (b) schools should be encouraged to take greater control over curriculum decisions, and (c) schools will not act independently but mesh their policies, plans and programmes with those of the national education system.

Some schools are already familiar to a degree with all of this – they include many of the schools where reorganization, amalgamation, contraction or expansion have led to a reappraisal of basic structures and new designs for the curriculum. New schools likewise know about the organizational problems of implementing new curricula. The adaptations, however, have often been modest; and frequently display a preference for the familiar. Even so, they have given rise to internal problems and have often caused concern to their protagonists through their demands on time, resources and human qualities like patience, commitment and ingenuity. Several of the *Readings* make this point and where school-level innovations are discussed (*Readings* Section 3) the need for forethought, planning, skills in design, group work techniques, management, careful monitoring and evaluative competence are apparent.

In school curriculum development, we cannot proceed on the basis either of a mystique of the teacher or of enthusiasm, hope and inspiration. As presented in this book, the concept of curriculum implies structure, developing the curriculum implies purposes, plans and goals, and curriculum designs infer rational procedures in which we can have confidence. All require a thorough appreciation of alternatives and new possibilities in teaching and learning. However, a great deal of the reflective and analytical literature in curriculum theory, design and development is critical and sceptical about our innovative capacity in education. Some of it is plainly hostile to attempts to define rational procedures for planning and designing curricula, impugning the motives and interests of those making these attempts as if their conscious or unconscious concerns were power politics. Policies are proposed – and reduced to shreds through critical analysis; theories about whole, common and core curriculum are enunciated – and demolished; evaluations of projects and programmes quickly focus the reader's – and the sponsor's – attention on 'what went wrong'. Teachers and school administrators are admonished to take on a new lease of life, abandoning their past customs and bad habits, but too much of this admonition evades the issue of modes of action that are appropriate to the different kinds of tasks we have in education – of which curriculum development is one of the most important for achieving our educational goals. Reflection is one thing, committing oneself to action is another. Both are required in curriculum development.

Curriculum development has engendered its own literature of failed innovations, leading to uncertainty about the status of curriculum theory, a reluctance to innovate and a discernible tide of reaction to many of the reforms in pedagogy and school organization of the postwar era: the integrated day, interdisciplinary teaching, unstreamed classes, school-based assessment, to name but a few. This reaction has led to the installation of new programmes – systemwide performance testing, improved examination techniques, vocational training are some of them – to make education more efficient, accountable and responsive to social demand. In turn, these reactions, which are often the consequence of our own educational muddles and prevarication, are shown to be inadequate or faulty. And so the process goes on.

The school is therefore challenged by these and related trends to take bolder initiatives: to equip itself as a centre of educational development; to restructure; to build itself into the educational system, not stand apart; and to achieve and demonstrate a practical capability for directing and organizing curriculum change. The focus of educational policy debates, for over a decade, has been the national system, and while this has been necessary, for reasons discussed in early chapters, it must turn to key development processes within the schools themselves. It is on these that the success of the system goals depend. Likewise, the school's claims for professional freedom and substantial curriculum autonomy must rest on its effective treatment of development issues at the school level. The emphasis here is on group and institutional actions, operations and performance. We can present arguments in principle for freedom and autonomy, but a successful bid for professional standing rests not on status or qualifications or position, nor even on knowledge and expertise, but on a practical and corporate capability in which those qualifications and qualities are clearly exhibited for all to see. Sound planning is both a condition and an outcome of that capability (Mitchell 1984). In curriculum terms, this means that the school itself, as a community, must have strong and convincing procedures, in operation, for all aspects of curriculum review, evaluation and development. While there is disagreement among curriculum developers, evaluators, teachers and others about the most appropriate and successful procedures to use – and we have discussed many of those disagreements already – it is necessary for the school to act. How, in the matter of curriculum development, is it to do so?

Problem solving and the uses of objectives

It should by now be obvious that there is no compelling logic or great unifying theme within curriculum development that obliges us to treat it as a hard and fast set of procedures with prescriptive roles and well-marked stages that all must follow. The processes of curriculum development are numerous, varied and intensely practical. The adaptation by a group of teachers of a new mathematics course, the construction by a teacher of a study programme built around work sheets, or a ten-year research and development programme in language learning with numerous subsidiary studies and projects: all fall within the compass of curriculum development. Does this justify an entirely eclectic stance – in the world of 'the practical' anything goes and there is no progress to be made in establishing general procedures and perhaps models that provide definite and useful guidance for within-school development? One kind of answer sometimes given and clearly influenced by Karl Popper's criticisms of holistic thinking and social planning (Popper 1962) is that the teachers, and perhaps the whole school, must learn to think reflectively – creatively as well as critically – about the curriculum, to deliberate upon the practical, everyday problems of schooling and to proceed in the curriculum as problem solvers, using an essentially piecemeal, incremental approach. From this, it is assumed that there will gradually emerge a momentum for action, the outcome of negotiation and the product of reflection, spreading beyond the initial steps but never becoming caught up in some kind of general strategy for development entailing the implementation of plans (Boomer 1978; Reid, W.A. 1978, 1981; Weston 1979; Westbury and Wilkof 1978). This approach has very considerable value both for individual teachers and for use with small groups of like-minded people, as in school working parties and in some of the action research networks in which teachers share their experience of small-scale research and development, such as the Cambridge Action Research Network (CARN) and a similar group centred on Deakin University in Australia (Cambridge Institute of Education 1977 onwards; McTaggart et al. 1982).

The concepts and procedures of piecemeal and incremental problem solving, of provisional agreements about elements of the curriculum growing out of collaborative efforts of small groups within schools, and of small-scale action research projects are a very large part of what many take school-based curriculum development to mean. I prefer to see them as one dimension, or perhaps as one related set of actions which are not, in themselves, sufficient. They need to be informed by more general and comprehensive curriculum designs and complemented by a planning mode. These are helpful to groups working in institutions not least because they specify types of task and relevant contexts outside as well as within the school. So far from the problem-solving and incremental approach being inconsistent with planning they can be integrated into planning and designing curricula which are highly adaptive to schools and to educational requirements.

The essence of the approach I have in mind is collaborative decision making in the school through the preparation of curriculum plans and designs which clearly express intentions and indicate how they are to be realized in action. Granted, this is a complex and variable process where much may occur that is not intended and where the realization of the plans and designs through the practical acts of teaching and learning requires judgement, flexibility and a readiness to respond to the unexpected. None of this relieves us from the responsibility of seeking ways of determining the general shape and character of the curriculum and of carefully appraising the results in practice. But we need definite and clear procedures which can be directed at the areas of greatest difficulty: involvement of the school as a whole; focus on whole curriculum not discrete subjects; mobilization of resources; strengthening professional capability; relating our educational values and goals to school realities.

In this chapter, we examine the objectives model, as a way of proceeding in curriculum design. It has been, for several decades, the most widely debated of all the procedures that have been proposed for designing and developing the curriculum. Despite its imperfections and limitations, this model seems to me of great value in addressing the problems just mentioned and to have most claim on our attention in thinking of ways of strengthening school roles in the curriculum. We shall therefore have to consider how far and in what ways it needs to be modified, in response to the criticisms and to serve practical purposes in the school environment.

The objectives model has been distinguished from a so-called process model which eschews prespecified objectives in curriculum planning, design and development. Instead of objectives, we are enjoined to search for procedures, principles and criteria to guide action (Stenhouse 1975, chapters 5–8). The distinction has some value in pointing up differences of emphasis and, in the hands of some writers, is used critically as a means of questioning the assumption that the fundamental purpose of education is behaviour modification (Stenhouse ibid.; Sockett 1976). Whatever the philosophical arguments may be, concerning the distinctions between action, intentionality and behaviour, the terminological separation of 'objectives' from 'processes' is unfortunate: *the objectives model itself refers to processes whereby aims are cast into specific objectives and these in turn are implemented and evaluated in practical situations.* Much confusion on this point has resulted from the illogical polarizing of objectives and processes in the curriculum.

Sometimes it is argued that the objectives model infers measurable outcomes *of* (things learnt), whereas the process model specifies contexts, conditions, criteria and activities *in* learning. There is value in this distinction, but it is erroneous to suggest that the objectives model is *necessarily* coupled with prespecified, measurable, specific items (facts, concepts, skills) or to imply that ascertainable learning outcomes are not important in discussing learning processes. A lot of extravagant and misleading claims have been made in the attempts to elevate the discussion of objectives and processes in the curriculum into a struggle between conflicting philosophical and political principles, ideas and practices.

Differences there are in underlying educational philosophies, but it is the purpose of this chapter to challenge the widely held assumption that they lead us inexorably towards either the 'objectives' or the 'process' model. There is, for school development work, value in the construction and critical use of objectives and no need thereby to abandon our concern for the processes of learning and teaching.

Ever since Ralph Tyler, in his short and highly influential book on curriculum, produced a succinct version of the objectives model for curriculum planning and design (the 'Tyler rationale') the nature and role of objectives has been fiercely debated (Tyler 1949, 1964). Good summaries of the criticisms are to be found in several writers (Davies 1976, chapter 4; Kelly 1982, chapter 4; Kliebard 1969–70; MacDonald-Ross 1973). The very word objectives invites controversy, in curriculum planning, development and evaluation. Criticism of the Tyler rationale and the Bloom/Krathwohl taxonomy has resulted in a too-hasty tendency to reject objectives in curriculum planning, instead of reappraising their uses, with well-drawn positions opposing the whole notion of building curricula by use of the objectives model except in what is often rather deprecatingly referred to as skills or vocational training. The role of objectives has been reassessed in teaching and learning and in some measure in curriculum design, with practical suggestions for their use

(Davies 1976, chapters 5–9). Less attention has been given to how we might build objectives into school-based curriculum development, where whole school planning and designing are needed. The critical literature helps us to determine limitations as well as uses of objectives; we need to refer to it in order to reconsider the objectives model for school use.

It almost seems as if we have, in the objectives debate, an Anglo-American divide: American supporters and English critics. In curriculum thinking, the recent interest in objectives derived very largely from the United States although there are antecedents, for example Herbart's steps in lesson preparation which had a great vogue in teacher training at the turn of the century (Connell 1980, chapter 2). Designing curricula by use of an objectives approach was strongly advocated and extensively discussed by Bobbitt, Charters and other American educators in the 1920s and 30s, and taken up in several cooperative educational programmes and projects (Bobbitt 1918, 1924; Charters 1923; Kliebard 1969–70). Curriculum planners and developers, teachers and examiners have been encouraged to set our curricula, teaching schemes and assessments according to clear and specific objectives.

Although 'objectives' are of several different kinds, what these advocates had in mind was the objective stated as *a particular learning activity or outcome*, rather than a very general statement of teacher intent. Objectives, thus, might range from specific items, such as discriminating between latitude and longitude, or accurately translating set passages from Molière, to more general ones, such as organizing a small group to conduct a social survey or producing a trend analysis in a country's foreign policy over a given time. In the 1920s and 30s, objectives were reduced to absurdity in some hands by being rendered into vast lists of discrete items of behaviour, predicated on a reflexive view of the school as an agency preparing children for society, as it was. Notwithstanding this reductionist tendency, which was accompanied by an overemphasis on education as preparation for future work and a faith that the whole enterprise could become a kind of science, this early interest was picked up again in the 1950s and 60s by Tyler, Bloom, Popham and others, built into educational technology and widely adopted in technical and vocational training programmes for young adults (Bloom et al. 1956; Davies 1976; Mager 1962; Popham 1969a, 1969b).

Opposition has come mainly, but not exclusively, from British curriculum writers and from a few prominent critics in other countries including the USA. In Britain, it is now difficult to find open support for objectives-based curriculum planning among the liberal and progressive mainstream writers in curriculum. In schools, however, many examples are to be found of courses and whole curricula set out on a kind of objectives basis (usually teacher, not student, focused), and there are a few writers, for example I.K. Davies, who have consistently argued for wider adoption of the objectives model as part of general education. I have already mentioned the situation in respect of technical and vocational education; in many schools, the interest in objectives is increasing as a result of external pressures for school review. Thus, despite the wider advocacy and use of objectives in curriculum planning in the USA than in Britain, it would be wrong to think that there is a sharp divide on national lines, or a profound split between liberal educators and trainers. It is nearer the truth to say that the division is an ideological one, blurred at the edges and, as I hope to show, unstable. If we can, as it were, put objectives into a new key, many of the objections and difficulties may disappear.

Given the extensive literature already referred to, there is no need to go into a lot of detail over the by now well-worn points of difference. But since I shall be arguing for the use of objectives in a process model of school-based curriculum development it is necessary to say something further about different types of objectives, their uses and limitations.

One of the problems about the debate has been the general assumption by critics that the objectives model is behaviouristic, in that it seeks to identify specific items of learning behaviour that are the intended results or outcomes ('products') of teaching, and that these behavioural outcomes are both prespecified in detail, in the planning phase, and measured through performance tests at the end of the cycle. None of these assumptions is required for the kind of objectives in the process model which is the subject of this chapter, so there is perhaps no need for us to enter the contest between the behaviourists and their critics. As Davies points out, the argument has moved away from the dogmatic claims that used to be made (and rejected) concerning prespecified bits of behaviour, to finding an appropriate form (and language) for general objectives in curriculum design (Davies 1976, chapter 4). Even in a more general form (concepts, strategies, values, dispositions and so on), objectives have worried their critics because they seem to put both learning and teaching into a straitjacket inhibiting flexibility and spontaneity. In the situations of flux and change common in education, they are said to give undue weight to preplanned decision making. They are criticized because they seem to lead to an overenthusiastic (and unreliable) pin-pointing of those 'performances' which embody or exemplify the general objectives. Emphasis is given to readily tested objectives, to the detriment of more profound and subtle ways of assessing learning. It is not only the critics of the underlying theory of the objectives model, but teachers and schools who are being encouraged to use it, that need to feel that such criticisms can be met.

Objectives: a hypothetical case

The uses – and the limitations – of course planning and design through objectives might become evident if we take an example. In planning a course in, say, the commercial growing and sale of potted plants, defining objectives in the form of clearly specified student learnings might seem relatively straightforward and uncontroversial. Let us suppose the course is being planned for people with known horticultural backgrounds – mainly those in cut-flower growing who wish to diversify – and that it is to take place in an institution of further education, over ten weeks, in two-hour sessions taught by a staff member. Course objectives might be written out by the teacher (or by a validating body); they would perhaps refer to certain kinds of knowledge to be gained, for example analysis of the relationship of daylight hours and temperature to flower production, or the effect on growth habits of particular chemicals, and application of this knowledge to relevant situations. Skills to be developed could be readily stated, within defined contexts of understanding: taking cuttings, or how and under what temperature and growing conditions to use chemical sprays. Such skills would be an extension or an enhancement of those already possessed by course members and could be defined in relation to existing skills. These kinds of knowledge and skills would lend themselves to clear and unambiguous, if perhaps rather superficial statements in the form of learning objectives, and a course could be constructed using such statements as a framework. Many more examples, of a more sophisticated kind, are to be found in the literature (Bloom et al. 1971; Davies 1976; Gagné and Briggs 1974; Schools Council 1969).

In our hypothetical case, course objectives seem to come from one source: a defined area of knowledge and skills structured according to a clear-cut situation of further training in horticulture. Teaching and study materials would be organized accordingly, that is to exercise the skills and build up the knowledge; and, if necessary, tests could be devised to establish whether or not, or in what degree, the knowledge and skills had been attained. These tests would complete the loop back to course objectives, and results, if carefully analysed, could assist the teacher in the review of the course and the teaching, and be a means of rewriting objectives for future courses. Course members could join in and, from their experience, contribute to course review and evaluation.

All this sounds relatively straightforward and, allowing for the simpli-fications, is not so very different from common practice in some parts of our educational system. It is helpful when teaching in this manner to consider course design as a means of thinking critically about practice as well as a sensible way of relating actions to aims in a rational sequence. There are indeed these advantages, and this helps to explain why so much curriculum thought and practice in further and technical education and training has moved in this direction, with manuals to guide teachers – and students – towards an objectives style of teaching and learning.

What, then, is the objection to extending this approach more widely throughout education? Returning to our horticultural example, closer inspection may suggest some complexities that the model in its simplest form could omit or disguise. In practice, things may be a little more complex: contrary to assumptions made in planning, students may show a surprising diversity in their existing knowledge and skills and their interest in the course, even though all are experienced horticulturalists who have elected, and not been required, to take it. Prespecified objectives, focused on content, seem to take the learner's course entry traits and characteristics too much for granted. Attempts to construct tests using the course objectives may throw up some interesting conundrums, as to just what is meant by 'knowing what the effects of a given chemical are' and 'how to ascertain skills'. There are examination techniques to help handle them but they still leave questions unanswered.

Difficulties, then, even in a simple application of the model, cannot be discounted. Yet there are in education innumerable courses based on the model just outlined, where prespecified course objectives stated in terms of specific knowledge and skill are to be found quite explicitly stated or may be inferred without difficulty. Despite the difficulties alluded to, there is no doubt that large parts of school learning could be divided up into short, intensive units of study, each with its own clearly defined objectives, and with satisfactory completion of one course a necessary entry condition for the next. Assessments could be phased, course-related and cumulative, yielding material of a developmental kind for student profiles or achievement records. Programmed learning makes use of this approach and growing interest in graded tests could result in widespread use of a simple objectives model in planning graded courses built on a unit-of-study system (Harrison 1982).

All this could be helpful to students, and be practical and manageable in school situations, leading to more conscious and deliberate course planning by the classroom teacher. By such means, the teacher could be said to be engaged in reflective problem solving, directing his energies to understanding and improving learning processes, and relating his work to the wider concerns of the institution and to education generally. There may be advantages, but they depend on whether there is an adequate context for action – one that fosters a wider and richer, not a narrower and more parochial form of education. If we consider the example further, we can see that not all aspects of the kinds of learning experiences provided or sought in schools can be stated so neatly and precisely as in our horticultural case. It is not desirable and is almost certainly not possible to treat the whole of the curriculum in this way, even if we accept that the quest for clarity, meaning, coherence and well-defined short-term learning targets in schools through a simple objectives model does not of necessity make us into crass mechanists and utilitarians!

Let us take the skills component in the case we have been considering: given that the course is itself designed to foster skills to be used once the course is finished, certain assumptions have to be made about the relationship between skills demonstrated in the course, in the tests and in subsequent use. This, let us note, is not a problem confined to objectives-based courses but is widespread in school education, including examinations practice. So much is taught – and justified – in terms of long-term effects whereas assessment techniques are seldom prospective or anticipatory and may yield only a very limited account of what has been learnt. The 'real' objective is not the skill here and now, it is the capability and the disposition to use the skill and its application in relevant life situations. But the assessment is in the here-and-now situation. That can be advantageous, of course, since, properly used, it can provide valuable information for teachers and taught on what to do next. The skill objective in our imaginary horticultural course, however, immediately assumes a double reference – its here-and-now demonstration in the course or the test and its longer-term application and development. Perhaps the objective is not so straightforward after all, if we are trying to set it in a context of education and its purposes. The construction of objectives to capture nuances and complexities in learning requires great care and has proved extremely difficult in practice.

Another question relates to what is often a tacit or unexamined dimension in training: the application of skills and knowledge commonly raises wider issues than factual and technical ones; commercial pot-plant culture in our society has become heavily dependent on a regime of synthesized chemicals, but these chemicals often have side or cumulative effects and, environmentally, their use is a contentious issue. Is the list of objectives in this knowledge and skills-based course to include at least an acknowledgement of these complexities? Are we justified in providing training courses that, for whatever good and practical reasons, avoid these issues? This question has come up, for example, in the Youth Training Scheme, where the Manpower Services Commission expressed the opinion that courses it was promoting or paying for should steer clear of controversial topics in civics and politics. Surely this is *educationally* dubious, as would be the avoidance of environmental and ethical issues in our horticultural case, and ought not to be accepted as a general curriculum principle in a democracy?

Then, again, courses are not just a matter of content, however refined: they are conducted in the social world of interpersonal relationships, something often played down or totally ignored in training manuals. It may be that the quality of even the skills component is dependent on the growth of these relationships within the course itself. Even if this cannot be directly demonstrated, we must not overlook the educative potential of the life of the group, which can be as important as any body of content. Ben Morris puts the matter as one of relationships and transactions in learning, both within the teacher and in the teaching-learning group. The teacher, he says,

> depends for his professional competence largely on the quality of the relationships he is able to develop with his pupils and colleagues, and these in turn depend on the integrity he has been able to develop within himself. The meaning of the . . . educational enterprise itself, can only be fully grasped when it is seen in this interpersonal context (Morris 1972, p. 119)

It would follow that in formulating objectives for the curriculum, we could not restrict ourselves to impersonal knowledge; likewise, in assessing the educational results of that curriculum we could not restrict ourselves to accounts of individual performances in terms of knowledge and skills. These transactional, interpersonal, values dimensions of education are often seen as the 'pastoral' or 'social' curriculum, or as features of teacher–school relations, not as part of the cognitive or academic curriculum. We have already seen how unsatisfactory is the bias of our educational system towards limited academic goals. Moreover, if it can be shown that the patterns of relationships are a condition of success or a significant outcome of academic and vocational education, then surely we would want to acknowledge this in the curriculum objectives? In practice, it is probably a general and typical objective of the teacher to 'create the right climate', or to 'establish good relationships', or to 'pursue fundamental educational values', even if these are never formulated as content or examination objectives. Is it sufficient, in curriculum design, to leave all this in the realm of the tacit – the teacher's special preserve, perhaps – or is it not better to try to produce more comprehensive, searching and educationally satisfying objectives which indicate how these worthy aspirations are to be reflected in the learning process? If our answer to this question is yes, what kinds of objectives do we have in mind for school curriculum planning and design?

Objectives in the school curriculum

We have seen that while it is quite possible, and is often desirable, to construct single courses using an objectives approach, the apparent simplicity of even that limited exercise disguises complicated, interesting and educationally controversial questions. Reverting from one-off specialized training courses to planning, designing and developing the whole school curriculum, we are struck immediately by the contrast in the scale and level of complexity. Our educational aims are broad and encompassing – schooling is a very large part of the life of the developing child and youth, and school curricula, in one way or another, relate to all aspects of development and are posited on the whole child or youth, not on discrete items of knowledge or skill to be acquired. Thus many more issues than those arising from our horticultural example would have to be addressed. Our objectives for school curricula would need to specify, even if only very generally: the expected or intended longer-term learnings, as well as the more precise and detailed short-term learnings; and the complex relations within and among learnings defined as knowledge, skills, understanding and relationship. 'Valuing', and not merely 'knowing' and 'doing', would somehow have to be captured or at least not washed out in some lengthy list of 'learning outcomes'; the range and diversity of students' interests, capabilities and background would need to figure in the definition of objectives rather than be taken for granted.

Finally, our school curriculum objectives would need to serve as clear yet flexible guides to learners, indicating to them and to their teachers the kinds of learnings they might reasonably expect to achieve, and therefore to aim for, in a given curriculum. The language of such objectives is a particular challenge, since it should fall in a range between qualities and dispositions (such as moral values, or intellectual honesty) and particular skills and facts (such as a specified set of facts about the results of electrolysis experiments, or competent use of a particular technique in pottery glazing). No single set of objectives for a school curriculum could embrace this range, thus we are faced with the prospect of several sets, one for the whole curriculum (school level) and others, perhaps, for areas of experience and others again for particular units or topics. American school students are familiar with this kind of approach, British ones less so, and there are arguments about its utility.

There are thus difficult challenges for curriculum designers to meet when adopting an objectives approach. In addition to those mentioned, the objectives produced would have to be seen to be of practical use, both in pointing clearly in directions which could actually be followed and in appealing to the concern sensitive and thoughtful teachers have for the uniqueness and individuality of their relations with students. These same teachers, using their professional skills and judgement and perhaps trying to foster in students enthusiasm for learning, creativity, reflective self-awareness, problem solving and mastery of a wide repertory of tools and techniques of learning, would need to feel that objectives in the curriculum actually facilitate all this. Unfortunately, the jejune and barren language to be found in the lists of behavioural objectives sometimes proffered to teachers has created a very different kind of image. It is no wonder, then, that objectives have come to be equated with a rather narrow and educationally limited style of curriculum planning. Objectives, however, can be helpful, and with the emphasis in national policy going towards them as a tool for analysis and development of the curriculum, it is worth while to look again at their possibilities as a planning procedure.

It may be objected at this point that, even if they can be shown to be of value, there are perhaps better ways of going about curriculum development in the school than constructing curriculum plans around objectives. It is not my intention to argue that an objectives model is the only valid one for schools to use in curriculum making. Other styles exist and have their advocates. Of special note is that the objectives model does declare a very definite interest in having *student learnings* – as distinct from *teacher actions* – clearly indicated. This emphasis on what the student knows, understands, values, believes and can do is the most important quality of the objectives model. It confuses the issue to dismiss all this as 'prespecified behavioural outcomes' when what we are searching for is ways of declaring our interest in quality, variety, and diversity of learning across the curriculum.

We have acknowledged that the construction of objectives that meet the criteria suggested and are focused on longer-term understanding and practical competence, instead of specific and isolated pieces of behaviour to be demonstrated in tests, is demanding and difficult. Progress is unlikely to be rapid even for experienced practitioners. There is much to be done, however, at the school level in improving what are often rather haphazard and woolly statements about the aims of the school and the objectives of the curriculum. Whether it is worth giving the time, energy and intellectual effort that are required to build strong curriculum objectives must be decided by schools and others in the light of their own assessment of priorities and alternatives. To put this slightly differently, by their practice, schools in fact declare their objectives, but often in a manner that is unclear to students, parents and members of staff.

School objectives in practice, however well or ill formulated they may be, can seem inadequate, partial, contradictory, for example by virtue of the tendency of mass schooling to obscure the needs of particular groups of students, or to give undue prominence to activities which are educationally dubious, just because there is pressure for them or in pursuit of opportunistic advantage. A *review* of practice, which includes an attempt to *evaluate* the objectives that lie behind that practice, is an important step towards educational improvement. The further step, of determining to develop the curriculum to overcome problems that have been identified, will be greatly enhanced by a willingness to specify student learning objectives that the school wishes to pursue and realize through its curriculum, organization, teaching methods and so on. If this specification includes the concepts, skills, values, information and ideas and interests of the students and not only what the teacher intends or expects, we shall have moved a long way forward.

The emphasis currently being given by the DES and LEAs to the review of curriculum aims and arrangements need not be regarded as an unwarranted intrusion, or a further set of bureaucratic requirements to meet. School principals, governors and senior staff can use it as a way of focusing the interests and energies of the whole school staff (and others beside) on self-evaluation, leading to the question of how aims are to be reformulated for action in the future. They can either be highly generalized, fine-sounding but rather uninformative statements which achieve nothing in practice, or more concrete, directional, action-focused statements about what is intended to be done, in and through the curriculum, to realize those aims in practice. Objectives predispose towards action and serve as a means of monitoring it.

Conversely, if in response to DES and LEA requests, schools present outlines of the arrangements for the curriculum that already exist in practice, the question of justifying those practices, or relating them to the broad aims of education and the purposes of the school will arise, as it did when a number of LEAs, in their first response to the government circular which sought authoritywide information on school curriculum practice, merely documented ways in which schools exercised curriculum responsibility (DES 1979a). Such information has its uses but they are quite limited and do not in and of themselves occasion any change. It does not advance the cause of curriculum development, or suggest that the schools and LEAs concerned have any great interest in planned change. A report on curriculum practice which endeavours to show the relationship of the practice to the objectives, offering a self-evaluation and indicating future developments, is a much sharper instrument and can often be the means of getting curriculum planning started.

We have emphasized that constructing good objectives is difficult and can be time consuming; we can go further and say that it is not something every teacher finds congenial or is interested or able to do. We are therefore presupposing, then, that a process model in which the specification of curriculum objectives is a component will be used in a number of different ways. Not all teachers and others who need to be involved will participate in the same way in curriculum planning. That need not disturb us, as homogeneity of interest and action would be an unattractive prospect even if workable. It may well be that detailed work on objectives, in many schools, will be carried out by small working parties or task forces. But it is important to recognize that participation in discussion of objectives in the curriculum is itself educative for teachers (and for pupils, parents, governors as well) and that there are risks in delegating the construction of objectives to a working party or management group. Teachers have frequently expressed a wish to take part in important curriculum decisions and are not content to leave them to principals and department heads (Cohen and Harrison 1977, 1978, 1979; Seddon 1981;

Weston 1979). The very expression 'management by objectives', which has been imported into education from business, suggests to many people technical and bureaucratic procedures whereby some members of the enterprise impose their will on all the rest. The processes and relationships of education – the *raison d'être* of the school – can be destroyed by the thoughtless application of procedures which may very well be of considerable value or utility in other sectors of society (Callahan 1962).

Our proposal is not 'management by objectives', but widespread discussion and examination of objectives and involvement in their implementation and evaluation, within the school community. The drafting of objectives, and arrangements for their review and evaluation can be, as with other aspects of curriculum design, properly placed in the hands of working parties and specialist groups. These ought to be representative of the school community, including outside interests, however, not just an aspect of middle and higher management.

Alternatives to the use of objectives?

The debate over objectives has resulted in a number of what are claimed to be alternative planning models being proposed. As stated at the beginning of the chapter, we need to examine them to see whether they really do depend upon a repudiation of objectives. Several of the better-known ones seem to waver or be unclear on this point. Perhaps the argument is less to do with the issue of thinking intentionally or through the use of objectives-based planning models than with the particular style of American behaviourism. In this section, we shall review several of the leading contemporary criticisms of the objectives model.

Lawrence Stenhouse, in his repudiation of the objectives model in all cases except perhaps for skills teaching, proposed that curriculum planning should be grounded in what, following Richard Peters, he termed *principles* – for the selection of content, the development of a teaching strategy, the making of decisions about sequence, and so on (Peters 1959). Using a Hirstian view of distinct forms of knowledge and subjects as his yardstick, Stenhouse claimed that curricula can – and should – be constructed by schools by selecting suitable content to exemplify the structure, content and criteria of the forms of knowledge. These structures, contents and criteria are not to be taught on the assumption of mastery of particular items of knowledge specified through objectives, but as problematic: 'They are the focus of speculation, not the object of mastery' (Stenhouse 1975, p. 85). It would be 'distorting' he said, to try to put all this into student performance terms. We should bring out the immanence of the subject, not set targets like standards of attainment in examinations.

We will consider, first, the claim that we should plan the curriculum within the 'forms of knowledge'. There are several difficulties in Stenhouse's position. As Hirst said, the analysis of forms is primarily epistemological and logical; it does not define the subjects or subject matter of the school curriculum. Determination of the curriculum does not rest on an analysis of the forms (even though we noted that Hirst himself often seemed to suggest that it did). Decisions as to what to teach – and especially the crucial curriculum decision of the school as an organization, namely what is the whole curriculum to comprise? – cannot be answered by reference to the forms of knowledge. We have already traversed this ground, in Chapter 2, where it was shown that larger issues arise, including the role of broad educational aims and the interrelationships of teaching and learning across the curriculum. Constructing a statement of objectives for the whole curriculum is a practical if demanding way of addressing these issues.

A second difficulty in Stenhouse's position, as in that of other critics of the objectives model, is his unwillingness to see that student learning in the curriculum is indeed a matter of 'performance' and that the justification of 'performances' (learning activities and their outcomes) takes us directly into a consideration of objectives. School learning is largely (although not exclusively) a mental activity which, it is true, we cannot directly observe or ascertain. In that respect it is like 'health' or 'well-being' where we also look for relevant performances – and symptoms – which serve as indicators of a condition and are themselves part of that condition. We are obliged to foster or facilitate the mental activity of learning by means of other kinds of activities than that mental activity itself. In education, the three main ways are: designing the curriculum; organizing and undertaking teaching; and providing material resources. All of these are themselves complex performances justified by the (testable) belief that they contribute to and facilitate student learning. It seems that the critics of a performance orientation to curriculum design do not object to performances (e.g. those of teachers) which effect learning, but only – in principle – object to performances that manifest learning. However, in teaching we are not satisfied merely with fostering or seeking to effect learning, we quite properly look for evidence that learning is occurring. The mental activity is not visible; indeed according to one school of thought – of which behaviourism is an extreme variant – it does not exist separately from observable physical activities. We need not adopt this position since it is sufficient to say that manifestations and evidence of learning can be found in particular actions of students. These include asking and answering questions, designing and completing projects, writing assignments, analysing problems, manipulating materials, playing instruments and so on. In all of these we are observing performances which we can – and do – adjudge to be more or less significant, using both our knowledge of the student, and educational principles, values – and objectives.

It is not necessary to suggest that 'mastery' is our goal in order to insist that qualities of performance are of vital concern to us in education. Nor is Stenhouse right in suggesting that 'speculation' is an alternative to 'mastery', or that we cannot set as an objective the fostering of a speculative stance in students. If we think that it is an important feature and outcome of education then surely we should set it as an objective and seek clarity about its meaning as well as knowledge of how it is to be best fostered and what forms it might take in different areas of the curriculum. That is, we need to understand how it would appear in the actions of students.

Was Tyler, then, whom Stenhouse criticized for his emphasis on the specification of student performances so mistaken in suggesting that curriculum planning ought, as far as practicable, to identify desirable performances in students? The implausibility of predicting detailed performances (when there can be unexpected outcomes) and the inherent freedom of the learner in an educative process are not reasons for supposing that we cannot or must not try to specify performance objectives. We can agree that student performances (a) cannot or should not be prespecified in detail and (b) are a part but not the whole of what we mean by education, but why should either of these considerations be inconsistent with stating objectives as the directions in which we are trying to guide student learnings?

The translation of broad aims into directions and structures for student learning is just what curriculum design is about. One of the reasons why there is so much justifiable dissatisfaction with schooling is that for large numbers of students this process is still missing out on what is important and valuable for them: by refusing to focus on sound objectives for all may we not be countenancing the continuance of an unfair and inadequate education system? We have already seen that broadly based, comprehensive objectives in the curriculum need not be confused with detailed inventories of pieces of behaviour. Likewise, to overlook the need to develop values, dispositions, styles and modes of action – human conduct, in short – would be to trivialize the objectives. To set objectives independently of learning situations and the activities of students, not to see them as directions, and negotiable directions at that, for activity (student and teacher) rather than as clear-cut endpoints, would be to commit serious educational blunders. Criticism of the behavioural objectives movement, by Stenhouse and others, reminds us of the dangers of and the absurdities of some uses and applications of objectives in curriculum design. What it has not done, however, is demonstrate that the model itself is erroneous or dangerous. On the contrary, a careful reading of Stenhouse's discussion of curriculum planning and his description of the alternative, so-called 'process model' suggests that his own position is not so far from some kind of objectives-based analysis. The language is different, and that is not without significance, but the tendency of thought is towards that projective, intentional, action mode where conditions for learning are defined and steps taken to establish them – in short, towards the same general type of enterprise as objectives planning in the curriculum. This should not be surprising since the modern conceptualization of curriculum, curriculum planning and curriculum development, including Stenhouse's own writings and achievements through the Humanities Curriculum Project and other innovatory projects, incorporates the fundamental tenet of the objectives model: curriculum is a matter of reflection on practice, taking thought for the future by indicating a range of learnings thought to be desirable and capable of being planned and organized, setting in motion the arrangements needed if these learnings are to be secured, and taking care to check whether what was intended has come about.

There *is* an alternative to all this, namely the libertarian or anarchic principle of leaving everything in education to the spontaneous and probably conflicting preferences and judgements of small groups of teachers and students, and it is perhaps towards this principle that the 'free' schools of the 1960s and 70s tried to move as did some progressive schools in an earlier period. Much can be learnt from the values and goals of this movement, including its elevation of a child-centred philosophy, its spiritual sense of the unity of experience and the wholeness of life, and the procedures adopted for achieving consensus out of conflict. But it has taught us relatively little about curriculum innovation or how to reform our system of public schooling. The curriculum cannot be left to the whims of individual teachers, however charismatic and brilliant, or to the child's preferences. It is the recognition of this that explains much of the structural orientation we find in modern curriculum development, including Stenhouse's own brilliant projects.

Another well-known critic of the objectives model is Maurice Holt, who finds in the advocacy of objectives in the curriculum a latter-day scientistic, utilitarian, rationalism which he believes is antipathetic to good teaching and a distraction in curriculum analysis. Holt is convinced that any kind of objectives approach will lead to the prespecification of observable, measurable bits of behaviour, a result which, if it were to occur, would be, as he rightly says, inimical to the true concerns of the educator. The specification of objectives, he argues, destroys the craft and intuition upon which good, imaginative teaching depends and results instead in a kind of 'painting by numbers' (Holt 1983, pp. 66–67). Instead of all this concern for front-end planning, and draftsmanship, Holt wants us enmeshed with the practical, the action itself.

In characteristically vigorous style, Holt demonstrates, in *Curriculum Workshop*, how 'deliberation' works in thinking about the curriculum: his notion of the workshop is itself a principle of small-group inquiry, sharply focused by the questioning of practice as revealed in school curriculum papers and of the plans and policies set forth in official documents. Holt is surely right to criticize the production of fine-sounding, political and bureaucratic documents on the curriculum if they are seen to be a substitute for professional engagement in the processes of curriculum review, evaluation and development. His strictures on some of the absurdities of prespecified behaviours which are sometimes given as the content of objectives are well made, as are his warnings about a gullible, scientist enthusiasm for technocratic models in place of conversation, tough-minded analysis and collaborative reflection on action.

Yet, when it comes to the point of what is to be done in curriculum planning and design, as distinct from review and evaluation, Holt's own remedies lead us towards the objectives model although not, I shall suggest, quite far enough for curriculum planning purposes. For example, secondary schools are advised, in taking a fresh look at the place and role of separate subjects in the curriculum, to seek 'greater coherence', to ensure that the subjects come to share 'a more clearly defined common purpose' (ibid. p. 99). Presumably, the desired coherence is for the sake of something that the students are intended to learn, not as an embellishment in a curriculum planning paper. It is right, therefore, to ask what the coherence is to consist of, how subject teaching is to bring it about, and how we are to recognize it in student learning. Otherwise, 'coherence' runs the risk of being a suitably stirring rallying cry which is soon forgotten once the workshop is over, and this is clearly not what Holt wants. If, in the spirit of Peters and Stenhouse, we are to define 'coherence' as a procedural principle, there would still seem little point in it unless it had some quantum of desirable consequences for student learning. This might take the form of a disposition by students to interrelate topics across subjects, or to make greater use of some methodologies, for example, problem solving across a broad range of subject matters. In thinking concretely about 'coherence' we begin our search for examples of student performance for which coherence can be quite properly made to serve as an objective – a student learning performance objective.

Another argument that Holt presents suggests that his position is not so different from the objectives model as it might appear. In presenting case studies of school curriculum planning, he refers in one instance to 'the underpinning *rationale* of the design'. His questions in these case studies infer that clear objectives for the curriculum, if not held, should be; and throughout the detailed discussion in the book, of what selected schools are doing, there is constant reference to what the curricula are or are not achieving in respect of student attitudes, values, knowledge and skills.

One criterion of a good curriculum design, therefore, which even the critics of objectives seem to concede, is clarity of objectives; another is that objectives should be educationally valid; a third, that they should take effect in the practice of learning. There are, though, two points of qualification to be made. First, much of Holt's discussion of schools and with school staffs is focused by questions which deal with the organization of the curriculum and other aspects of school management. It is to be expected that substantive curriculum objectives would often be raised in an incidental and indirect fashion. Second, the *manner* in which objectives are handled in curriculum review, evaluation and development is of crucial importance and Holt's critique of the behavioural model very effectively pin-points the gap between the managerial jargon of behavioural objectives and the school culture. Objectives have been reified as a peculiar kind of entity which comes to notice at a particular 'stage' of a continuing process of reflective inquiry and planning. This, and the harsh language of 'prespecified behaviour changes', may very largely account for the pervasive disquiet of the critics of the objectives approach.

We have examined two proposed alternatives to the objectives model and found them less alternatives than different ways of getting at a common, if not fully articulated, set of concerns in curriculum development. We need not attempt to take in all of the main kinds of alternatives proposed but we do need to pay particular attention to those which, on the one hand, envisage a kind of rational curriculum planning for school curriculum development and, on the other, explicitly reject the objectives model as useful for this purpose. In his justly popular writings on curriculum theory and practice, Vic Kelly has made a comprehensive review and strong criticism of the objectives movement. He concluded that in the school curriculum our primary concern must be a broad concept of education, and not instruction and training. From this conclusion he is led to eschew the objectives model (Kelly 1982, pp. 86ff.).

Kelly assimilates all forms of the objectives model to prespecified behavioural objectives. This is unfortunate, begging the very question which is at issue. He accepts, as all critics of the model seem to, a place for prespecified objectives *in training*. This qualification occurs so frequently in criticisms of the objectives model that it deserves comment. Training and instruction have a place in education, including general education and the core curriculum, which is not always properly appreciated or understood. There is no inherent reason why training should be narrow, doctrinal, inflexible, propagandist and inimical to the overall development of the student just because it is precise and highly structured learning: it may serve broad educational purposes quite well. That training is 'utilitarian' is not a condemnation unless we think there is no place in education for knowledge and skills that are justified because of their direct usefulness in personal and social life or as a means to some other end, as, for example, using a chisel skilfully is a means towards the end of cabinet-making. Instruction, too, may be educative or noneducative according to the manner in which it is conducted and the aims being pursued. Despite these educational values and applications of training and instruction, they may be and sometimes are practised in a way that is hostile to educational ends. This does not lead us to the conclusion that there is a fundamental conceptual difference between them and 'education'. Practices in schools which are defended on grounds other than their training or instructional value may equally fail to meet educational criteria. The training–instruction–education distinction is notoriously unclear and because of the ambiguities of the term 'education', can be quite confusing. It is generally admitted that some kinds of education incorporate a degree of training and instruction. Education is a polymorphous concept, and training and instruction are among its branches. It seems that for some critics objectives may be acceptable for 'training' that is clear and definite but not for 'education' which is less clear or definite – either because it is more open and general or because it is vague and uncertain. This is surely an odd conclusion, since it overlooks the reasonable claims that may be made for including training within our concept of education. Furthermore, there might be an even stronger case for thinking out our objectives for those educational processes where we are unclear or where there is scope for variety, diversity, the unknown and so on, than where we know in advance what the training requirement is.

Without going back over ground already covered, we may accept Kelly's proviso that his criticism refers to the tendency to use a narrow, behaviouristic style of objectives planning where it is neither relevant nor helpful. What, then, is the alternative 'process' model that Kelly offers? It seems that he does need one for, after a very careful and informative review of the several refinements that have been made in the objectives model in order to fortify it against criticism – such as Elliot Eisner's acceptance of a new class of expressive, or more open-ended objectives in addition to the tighter, less flexible behavioural objectives (Eisner 1969), or the adoption of a progressive-modification of objectives in the course of teaching – Kelly concludes that it is, fundamentally, an antieducational approach. This is notwithstanding his earlier concession on its usefulness in training. Like Peters and Stenhouse, he wants us instead to adopt a model of change that is centred on the professional judgement of the teacher, which in turn is to be sustained by well thought out general aims for education and principles of procedure.

As with the other 'alternatives' we have considered, this concept of aims combined with professional judgement is presented as radically different from an objectives model. It is not clear, however, from Kelly's account, that the differences would be marked at the level of practical planning and design even if they were to hold up conceptually. What we seem to have, as in so much of the criticism of objectives-based planning, is a vehemence arising from unease over where, if it were taken to extremes and reduced to absurdity, interest in the objectives approach might lead us. The objections and criticisms, as we have seen, indicate preferences for other ways of looking at the curriculum, but they do not destroy the case for the use of objectives. Thus Kelly concedes that we cannot overlook, in our planning, the outcomes that are sought or desired for student learning and he allows that we can emphasize (but not set as an objective) intellectual development, cognitive functioning and other dynamic elements in learning, provided we don't give prominence to 'quantities of knowledge absorbed or changes of behavioural performance' (ibid. p. 120). But as soon as we try to render this into learning activities and once the teacher sets about assessing the 'cognitive development' a definite relationship between general aims, curriculum objectives, teaching processes and learning activities has been foreshadowed if not explicitly identified. Making that relationship clear and trying to ensure its effectiveness is what a focus on objectives will bring about.

Kelly also shows that we may formulate our aims, as broad procedural principles, for the guidance of teachers. This is precisely one of the purposes of curriculum objectives, but they go further to identify what are professionally judged (not mechanically predetermined) to be appropriate learning activities and outcomes. Like others engaged in this debate, Kelly is committed to the kind of reflective inquiry within and through which plans and proposals for the curriculum are projected. Reluctance to express this in the form of general curriculum objectives may be a matter of taste, convenience or practical utility, it is not ruled out by the arguments given.

The three critiques and proposed 'alternatives to objectives' that we have considered are alternative in the sense of being different in language and strategy of analysis from the style of curriculum planning adopted by Tyler, Popham, Davies and those numerous curriculum developers who have structured their projects through the use of learner-related objectives. But these differences can be exaggerated and it is misleading to present them as if they were grounded in contradictory philosophical positions.

Perhaps there is another noteworthy difference, in that the critics of the objectives model, on the whole, seem to place a higher value than many of its advocates on the informed, but predictable, professional judgement of the teacher. The very interest in systems, in a progression from aims to objectives to classroom action suggests, to the critics, more formality and less flexibility in teacher action than they think desirable. Stenhouse's theories are of special interest here since they place teacher action, reflection and research at the very centre of educational reform (Skilbeck 1983a). Is there, then, a basic inconsistency between *any* form of the objectives model and teacher freedom, initiative and spontaneity? In an earlier period, this is the question that was asked of planning. Is sound planning, of its nature or in its characteristic forms, hostile to individual freedom and inimical to flexibility and adaptability to changing situations? The answer given by Karl Mannheim, John Dewey and others who believe in purposeful democratic action, is that freedom of action in social systems and organizations, so far from being within the reach of spontaneously acting individuals (professional or otherwise), requires both collaboration ('community') and the adoption of procedures where, amongst other things, participants not only try to reach agreement on their objectives but also work out the kinds of action needed to achieve them (rational planning) – (Dewey 1916, chapters VIII, IX; Mannheim 1943, chapter 1). We need not assume that the use of objectives in planning and design prevents us from using them flexibly and imaginatively.

What the critics of the objectives model do not show, is either the inadequacy of the model in *any* form or the undesirability of its continued development and refinement as one of our most useful instruments of curriculum analysis and development. They fear its inhibiting effects, and this is perhaps salutary if surprising, but do not show why schools should not use it with discrimination and sensitivity as a typical mode of practical curriculum development.

Due to the critical onslaught against objectives, for some two decades and more, we have had battle-lines drawn and only the unwary or the brave have come forward with their objectives built into curriculum plans and programmes. Over the next decade, this is very likely to change as increasing numbers of schools become familiar with curriculum planning, the analysis and determination of aims, the overhaul of assessment procedures and the need to communicate the what and the how of their curricula to parents and the community at large. In this new environment of renewed, school-level curriculum activity we may very well find ourselves turning to the systematic review, evaluation and development of the curriculum through the use of simple, powerful and economic objectives design models. The practice and issues arising from it may be expected to lead to a revision of recommended procedures for that practice, and a realignment of theoretical positions.

A design model for school-based curriculum development

We have considered the question of objectives at length, because the opposition to objectives has been intense and widespread, not to say intimidating. It is time for us to change course. The criticisms have meant an uneasiness and ambivalence about objectives which has obscured the issue of how planning and designing the curriculum are to proceed. We may not wish to reduce all of this to models for curriculum development. Yet general planning and design models are undoubtedly valuable, in identifying and interrelating significant areas of action, providing a momentum for action by pointing the way ahead, and indicating where monitoring and evaluation are required. Inevitable simplifications and distortions can be put to further use, as they can be the means of critical analysis and the improvement of the curriculum plans and designs.

In the remaining part of this chapter I shall outline an approach to school-based curriculum development which I first became interested in and adopted several years ago. As formulated in some of my own papers, it has been widely used, often with liberal variations and adaptations, in many different school settings. Discerning readers will have no difficulty in identifying its sources and antecedents. It is set out in Table 8.1, as an outline of the kinds of action to be taken in curriculum development, conceived as a process of collaborative, structured decision making.

Table 8.1

Analyse the situation
↓
Define objectives
↓
Design the teaching–learning programme
↓
Interpret and implement the programme
↓
Assess and evaluate

It scarcely needs saying that such a diagrammatic representation of the processes of curriculum making must simplify and risk distortion by its very brevity and apparent orderliness. What should also be obvious is that sequential and cyclical models of human action suffer from the disadvantage of imposing the logic of projected forward motion and anticipation on decisions that may oscillate rather than progress and on activities that may diverge or reverse as often as they seem to 'move on'. Let us accept at the outset certain limitations in all such proposals and be ready, in this one, to take concurrently or even in reverse what may suggest themselves to the orderly-minded as items for step-by-step progression. By way of illustration, evaluation is a discrete step in a design process, a set of procedures – and also a cast of mind, a way of reflecting on data and decisions which should be apparent throughout a planning programme; again, objectives need to be modified in the light of experience, they are not set down, once for all at the beginning, but are to be thought of as a succession of approximations and in this sense as organic rather than extrinsic, belonging *to* the curriculum in action, not projecting it *from* outside. What uses has this sequence of actions in curriculum planning and design? First, we may use it to provide a résumé, a kind of prospectus of tasks to be accomplished. Second, it can be the basis of agreed action and hence help in reducing arbitrary or authoritarian decisions, a matter of some importance when hierarchies may feel challenged by unstructured reviews and evaluations. Third, it will be useful if it encompasses, in simplified ways, crucial and productive kinds of action. There is some risk of circularity here which can be reduced if we are able to show that the approach proposed captures what curriculum planners, designers, teachers and others have found through experience to be the tasks that need to be carried out. Fourth, what is proposed is useful if it helps in the presentation and communication to interested parties of what is planned and is happening in the curriculum. In summary, the kinds of action represented in Table 8.1 are those required in an integrated programme for planning and undertaking curriculum development, evaluating it and communicating with interested parties. They constitute a guide to reflective action in the curriculum. We may better appreciate this by considering the five distinct elements in a little more detail.

1.   Analyse the situation

A proposal for curriculum review, evaluation or development always presupposes 'a situation': this may be as large as 'the country's primary schools' or 'music teaching in this LEA's secondary schools', or as limited as 'opportunities for second language learning in this school's option system'. Taking the DES cue (*The School Curriculum*, Circulars 6/81 and 8/83), 'the situation' for schools in contemporary Britain might be the whole, existing curriculum of a given school, its assumptions, characteristics and social relations, in the context of emerging national and LEA curriculum policy plans and priorities. In analysing this situation we have, to start with, to find ways of describing what the school's curriculum is –

not only the general statements of intent, syllabus outlines, etc., but what the Schools Council called 'the effective curriculum', that is what students are learning, in or out of the classroom, formally or informally. The Schools Council's handbook, *The Practical Curriculum*, suggests ways of doing all this, by monitoring children's learning experiences (difficult in practice – time consuming and with much inbuilt redundancy of effort); drawing up detailed schemes of work; preparing a visual account of the school's activities, etc. Similarly, there are helpful suggestions for the equally difficult task of gaining a general profile of the students (Schools Council 1981, chapters III and IV).

Comprehensive schemes of this nature exist in many schools already and reference may be made to them for guidance on factors that need to be taken into account and examples of teacher-organized analyses of the context, conditions and evidence of learning (Blenkin and Kelly 1983, chapters 2–7; Galton et al. 1980; Gammage 1982, chapters 2 and 7; Mitchell 1984; Rowntree 1977).

The 'situation' we are referring to, however, embraces not only the teachers' (parent-community-student) perceptions of the curriculum, but the teacher's own reflective self-awareness. Young teachers, especially, have to come to terms with their own situation and the curriculum is often an extension of their own values and concerns, which they need to address (Dow 1982).

But what, also, of the so-called 'hidden curriculum' (an overused and vague term!)? How do we get to the underlying value structures of the school, the message system of rules, rituals, relationships, and the 'sets' toward learning, values and other people that students bring with them to school? There is a growing and sometimes rather excitable literature on this subject, to some of which we referred in Chapter 2. It is surprising, though, how little has been said about what – other than know of its existence, or perhaps regret it – teachers and schools are meant to *do* about the 'hidden curriculum'. Generally the concept has been used as a critical weapon against schools and schooling; its heuristic potential in curriculum development has yet to be brought out. As a kind of negative capability, knowing about the assorted items covered by the term 'hidden curriculum' has value; planning the curriculum in the light of this knowledge ought to be more intelligent than planning based on ignorance. There is something paradoxical, though, in the prospect of the planned curriculum being directed against some aspect of the hidden curriculum. In making a situational analysis, we treat the hidden curriculum as part of the data for planning, neither ignored nor unwittingly reproduced but 'appraised' for its educational significance and possible utility.

Let us try to summarize some of the key questions to ask – and answer – in a situational analysis. These questions can form an agenda for curriculum review within the school. Reference to several of the Section 3 *Readings* shows how such questions are identified and addressed – or sometimes lost to sight – in the course of school curriculum development.

Within the school:

1. What is the existing curriculum including the school rules, rituals and value sets?
2. What is the students' experience of (performance in, perception of) the curriculum?
3. What is the curriculum context within the school (i.e. social climate, patterns of conduct etc.)?
4. What are the strengths and capabilities of the staff?
5. What are the available resources for the curriculum?

Wider environment:

6. What kind of neighbourhood, community, society are we serving?
7. What are the key educational policies to which we should be responding (LEA, national)?
8. What kinds of resource/support can we draw upon (LEAs, teachers' centres, community, teacher education, research etc.)?
9. What are some of the changes, proposals and developments in curriculum practice and ideas that could be useful for us here?

In short, the question we must ask is: 'What are our curriculum problems and needs and how can we meet them?'

2. Define objectives

We have already observed that defining objectives is neither a once-for-all matter nor a step that occurs only at the front end of a planning model in a defined 'stage'. The situational analysis will undoubtedly lead into a discussion of objectives; indeed, being clear about problems and needs presupposes at least some sense of purpose, an implicit aim that is not being fulfilled, a sense that things could be different and that something might and ought to be done to make them so. We have already discussed objectives at considerable length. Three or four additional points need to be made here.

1. Objectives in a curriculum should be stated as desirable student learnings and as actions to be undertaken by teachers and those associated with them to affect, influence or bring about these learnings; they need to be clear, concise and to be capable of being understood by the learners themselves.
2. Objectives are directional and dynamic in that they must be reviewed, modified and if necessary reformulated progressively as the teaching-learning process unfolds.
3. Objectives gain their legitimacy by being related systematically both to general aims and to the practicalities of teaching and learning, and by the manner of their construction and adoption in the school (see 5 below). There are problems here but it is nevertheless desirable to try to show that the objectives have a rational and legitimate basis.
4. There are several types of objectives: broad and general – specific; long and short term; higher order cognitive – lower order informational; subject-specific – global; and so on. Working groups, as Davies shows, need to select and plot types of objectives (Davies 1976, chapters 6–9).
5. The construction of curriculum objectives has to be participatory, involving students as well as teachers, parents and community as well as professionals. This is too large an issue to discuss here – we return to it in the next chapter.

3. Design the teaching-learning programme

We may think schematically of the design of the programme – what is to be taught and learnt – under a few general headings. For their elaboration it is necessary to consult the detailed and often subject-specific literature on this topic. We are considering the general, procedural principles here, not the detail. Design of the programme of teaching and learning refers to decisions about:

1. the fundamental orientation of the curriculum, as for example areas of experience in a core curriculum, or academic specialization or leisure interests in the electives part of the curriculum;
2. the groupings and combinations of subject matter;
3. the groupings of students, for example mixed ability, or special interest groups;
4. the relationship of learning in the different subject areas to the overall objectives of the curriculum – a particularly important and often neglected matter in planning;

5. the scope, sequence and structure of teaching content;
6. space, resources, materials, equipment;
7. the proposed methods of teaching and learning;
8. staffing needs and allocations;
9. timetabling and scheduling.

Examples of how decisions such as the foregoing may be prepared for and taken are given in the *Readings* and in the literature on the selection and organization of curriculum experiences (Cohen and Harrison 1977, 1978, 1979; Galton et al. 1980; Gray 1974; Taba 1962, chapters 17 and 18).

In our discussion of the core curriculum in Chapter 7, we defined nine 'areas of experience' with reference to which, we argued, the core ought to be constructed at the school level. Taking this as an example, the design of teaching-learning programmes according to the decisions listed above would, in the distinctive and individual situations emerging from the first stage of our model, undoubtedly yield a considerable variety of school-based core curricula. This variety would reflect not only the diversity of students, school buildings, equipment, locations etc., but also the different interpretations that inevitably arise in group decision making.

It comes as a surprise to some critics of core to realize that it is not monolithic or directive when used as a *strategy* rather than a *blueprint* within a national curriculum framework approach where school decision making in the curriculum has a prominent place. Use of the planning procedures proposed here for school-based curriculum development, and drawing in national policy guidelines and a design for core curriculum, need not result in external control and manipulation of the school curriculum. Curriculum decisions by schools, when orderly and skilfully executed, can facilitate their own freedom: schools can – and should – set objectives and work out teaching and learning programmes in and for their own individually defined situations; they can – and should – use their own judgement in interpreting and implementing these programmes, in assessing students and in evaluating their overall performance in planning, designing and implementing the curriculum. Time and effort given to the decisions in designing teaching and learning programmes, as enumerated above, are justified by the results in student learning and by the school's demonstration of its own capability in curriculum development.

4. Interpret and implement the programme

Unless we are engaged in training and simulations, our purpose in planning and designing curricula is to implement them in particular settings and evaluate results. The ultimate justification for all this projective activity is to be found in the satisfactory teaching and learning that take place. No plan or design can guarantee this. The underlying structures of rationality, foresight, and preparatory organization must be combined with teacher professionalism and supported by regular monitoring, review and evaluation. Will the planning and designing be worth while? Will things happen as intended? Will there be results and benefits? Schools are in principle no different from the wider educational environment when change is being proposed: the problems of acceptance, implementation, achieving what was envisaged, coping with the uncertainty, confusion, resistance perhaps or indifference, being flexible enough to adjust and modify according to circumstances, apply within schools, as they do when national projects are being implemented. The location of major responsibilities for the curriculum and decisions in the school is not a panacea. Several of the reports on school experience in Section 3 of the *Readings* make just this point. Curriculum development in the school is often carried out on the initiative of innovators and enthusiasts – perhaps a director of studies, departmental or year head, or a strong-minded primary school principal. Problems of communication, shared values and expectations, of differences of interpretation, of inadequate implementation, frequently arise.

There are one or two crucial differences between schools and educational systems which should – but do not always – ensure that the plans made by the school will be honestly implemented by the school. For several good reasons, we have accepted that the curriculum ought to be planned and designed in detail by those in the school, including teachers with their intimate knowledge of the students for whom it is intended, to ensure a good match with their characteristics and needs. The curriculum, we have also argued, ought to be designed in major part by those responsible for teaching it to ensure their commitment and practical engagement and a good match with their capabilities. Interpretation and implementation by teachers of a curriculum in whose design they have prominently figured ought to be better than other styles of curriculum development, even if the role of the school is primarily adaptive with respect to an externally produced plan and design, and if the curriculum materials are very largely of external origins. The school moreover is not, like national curriculum projects, a temporary system. The curriculum is not an accidental extra but is of the essence of the institution. In spite of these advantages, we cannot take successful implementation of well-designed curricula for granted, and must, as part of the planning process, undertake a fifth step.

5. Assess and evaluate

Assessment and evaluation are large topics and we have already referred to them (see Chapters 2 and 5). Our interest here is in the function of assessment and evaluation in the curriculum development cycle, not in detailed procedures which are dealt with in more specialist literature (see for example Rowntree 1977, and the bibliography in Skilbeck 1984c).

Assessment and evaluation are not the same but they are closely related. For our purposes, *assessment in the curriculum is a process of determining and passing judgements on students' learning potential and performance; evaluation means assembling evidence on and making judgements about the curriculum including the processes of planning, designing and implementing it.* Evaluation of the curriculum ought not to ignore student performances, (although it often does) both because those performances are part of the curriculum as experienced and because their quality tells us something about the quality of the curriculum. For practical purposes, the two processes are often kept apart: assessment (of performance) is the business of defining and agreeing attainment standards, setting tasks, observing and recording work, examining and reporting. As Henry Macintosh and John Stephenson argue in the *Readings*, there is plenty of room for improvement in all of this in schools, and for reducing the excessive weight given to external examination results as 'the final verdict' on student performance. Similarly, much can be done, and is being done, in the development of procedures for curriculum evaluation for use within the school (Eraut 1984; Mitchell 1984). From a curriculum perspective, varied, comprehensive and continuous (as distinct from 'terminal') assessment of student performance is indispensable and can be very effectively used in the curriculum review process. This requires us to shift the emphasis from assessment as a summative activity to assessment as prognostic in respect both of the learner and of the curriculum designer. Similarly, with evaluation, the cyclic nature of our curriculum development model demonstrates a crucial feature of the function of evaluation in focusing discussion, reflection and action – its contribution to the continuity of the whole planning cycle.

Just as we need well-prepared and practically useful schedules for the observation and assessment of students (including their self-assessment) so we need schedules which structure and facilitate evaluation of the curriculum. Their construction has been attempted but the widespread practice, in schools, of occasional or periodic or partial curriculum evaluation – or none at all – suggests that available instruments and procedures are unsuitable. There is a role here for schools, as in any other aspect of curriculum planning and design, to experiment with and develop these instruments and procedures.

So much for an outline of the steps in the curriculum development model. It may be, as Michael Marland remarks, that 'In the British school the main burden of curriculum planning is placed on the heads of departments, and their task is expressed in the department's syllabus' (Marland 1981, p. 88). He quickly makes it clear, however, that by syllabus he means a great deal more than topic outlines and that the head of department is expected to share the 'burden' with his colleagues. This is still (and allowing for the assumption of the secondary sector) a narrower conception of the nature of the curriculum development task than the one we have been discussing. Partly, this is because what the department in the secondary school or the class teacher in the primary school does in constructing a scheme of work is not the whole of what is generally understood – and accepted – as the school's curriculum responsibilities.

We have given excessive emphasis, in British education, to the relationship of curriculum decisions to the roles of departments and class teachers, and paid too little attention to the curriculum conceived as the whole range and variety of school learning experiences. One of the purposes of this chapter is to redress this by discussing modes suitable for whole school curriculum development – within and towards which there are vital, but not exhaustive, contributions to be made by the individual subject departments and class teachers. Thus, the objectives component infers objectives for the whole curriculum, in context – the context of the school and of the education system. Correspondingly, our assessment component must not be limited to class learnings and performances in departmental schemes of work but must reach out to encompass that wide spectrum of learnings that the good school facilitates for all its members. It follows that the evaluation of the curriculum entails judgements on the whole life of the school and the quality of experience it provides.

Summary

For the school to perform the curriculum roles that are widely expected and claimed, it needs to decide how the curriculum is to be reviewed, evaluated and developed. Curriculum planning and design within the school involve many different procedures which cannot be undertaken indiscriminately but require different kinds of ordering and articulation. Reflective problem solving, using individual and small-group studies and inquiries and incremental change strategies are not inconsistent with more comprehensive planning approaches. Both are needed in curriculum development. Their combination produces a model for curriculum development comprising the five interrelated processes of:

   situational analysis
   definition of objectives
   programme design
   implementation
   assessment and evaluation

This approach to school-based curriculum development accepts that well-constructed objectives are crucial for planning, and designing, the curriculum. They figure equally in evaluation and help structure teaching. Disagreements among curriculum theorists and others over the value of attempting to define objectives for the whole curriculum, the nature and level of specificity of objectives and the implications of constructing curriculum designs using objectives, have obscured points of similarity between the several positions taken and magnified differences. It is more helpful to schools to address these issues constructively than to adopt entrenched ideological positions.

Objectives are widely if often inadequately used in curriculum planning and design in schools and colleges and improvements are possible through a reappraisal of how objectives can be incorporated into the curriculum. Weaknesses of the earlier, behaviouristic attempts to define and articulate objectives have been revealed through a succession of critical appraisals. Different forms and styles of objectives have emerged to meet these criticisms.

For whole school development and for more specialized work in particular aspects of the curriculum, the five-stage design model can be used in reaching decisions and determining action to carry them through in the practice of teaching and learning. Decisions need to be collaborative and to be tested in action: the curriculum development model that is proposed is reflexive and developmental in that, by its continuous application, progressive modifications can be made to the curriculum by all the partners and in the light of experience.

CHAPTER 9

PARTICIPATION

'A boy who had just left school was asked by his former headmaster what he thought of the new buildings. "It could all be marble, sir," he replied, "but it would still be a bloody school".' (Central Advisory Council, *Half Our Future*)

In our discussion of the nature of the curriculum and of the school, in earlier chapters, the active roles of teachers – all teachers – have been seen as fundamental in any programme of school-based curriculum development. How these roles are best exercised is a question that cannot be answered unless we give consideration to other relevant participants, both outside and within the school. Our argument in Chapter 3 was that a major new factor since the mid-70s has been the resurgence of national curriculum roles, mainly those of officials in the Department of Education and Science (and to a growing extent in Industry and Employment), HMI and the Government. These roles are not confined to general policy determinations and resource allocations but, as we saw, extend into many areas of the curriculum itself, previously assumed to be distinctively professional, that is, the preserve of teachers and allied groups. Although the exercise of these official and political roles has not driven out other national interests with a strong professional character, such as national curriculum agencies, they do constitute an important factor in any review of who participates in curriculum making and of their claims to do so.

In this same period we have also noted growing parental and community interest in the curriculum of the school with evidence of an enlargement of formal roles, as in the strengthening of the curriculum role of school governing bodies (parents, local community, local politicians) enhanced statutory rights of access to and knowledge about the curriculum, the active exercise of choice, and so forth. Finally, with the expansion of teacher education and many different types of professional development, in-service and advanced study programmes for teachers, there has been a growing interest within the education profession itself in the ways teachers, those holding posts of responsibility and principals might participate more actively and effectively in curriculum decisions, not only within particular parts of the curriculum but in the school as a whole.

This enlargement of professional roles at the school level has been accompanied by an elaboration of the apparatus of support, consultancy and advice at the LEA and national levels, including, of course, the teachers' centres and professional centre movement (Bradley et al. 1981; Bolam et al. 1978; OECD/CERI 1982). Although, by the early 1980s, much of this expansion had come to an end and there have since been cuts in many areas, the exercise of professional roles in the school curriculum necessarily calls into play quite an elaborate network of local, regional and national agencies. For example, in primary education, local advisers and teachers' centres play a very active and often quite an intimate role in individual school decisions about the introduction of new areas of study, choice of student materials and curriculum review. Terence Joyes gives an example of this in the *Readings*. In the secondary school, any form of reorganization or major new development in the curriculum will normally bring the local advisory service into play; in the upper secondary school, curriculum change of any substance will almost invariably be related to the apparatus of external examinations.

Thus the definition of roles in school curriculum development cannot be assumed to be a fairly simple matter of relating tasks and responsibilities to particular position holders and class teachers in the school. As our discussion of 'situational analysis' in the preceding chapter shows, a wider review of the situation is called for and this will show how a network of decisions and responsibilities operates, what its strengths and weaknesses are, and how it might be used and improved in the curriculum development process itself.

There has been a lot of recent discussion of teacher roles and responsibilities in curriculum making. I have already alluded to some of the literature. The only point I wish to make in addition is that in seeking ways to involve all teachers in the school in the curriculum planning process we have not only to consider how that involvement best 'fits' the wider structures beyond the school, but also to define the scope, nature and limits of teacher freedom. The move towards greater participation challenges older assumptions about authority and requires us to redefine authority relationships. For example, what, precisely, is to be the principal's authority and power in relation to decisions taken by teacher working parties? This question is raised in the *Readings*, for example by Elsa Davies and Colin Bayne-Jardine, as principals, and by Robert Crone. It is not sufficiently answered by the conventional remark that as the principal is responsible (to whom?) the ultimate decision must rest there. Responsibility itself needs to be carefully considered, since there are several lines – to the governors, the LEA, the teaching staff, the students, the parents, the wider education profession. In curriculum development, where particular kinds of professional expertise are very important (e.g. subject matter specialization; pedagogical expertise; organizational skill; selection, adaptation and creation of materials; assessment and evaluation) the exercise of responsibility by authority figures is a delicate matter. There is usually, in undertaking curriculum development, the need for an appraisal of structures for decision making and the allocation and exercise of roles and, generally, for a clear understanding by all concerned of the lines of decision and responsibility for them. Equally, there is need to avoid the extravagant and tiresome mini-bureaucracies that often surround the group and committee work required for collaborative development. The rule seems to be: careful analysis and appraisal of the kinds of questions we have been raising and simple structures with well-understood, agreed roles and responsibilities.

It is more important that agreeable and productive relationships characterize decision making and that the work itself is successful, than that perfection is achieved – or sought – in the structures themselves. In trying to ensure that all is done well and effectively, we should aim to involve in the development process itself those who have a right to be there, those who can contribute and those whose absence could create difficulties. Do *students* belong to any of these categories?

The student and the curriculum

In this chapter, we address a frequently neglected issue and take a stand: a participatory style of curriculum development necessarily involves students. That involvement is, however, difficult to be clear about given the position of the student as the learner, the initiate, the one for whom the curriculum is constructed in the first place. The very suggestion that students – as students – have curriculum roles, over and above those of dependent learners, raises questions about the nature of authority in education and about how the student should participate in school life. These questions are usually implicitly answered in the way the curriculum is conceptualized, as a design for learning *for* students. Further reflection shows that there are problems in this answer and closer consideration of the student in relation to the curriculum will indicate that the assumption that the student is the recipient of the curriculum is unsatisfactory in several important ways.

Of all the major groups over and above teachers with a definite – if often unacknowledged – curriculum role the least discussed is the student group. Is this because, by tacit agreement, their involvement in decisions about the curriculum is properly confined to that of recipients? Should we not, however, regard them as partners in learning? For many teachers, there is something odd about the suggestion that their students, those for whom they are responsible and over whom they exert authority, could, in their immaturity and inexperience, contribute to or gain from participation in curriculum decisions. Surely their role is that of learner; let the larger decisions be made by those who are employed for that purpose!

But what is a learner and what are the roles in the curriculum that are proper to a learner? We cannot be satisfied with the suggestion that the learner simply 'receives' the curriculum. The learner must be active, responsible and engaged with the learning task. These pedagogical needs, combined with a general trend towards greater independence for young people and wider access, even for very young children, to new ideas about the scope of personal freedom, compel us to think again about the connections between students and decision making in the curriculum.

Since, as we have seen, curriculum extends to the whole life of the school, including out-of-class activities in some of which at least (such as clubs, sports or field excursions) students may well play a prominent decision-making role, the almost instinctive response – that students do not have a significant decision-making role in the curriculum – is inappropriate. Such a response is also inadequate, for reasons to be discussed, in relation to what is often taken to be the teacher's special preserve: the format and content of the teaching syllabuses. Participation in learning, with active roles for students, cannot be achieved if we simply put whole areas of the curriculum, including curriculum decision making, in a zone where entry is restricted in this manner.

There are good educational reasons for setting as one of our professional goals a wide participation in the continuing review, evaluation and development of curricula and for building into the organization of school life procedures that are necessary for participation to become a reality. From experience of many different kinds, ranging from very limited, highly focused classroom innovations to large-scale national projects, we have learned a great deal about how, in a participatory way, to set about planning curriculum change, designing programmes and projects, reviewing and assessing progress, and making the decisions needed to handle change successfully in complex organizations. But participation remains something of a slogan and is seldom addressed from a student perspective. Is the learner really the centre of the educational process?

A case for student participation

We engage in curriculum development primarily in the belief and expectation that this is for the benefit of the students in schools. Other considerations are real enough, but they are, or ought to be, subsidiary. The wider issue of participation of all the partners in decision making about the curriculum needs to be addressed with several aspects of curriculum and schooling in mind. These include organization and procedures, interpersonal relationships, efficient and effective use of time, opportunity costs, political principles and the types of participants and their rights and responsibilities. But if we focus on the student role, these considerations in the school environment should be secondary to a principle: student roles in the curriculum must have a clear educative value for students themselves. If we are to justify greater student participation in wider aspects of curriculum – over and above their involvement as active partners in classroom learning – we shall need to have reasons, relating centrally to the growth and development of the students themselves. Student roles in the curriculum are not easy to define and we must be careful in spelling them out to try to show their potential value to student learning, even if we cannot always be confident that this potential can be achieved in the varying practical circumstances of schooling.

Students are, of course, the principal reference points in the construction of the aims, plans, designs, learning programmes, and processes of curriculum development. It does not follow that their roles are adequately acknowledged when these activities are carried out. The curriculum is affirmed to be for the students, even if it is not commonly thought to be something they need or indeed are able to be involved in except as the end point of all the plans and programmes. It is therefore surprising that in a great deal of curriculum writing they are either taken for granted or overlooked altogether. Quite frequently, they are passed over in some perfunctory statements about meeting their needs or ensuring their active involvement in the learning process. This is all too common in the professions generally, where because clients are recipients, not partners, they are commonly excluded from the decisions that vitally affect them.

Consumer movements have sprung up to protect consumer rights but also to bring consumers/clients into some kind of partnership – albeit mostly an unequal one – with the providers and producers. Behind this lies a theory of alienation: that individuals, groups, whole nations are split or separated from the products of their own activity and denied access to the situations where decisions about that activity are taken, living in a world whose central activities are so conducted as to make them feel outsiders. The phenomenon of the alienation of youth when related to curriculum planning can be formulated thus: the curriculum is a plan of action for learners in whose construction they play little if any part and whose outcomes are judged in ways that exclude their self-assessments. On this analysis, alienation is both a problem *for* schools (since it is a societywide phenomenon) and a problem *of* schools (since the major school structure, the curriculum, excludes students in the manner indicated). Some writers regard alienation as inevitable, part of the human condition (Kaufmann 1971). Even according to this view, however, where alienation is seen as a condition to be coped with, an educational process would have to assist in providing the means to do so. This it can scarcely do if students feel themselves to be objects of it, and objects of its judgements, rather than members and partners in its decisions and assessments.

Perhaps we can think of students as clients. But, if so, we must ensure that the role itself does not become the means of alienating them from the curriculum. In a very unequal relationship, this can easily follow. Yet, properly speaking, clients have standing, expectations, rights, which may or may not be formally established: for example the right of appeal to professional bodies, to take their custom elsewhere, to associate with others in support of their common interests, and the right to judge provision of the service. Normally, we think of parents as clients of the school – but so too is the community and groups within it, for example employers. What we have said about students is also relevant to parents, with acknowledgement of their role as parents.

It is clear enough that in one sense at least the curriculum is for the students – designed and provided for them. But these remarks about partnership and clients remind us that it is also a social artifact, which is in some sense or other 'for' society at large, and for parents as well as students and teachers. There is confusion and disagreement about the roles of various groups; also, there is no clear-cut division between 'providers' and 'receivers'. It is perhaps unhelpful, therefore, to seek a sharp definition of 'clients' or 'recipients' and their roles. It is difficult, too, to pin down participation and responsibility to a few specific items to act on where these take many different forms and where there are serious practical obstacles to face. Since our primary concern in this chapter is with the student group, by a more detailed consideration of *their* roles we may gain a better understanding of participation in general. Ostensibly the recipients but, as I have suggested, with rather a larger role than this, the students are a good focal point. I have mentioned that not much has been said about student roles by contemporary curriculum theorists. A survey of the most prominent and widely read English books on general curriculum theory (including those which discuss all the major aspects and phases of planning and design and draw heavily upon school brochures and policy documents) that have been published in England over the past decade has some interesting results:

1. In many books there are neither index entries nor chapter headings or subheadings referring to children, pupils, learners, students, pupil-teacher relations, participation. Students are part of the taken-for-granted world, whereas policies, plans, government proposals, aims and objectives, teacher action, evaluation and strategies for change are given close attention. There seems to be a general assumption that students will receive and respond well to the curriculum designs that are prepared for them or for their teachers. Meeting their needs is the ultimate goal of the curriculum analysis, but it is often an implicit one.
2. Where there are references to and discussion of learners (often very brief), the following items receive attention:
   - ways of observing and assessing students, especially their learning performances
   - examinations and students
   - defining student needs
   - involving children in their own learning
   - activity learning methods

In these discussions, the student is normally treated as the object of concern, as for example when (in a published school curriculum document) it is said that 'the curriculum must take account of individual children', or that children can be involved (in primary school topic work) through a visit, or a film/slide show, or that the curriculum should be responsive to children's interests rather than directive of them. The assumption here is that planners, whether teachers or others, will make independent judgements about what students need and are interested in. The students' contributions – if any – to these judgements, would be made in the immediate, face-to-face situations of teaching and perhaps, from there, relayed back to the curriculum planners.

3. Where important political issues and decision points in curriculum planning, design and development are discussed, or where 'interest groups' that ought to be involved are singled out, or where participation and involvement are mentioned, it is only rarely that students are recognized as a definable interest group with any definite rights, roles and responsibilities of their own in the curriculum process. Thus, when the well-known negotiation thesis – that curriculum decisions including decisions about evaluation of the curriculum must be effected through agreement – is under consideration, children and students (and often parents and community as well) are commonly not mentioned. 'Negotiation' is between and among the professionals: project workers, evaluators, paymasters, government officials and so forth. Thus in their book on the project-based curriculum development movement, MacDonald and Walker treat negotiation as interactions among adult power groups (developers, teachers, professional bodies, publishers etc. (MacDonald and Walker 1976, chapter 3). This is the common practice of curriculum evaluators and the moves to construct a democratic theory of evaluation of the curriculum have focused on these groups with little attention, as yet, to students. Similarly, in many critiques of schooling which point the way towards a substantial reorientation of the curriculum, such as David Hargreaves' argument for a community-oriented curriculum that does justice to the cultural experience of all students (Hargreaves 1982, chapter 8), the reforms are to be managed by teachers on behalf of the students: we do not find out what the students themselves want or how they are to be involved in the negotiations leading to the new curriculum.

4. Where exceptions to the foregoing have occurred, it is usually the

authority relationships between students and teachers that are singled out, authors recommending a gradual reduction, with increasing age or maturity of students, of the scope of the teacher's authority over them (Moore and Lawton 1982).

5. It is mainly in the small number of writings in the progressive and deschooling tradition that we encounter, as we should expect, an explicit and usually quite strong case for student decision making as a major determiner of what the curriculum shall be. The authority question is again central – students should be free to make choices from an early age – but often this is combined with a general indifference towards the curriculum conceived as a design for learning. Either the school is regarded as quite incidental or even an obstacle (as with American deschoolers such as Goodman and Reimer) or as a way of life which students should help to govern. In British education, the writings of A.S. Neill (1960) give the most sustained support for the principle of student-led schooling, but relatively little attention has been given to his ideas in curriculum development projects or studies, probably because Neill seldom discusses how or on what principles the curriculum is to be planned and designed, as distinct from how the school is to be run or the pattern of relations between students and teacher. These have important implications for systematic curriculum development which have been taken up only occasionally and sometimes with unfortunate results.

By way of contrast with the usual British practice, it is common for American writings in curriculum and increasingly those in some other countries to give a prominent place to students and to parent and community roles. This is no doubt due to the administrative pattern of local school districts in the USA, but also to the interpretation given to democracy in that country, where involvement or participation of the community in schooling has been for more than two centuries espoused as a social principle.

We have mentioned the important changes in Britain through recent legislation referring to parent rights and through the DES curriculum documents where, increasingly, parent and community roles are singled out. Both in official documents here, and in the professional curriculum literature, however, when 'involvement' is being discussed the theme is usually the individual child and ways of relating the curriculum *to* the child. Thus, in their book on *The Primary Curriculum* (1981) Geva Blenkin and Vic Kelly draw out, as the single most important imperative in planning the curriculum of the primary age child, the need to focus on the child – its development and activities – and to build the curriculum through a careful (teacher-determined) analysis of ways of fostering development and involving the learner. No mention is made of the children themselves, or parents, engaging in curriculum making as distinct from learning tasks, even when the issue of the accountability of the school is reviewed. By contrast the American writers, John Lounsbury and Gordon Vars, in their by no means untypical book on curriculum for the middle years, when discussing student and parent roles, say:

> Middle school youngsters or their parents are not as continuously and actively involved in curriculum improvements as teachers, but it would be a great mistake to assume that they have no role. Students are the *raison d'être* of the institution itself. Their parents have more of a vested interest than any other groups. Though one group is young and somewhat immature and the other is a 'lay' group, they both can and should be brought into the curriculum improvement process. The initiative for their involvement lies necessarily with the faculty and administration. (Lounsbury and Vars 1978, pp. 117–118.)

The American middle school covers the age span of 10 or 11 to 13 or 14 years, so the difference with Britain is scarcely one of the age and maturity of students, nor is it due to differences in declared national policies or schooling structures. Given the general omission of student roles in 'the curriculum improvement process' in British literature generally, the explanation is likely to be found in differences in the values, assumptions and expectations of the two societies. Is this then a cultural difference of some importance deeply rooted in the differing historical experience of two countries? Even if this were true, we could still suppose that curriculum specialists in Britain have been overlooking an important issue. There are indeed cultural differences to respect, but they are not clear-cut and are now less sharp than in the past. During the period since the mid-70s, Britain has moved towards a style of curriculum debate and decision making where parents and community are gradually coming to the fore.

It is likely that as schools become more extensively engaged in curriculum review, evaluation and development, and as more effort goes into producing policy statements, locally and nationally, the issue of participant roles in curriculum making will receive more attention. As this happens, the question of student roles will emerge, and we shall no longer be satisfied with a view of the student in the learning process that is, for all its liberal and humanistic assumptions, educationally patronizing and socially too narrow and backward looking. On the other hand, we are unlikely to experience a radical and dramatic reversal of common practices when they seem to be grounded in a mixture of long-established views of the child's place in the world and school arrangements that assume the learner to be in all essential respects the recipient of a professionally designed curriculum.

What we might hope to achieve, in this situation, is a gradual shift, with all schools moving by degrees towards a more participatory style in the curriculum but at different rates and in different ways. Changes of this kind are happening in other countries. In Australia, for example, where curriculum decision making has traditionally been highly centralized in large, hierarchical state departments of education, moves towards region-alization and school-based curriculum development have identified new roles for parents, local communities, school boards and students (Kemmis et al. 1983, chapters 3 and 4; Schools Commission 1978). In the more progressive systems, students are full members of school councils and in one, the ACT, of the individual boards which are responsible for running the schools. Increasingly, they are involved in school reviews, which are a normal feature of some systems. These are beginnings, from which it is likely that student membership of the formal decision-making structures of the school will gain general acceptance. It will still be a considerable step from there to active roles in curriculum construction.

Thus, it is gradually being conceded, in education systems traditionally dominated by officials and education professionals, that schools need to encourage and provide the means for greater parental, community and student participation. The most obvious mechanism is the governing body, which must first become much more curriculum-conscious than it has been in the past, and then, with the staff of the school, explore practical ways of bringing parents and community groups into closer dialogue about the aims and directions of the curriculum. This does not answer our earlier question about how roles are to be defined and the nature of the responsibility that is to be shared. These will be hammered out at the local authority and school level, within the broad national framework of legislation and policy. The student issue must not be neglected as new authority relations are established. But, with so little attention being given to student roles in the curriculum, we can at best consider some of the needs and issues in relations between students and the curriculum to see how far and in what ways these might conceivably be modified in the course of school-level curriculum development.

'Participation' does not capture adequately all the relationships between the curriculum and the learner that are of interest to us. Terms like 'involvement in', 'engagement with', 'activity learning', 'children's interests', 'needs-based curricula' are also part of what we are getting at. Consequently, the issue is not simply one of efficient structures or of motivation: it arises from different perspectives on educational goals and values. The limits to feasible student (or parent and community) participation in the curriculum process are quickly reached where curricula are determined in detail by central ministries, or schools are dominated by external examining boards, or a narrow academic curriculum is being transmitted.

Forms of student participation

If, for the sake of the discussion, we disregard those curriculum arrangements which are inherently resistant to participatory processes within the school, there are three forms of student curriculum participation to be examined:

1. deliberate and systematic efforts to define curricula with reference to ascertained (a) learner interests, needs and values, and (b) styles and strategies of learning, thinking and behaving – a child-centred curriculum in a primary school, for example, or a special extension or transition year programme for 16–17 year olds;
2. curricula designed in such a way as to foster active, student-initiated engagement with learning, including tasks and projects chosen, devised and managed by students – as in project work, field trips and so on;
3. curricula designed by groups and teams with full and active student membership – whether through formal decision-making bodies or in working parties and discussion groups.

These three do not exhaust the possibilities but they are helpful in pointing up different aspects and meanings of participation. They do not constitute a sequence or progression although it is likely that the third type will assimilate the other two and that the second type will be found within both of the others. Neither is it implied that there is a chronological progression since, although the third type might seem irrelevant or unrealistic for younger students, the first will be relevant and practicable for students at any stage of their development.

1. Determining student interests

Taking the first of these three types of participation, we may observe that despite the numerous differences – as for example between supporters of curricula built around children's interests and those which have as their source knowledge structures or social demands – there is very general agreement that curriculum planning inevitably should have some means for determining and assessing, and not merely making assumptions about, children's learning characteristics, or affirmations of what they need. But, beyond this important yet elementary point, we seem to have made little progress in working out just how, in curriculum planning, design and development we are to make these assumptions more explicit and to incorporate, in a systematic way, knowledge about students as learners.

In the psychological literature and in studies of child-centred education there are numerous discussions of learner characteristics and of the value – and limitations – of building the curriculum around the child's values and interests. This is useful material but, as Harold Entwistle wryly remarks: 'One of the interesting things about curricula devised in terms of the interests and needs of children is the way in which these often merely reflect adult assumption about what children *ought* to be interested in, often completely ignoring obvious manifestations of children's interest' (Entwistle 1970, p. 116). He instances children's vocational interest, a point which other commentators have made the basis of their criticisms of the ways adults – teachers included – attribute values to children without trying to establish children's own views (Raven 1980).

In practice, characteristics or traits are frequently attributed to children and they are invested with 'needs' which, it is affirmed, the school has a duty to help meet. Sometimes, but not often, the curriculum designers and developers suggest ways in which these characteristics and traits might be derived from studies or observations of children, including occasions for children to speak of their own needs. Far more common, is a tacit acceptance either that in curriculum design we 'know' who the students are and what they need or that impressionistic accounts by teachers will give us that knowledge. Often, 'needs' are affirmed in the light of some claim about the universal human condition or about the aims and values or, more often nowadays, the economic needs of a particular society.

Can we be confident about the basis on which these affirmations of social or economic need are made, and how do we bring about a relationship between such generalizations, even if valid, and the immediacy of students in schools? There are some very real problems here for schools and the curriculum community generally to take up. In curriculum planning we must look for better ways of ascertaining student learner characteristics and traits and for defining their needs as learners, as part of the curriculum process. In Chapter 8 we suggested that use of a process model of curriculum development is a way of listing relevant questions, indicating means of answering them and using the results in the planning process. Philip Gammage, in the *Readings*, makes suggestions for teachers on ways of identifying characteristics and interests, not so much by bringing in batteries of tests (although these can pin-point particular characteristics) as by being more careful and reflective in their everyday judgements. Curriculum development at the whole-school level, or for units larger than the single-class group, requires us to be more systematic in the future than we have been in using assessments. A good example of this is given by Peter Mitchell, describing a complex but efficient set of procedures in his own school (Mitchell 1984).

The organization of the school and of curriculum planning to act on suggestions of this sort will require changes in subject-based and whole-class groupings since the greatest obstacle to child-centred curricula is not a school structure which provides only very limited opportunity – and resources – for child study, but our orientation towards educational goals and values. The question is whether teachers themselves are as interested in the psychology of learning as in the logic of subject matter and classroom organization and management. There are practical ways of expressing this interest which many teachers use. Systematic observation during teaching, the sharing of the worlds of the teacher and the student in conversation, plenty of opportunity to listen to and observe students, close home–school relationships, and the use of profiles detailing the students' overall participation in school life, are examples of ways of identifying student interests within present resources and arrangements.

Externally produced guides for identifying student interests and capabilities, including diagnostic and attainments tests, are in widespread use, more with younger than older students. They are often helpful to schools, yet there is no alternative, in school-based curriculum development, to systematic appraisal, and record keeping, within the school, of the student population. The Schools Council, in *The Practical Curriculum* (1981) and *Primary Practice* (1983b) suggests ways teachers can, in the course of teaching, observe students, showing how these can provide a basis for more structured profiles. At another level of generality, the Piagetian stage model of development, or the findings of attainment surveys, including APU, or interest surveys, provide schools with expectations and hypotheses to test (APU 1984a, 1984b, 1984c; Biggs and Collis 1982; Dawson 1984; Ginsburg and Opper 1979). What they do not do is provide norms which set a standard for a school so we must be careful, in using them, to avoid this trap. Their chief value is in providing constructs and comparative data on learning processes and achievements, and in suggesting ways in which schools might carry out their own, small-scale observations and questioning. Much of this kind of research, however, is still presented in a form where its potential use in schools is greatly limited. We need more of the reviews and résumés that some teachers' centres, education authorities and information centres provide. APU has begun to take a step in this direction with its Science Reports for Teachers (APU 1984a, 1984b, 1984c; Black et al. 1984).

Drawing upon such outside resources as seem helpful, the school must move towards carrying out its own studies and inquiries. The organization of the school to achieve this is the responsibility of middle and senior management in the larger school, of the principal and those holding posts of responsiblity in the smaller school. The provision of LEA support and of specialized in-service training for these purposes has been insufficient and it is to be hoped that in the new national schemes for training heads and senior staff this important area will not continue to be neglected. The curriculum is, of all aspects of schooling, the most important and its successful management and organization in the future will require far better ways than we have at present for linking curriculum planning with ascertained traits and characteristics of students.

In seeking to relate curriculum development to ascertained student characteristics, their values and needs as they perceive them, we cannot avoid the potential conflicts that John Dewey detected between assessments of the needs of the child, the society and the established curriculum. Dewey's answer is particularly interesting for curriculum developers: if we take the notion of *experience*, he said, we can find a common ground: the dynamic and fluid experience of the child; the curriculum conceived as an embodiment of the experience of the society (Dewey 1902a). The design of the curriculum and the acts of teaching, properly conducted, can themselves provide us with a way of bringing into focus our subject knowledge, social knowledge and the experience of the child. This calls for an acute sense of both the psychological and the logical dimensions of subject matter and the social organization of experience.

Our argument has been that, in the design of the core curriculum, precisely these issues are raised and in such a manner that the experience and understanding of teachers can be drawn upon. But we need to ensure that in the competition of interests that occurs when curriculum development occurs, learner interests are central. The organization of the curriculum, to achieve educative growth and development for all students, is a practical contribution. It needs to be supported by the close study of students, communication with them, and the translation of curriculum plans and designs into student-centred learning situations. In this context, a successful curriculum design is one which shows the interrelationship and interdependence of student interests and traits, subject matter and social life.

2. The active involvement of students

We turn now to what we identified earlier in the chapter as a second form of student participation in the curriculum: the principle that the student should be actively involved in and engaged with learning. This sounds obvious enough – until we reflect that there are degrees of involvement, from the deep engrossment of students with problems they have themselves defined, to the reluctant memorization of commercial cribs for external examinations. Both entail 'active involvement' but of very different kinds. Too much of the learning called for in tests and examinations – our most prestigious ways of assessing learning – whether constructed in or out of school, belongs to that end of the spectrum where we find question-spotting, the performance of tricks, memorization of isolated facts, formulae and techniques, regurgitation of other people's interpretations and opinions, and the reproduction of schemata whose meaning is lost on the learners because they are not used. This little catalogue could apply to a great deal of our assessed learnings, and hence to what students and teachers alike will tend to see as the 'real' purpose of the curriculum. There are alternatives which emphasize insight, meaning and understanding. David Ausubel, by no means a radical educationist, deplored the neglect in schools of 'meaningful verbal learning', and was followed by other cognitive psychologists, including J.S. Bruner, who showed how student structuring of learning tasks and the design of curricula to demonstrate the patterns, hierarchies and structures of concepts and ideas, not only the factual and skill elements of subjects, can help to overcome this widespread problem (Ausubel 1963, 1978; Bruner 1966, 1972).

There is, of course, a place in the curriculum for learning tasks not of the learner's own choosing and not of immediate interest to him, and not all learning tasks can be set out so that their elements are interrelated and the student can perceive their place in a general logic of the subject or area of experience. Structured tasks, including text materials and explanations and illustrations of how a piece of learning 'fits' in a sequence or a wider pattern are, however, part of good teaching and need to figure prominently in curriculum designs.

On examinations, there may be a justification for cramming if that is the most efficient way of surmounting an unavoidable barrier to further study and providing that it is not a substitute for a richer educational experience, but it cannot be regarded as an educational experience of any worth and no one could seriously propose a curriculum which set these as primary targets. Indeed, reference to our discussion (page 131) shows that this would be contradictory and self-defeating. What is necessary for the school in curriculum planning and design is to include in all stages of the design model itself procedures whereby students' active involvement and engagement are clearly and definitely stated. What does this mean in practice? Would it suffice to write this in as a general criterion and then – as often happens – simply to get on with the business of setting forth the topics, subjects and themes to be studied, ensuring that they were of a kind that would 'interest' or 'be of use to' students? Active participation in the curriculum would not be achieved in this fashion. What is meant by activity learning can scarcely be summarized in a sentence or two, but some basic conditions can be specified. First, there must be a wholehearted commitment and engagement with the learning task, and this requires a realization of how that task relates to other learnings and an appreciation of its value and significance. Second, the activity must have an element of student volition, having or fostering interest, with opportunity for free choice and scope for freely chosen further learning. Third, active participation in the curriculum is taken to mean some responsibility for it: the learner not only has some control over the learning but recognizes that an obligation is being entered into – a sense of duty towards the object of study. Put in this way, active participation is no soft option but is one of the most difficult of educational goals, for students and teachers alike.

Difficult goals, of the kind we have just been considering, need to be reduced to manageable propositions. How can we increase the likelihood of procuring the student's active participation in the curriculum? First, planning should aim to provide diverse and varied types of learning opportunities and experiences. These constitute invitations to get inside the curriculum. Second, in the design of the curriculum we have to focus on student interest and motivation and be ready to question whether or not the curriculum is succeeding in this respect. Third, the curriculum should provide scope for student choice and decision making, with definite statements made as to what this all means in different situations and areas of the curriculum and at different stages of schooling. Fourth, the language of our curriculum plans and syllabuses needs to change, from the barren specification of themes and topics as so much 'ground to be covered' to a structure of activities, questions and issues. These need to be stated in content terms, but in an active mode: doing, making, constructing, observing, testing, reading, discussing, and so forth.

In the implementation of the curriculum, other questions would need to be addressed. For example, are all the students in practice gaining access to the curriculum, or is it so designed as to be engaging and engrossing for some, possibly a majority while there is still a significant minority of alienated or dispossessed students? There is some evidence, although it is controversial, that for particular groups of students quite different regimens of learning are more appropriate than others: that is, more or less visibly structured and directional. For students with special learning difficulties, for example, greater teacher structuring and less openness of learning situations may be recommended (DES 1978a).

This example, however, reminds us of a new challenge, arising from the implementation of the 1981 Education Act, which is requiring schools to 'mainstream' students with special learning difficulties. Attention is being given to students with designated 'special needs' and research and development projects now under way could be of great value to schools in indicating how new forms of general curriculum organization can help meet these needs.

The problem of universal schooling, however, is less that of particular groups who can be shown to have 'special needs' than of large numbers who become progressively disenchanted with schooling and either indifferent or hostile to the school curriculum (Hargreaves, D.H. 1982, chapter 1; Raven 1982; Willis 1979). It is becoming obvious to all concerned that the whole basis of the school curriculum, with its profound bias towards academic disciplines geared to half or less of the school population, has to be changed. As James Hemming points out in the *Readings* student needs are not being met and social losses are one result of this.

The concept of the activity curriculum is relevant here, since reviewing and changing the whole curriculum are useless exercises unless we are prepared to work out, in highly practical ways, designs that students can feel are at one with their ideas, aspirations, experiences and needs. Their active engagement with the curriculum depends on the capability of the curriculum designers to find the right kinds of experiences and situations. In Chapters 6 and 7 I proposed that these should be drawn up, not by taking the apparently easy but in fact quite disastrous course of finding some weak form of popular or mass curriculum for the majority, leaving the academic curriculum intact for the minority, but by recasting the common core for all students. If this is to be a successful direction to follow, that recasting must set students' active involvement as a primary target. Later in this chapter, I suggest that to achieve this, especially with the young adolescent, we must make provision for the student to be not only an active but also an equal partner in the curriculum.

It follows from this that the ability and readiness of teachers to provide learnable, interesting and involving curricula for all students is vital. Recommendations and proposals for interest or activity-based, participatory learning are of little value unless the whole teaching staff of a school have the willingness and capability to organize and provide appropriate learning environments which reach out to all students. This is partly a matter of teaching style, sometimes thought to be unchangeable, but we need not assume that teachers are unable or unwilling to deploy a range of styles over and above what they find most 'natural' or 'comfortable'. If universal schooling is to work, very substantial changes must be made and these can only happen if teachers lead the way. But they need support. In other words, it is because the student's active involvement in school learning is in many subtle ways dependent on the teacher that we have to ensure that the curriculum plan itself provides for support of teachers, including cooperative or team teaching, resource-based teaching and in-service training where this proves to be necessary. The intimate relationship of curriculum development and the professional development of the teacher is discussed in the *Readings* by Jean Rudduck, Neil Russell, Glen Evans and Agnes McMahon with particular concern for school roles in in-service education, evaluation and systematic research and development.

3. Sharing the decisions

Thus far we have looked at the curriculum as a way of bringing the student into the centre of the learning process. The assumption has been that the curriculum plan, professionally prepared, defines the targets, specifies the activities, legislates the tasks and assembles the resources: the student's role is to enter this well-structured environment and participate in it. The curriculum is still likely to display serious flaws if the matter is left to rest there. However elegant the design, it lacks what must surely be an essential component, namely the participation of the learner in the definition of the learning situation and the tasks therein. Why is this to be treated as essential and how, if it is, can we provide for it? We have already answered the first question in part. To recapitulate and to develop the argument further: students in the educational process are subjects, not objects; affirmation of one's own self and one's own needs are primary conditions of human life; the fundamental rights of the student as a human being include the right to such self-determination as is consistent with the need to grow, develop and mature and relate constructively and harmoniously to other people. There is no age where this 'starts'. It is a matter of finding appropriate ways and means at any age. Needs cannot be wholly attributed but must be determined through some interchange, through mutual determination. Freedom, in the dual sense of absence of constraints and fulfilment, can be attained only where there is mutuality between adults and children, teachers and taught in the determination of needs. Attending school is compulsory, but the experience of schooling provides rich opportunity for discussion, negotiation and agreement on the nature of that experience. Participation of some sort in the planning, designing and organizing of the curriculum is one suitable and important way of making school experience more equitable, fulfilling and educative.

As we have tried to show, there need be no great difficulty of principle, at the classroom level but often the reality is different. How can we achieve all this in practice? There are many ways whereby the student can define or help define parts of the curriculum: in the choice of reading materials, the selection of projects and topic work, opting for particular specializations, choosing additional materials for enrichment and so on. Curriculum development projects are only one of the many sources of ideas and resources for these kinds of creative encounters between students and teachers whereby we can say that in the day-to-day experience of teaching and learning the students are indeed participants. The whole style of resource-based learning, which Philip Waterhouse discusses in the *Readings*, is another illustration of this point. It has as one of its virtues the scope it gives to student initiative – their self-chosen means to study. Can we go further still? Should we attempt to do so? I believe we can and ought to go a good deal further.

The greater the use in schools of self-directed or self-organized learning – whether individually or in small groups, in workshop projects or field excursions, in self-initiated study assignments or in programmes combining work and study – the more evident it is that students need to have a positive role in the planning of the curriculum. They are being called upon to exercise choice, discrimination and judgement, and these qualities cannot be confined but become self-generating. This point may be conceded for pedagogical practice, but what about the planning of the curriculum? In arguing that a general framework for the curriculum, including a core of required areas of study, ought to be constructed on a national basis, I tried to show how schools could play their part in the whole enterprise. Major planning and development roles in core curriculum belong to the school. The construction of the curriculum as a concrete programme of learning experience is properly a school responsibility and cannot sensibly be carried out anywhere else. But the school is a community in which the students are the major part – for whom the institution exists – and it would be a mistake to assume that they lack the interest, capability or materials to participate in the planning of the curriculum at the school level. It would not only be a mistake, it is wrong and a primary source of the disaffection with schooling and the inadequate level of general education in our society. Not to involve students is thus to miss excellent opportunities for the exercise of initiative and responsibility, for learning about school responsibility, for taking decisions and for relating their own views of themselves and the world to the activities in which they will be engaged on a daily basis.

Let us take some examples of what is being done or could be achieved: students of any age can help to decide how their performances are to be assessed and can join in discussions of these assessments; as they get older, these discussions are likely to bring into question some aspects of what is taught and how it is taught. Children of any age can also join in discussions of what they need. Not to involve children in such discussions is to suppose that 'need' can be determined independently of the views of those to whom the need is attributed and I have questioned the rightness of that. While it is true that there are some needs which adults must judge and determine, by the time children are of school age there are many areas of need for which their subjective views must be sought, and room ought to be provided in curriculum planning for reports on how children have assessed and discussed their own needs.

Schools sometimes make questionable claims and assumptions about need. Researchers, of whom John Raven is one of the most critical, have pointed to the disparities between what schools do (based on their judgements of need) and what various groups in society, including students, regard as need (Raven 1980, 1982). Is it sensible for us to try to maintain curriculum policies and practices that do not at least address the gravity of these issues? Needs assessments in human groups will always differ but this is not a reason for a school assimilationist policy which neglects to bring the students' own assessments of what they need into the reckoning and to address openly the issues arising.

Students are not isolated individuals but belong to families, communities and cultural groups outside the school. Although there is now a tendency to give those groups some kind of a say – but seldom an adequate one – in education, we must not assume that the group determination of the 'needs' of its members is sufficient. This point has to be handled very carefully in a multiethnic, multireligious society where there may be conflict of values, customs and mores between groups and across the generations within groups. This issue is, of course, central to the debate over core curriculum. It is equally relevant when considering how students are to participate in the curriculum.

We need a negotiated curriculum, but lack the machinery and procedures to achieve it. To move in this direction would go a long way towards meeting the recurring criticism of schooling, that it is often 'out of touch' with social trends and requirements and that it is not motivating for large numbers of students. However, we must not suppose that the negotiated curriculum will escape criticism on other counts. The affirmation of student rights along the lines I have suggested will not eliminate conflict, but it will ensure that the student's voice is heard.

Two examples of ways already in use of strengthening student participation in the curriculum, without any major change to school decision-taking procedures, are given by Jean Cosslett and Carole Ann Eastgate in the *Readings*. Their common aim is to help students objectify the curriculum and, in seeing it as a whole, to understand its value and potential for them as learners. For older students in the secondary school, this becomes much easier when they are faced with the necessity of making major choices, for example over optional courses. But their scope is rather restricted, to deciding whether to study a particular subject or combination of subjects. Is it not possible for them to be encouraged to think about and assess the curriculum as a whole and thereby to contribute suggestions for its modification or improvement? Jean Cosslett has shown that this can be done and that the imputed difficulties (students reject whole areas of the curriculum as 'irrelevant' or 'boring'; students make invidious comments about teachers and teaching) are more imaginary than real and can be adequately handled by the experienced teacher. Her interest is less in the use of such studies as a guide to curriculum planning than in their pedagogical value as a way of motivating and involving students in the existing curriculum. Nevertheless, the methods proposed could have wider applications in planning and design.

Many other instances might be given: inviting students to review their textbooks is one, and a small-scale study where students evaluated textbooks about the modern world makes an instructive contrast with how academic specialists and teachers evaluate materials (Wright 1983). Such exercises can be readily organized in any classroom and be the starting point for a more objective relationship between students and the materials they study.

What are the obstacles?

Perhaps because so few opportunities are taken at an earlier stage, as students get older, schools do not necessarily provide greater scope for their participation in curriculum planning and design, although there are very encouraging developments in British secondary schools in innovative post-16 courses (Further Education Curriculum Review and Development Unit 1981; Schools Council 1983a). What frequently happens in the school up to age 16 is that students make more and more (but not necessarily better) choices, rather as they do in options systems, regarding areas and types of study. There is a great waste of talent and experience here because, with so much of assessment and examining at this stage being summative, there is far too little feedback into courses and course planning of what the learners themselves have gained from or thought about their studies. Even the freedom they have in making choices about the curriculum is, in our system, circumscribed or trivialized by the confused and impenetrable tangle of courses and programmes for the middle and upper adolescent. Symptomatic of this confusion is an attempt, sponsored by the Schools Council and other bodies, to produce a 'map' of courses and programmes at 16+ which had to be curtailed because the authors, baffled by the complexity of it all, could find no consistent way of describing and relating them (Locke and Bloomfield 1982).

For inexperienced students seeking to map out study programmes that are available to them and would be of most relevance and interest, this situation is clearly unsatisfactory. Since the Schools Council project was attempted, it has become exacerbated by the proliferation of courses and structures under the Technical and Vocational Education Initiative, the Youth Training Scheme and the further expansion of the empire of external examinations. Doubtless there are programmes and activities of educational value emerging from all this, although they have not been in operation long enough to have been properly evaluated – and many more are likely to emerge over the next few years. So far from enlarging freedom of choice and improving student participation in the curriculum, expansion of this sort, a rapid proliferation driven very largely by noneducational concerns, at one and the same time produces a severe imbalance and complicates still further the student's task in decision making. Individual schools and colleges, participating in these programmes can do a great deal to improve matters here, by increasingly, as students mature, treating the curriculum as a joint exercise – the planning and design of learning situations.

It will be objected that the largest single constraint on all of this is the determining influence of external examinations over all kinds of curriculum decisions for the post-14 age group. This is undeniably a very real obstacle and teachers often feel obliged to accept the constraints of the examination because of their own career aspirations – and also, it has been suggested, because they serve as an aid to order and discipline (Mortimore and Mortimore 1984, chapters 2 and 6). It may not be the examinations themselves but their place and use in school life that is the problem. We ought not to accept that the pressures on the curriculum from examinations at age 16 and beyond will determine our fundamental stance towards curriculum making at any stage in the schooling process. Apart from the scope provided by exam boards for some degree of teacher involvement, there would be something odd about a situation where we submit overall curriculum planning and design to the particular demands in single subjects. There are too, as Henry Macintosh and John Stephenson point out in the *Readings*, ways around the present incubus of examinations.

It would be implausible, therefore, to invoke the examinations as a decisive constraint on student participation in the curriculum. The programme of the school still has to be constructed in such a way that choices and opportunities are maximized at the same time as general education for all students is provided. It is here that the most mature, experienced and capable students can make important schoolwide contributions as well as joining in the decisions over their own individual programmes. For this to happen, students must, as a matter of course, be brought into the decision-making process through buzz sessions, working parties, planning groups, meetings and conferences – in varying degrees and ways that acknowledge and respect their limitations as well as their strengths.

There is, finally, a humanistic principle which might lead us to take student participation in curriculum decisions more seriously than we commonly do at present. In its simplest form, the principle is that what we do for people we must as far as practicable do with them. Gaining ground at present is the expression of the principle in the teacher-as-researcher or school-based action research and evaluation movements, as discussed by Jean Rudduck in the *Readings*. In all of these cases, the role of the teacher as subject, not object, is the key theme. Self-reflection, the self-critical and socially critical school, the teachers doing the researching and the evaluating: all of these are, of course, entirely consistent with – indeed part of – the general movement towards enhanced school responsibility in education. It is worth recalling Lawrence Stenhouse's dicta: teachers must do research, not merely (or only) have research done on them; pupils must become students, i.e. take more responsibility for their own learning (Stenhouse 1971, 1975, chapter 10). These statements bring out the freedom, responsibility and centrality of the actor, whether teacher or student, in the educational process. Applying this to curriculum planning and design we can find ample scope and justification for student participation. The *application* of these principles is another matter. They can easily become perfunctory, routinized – reduced to a formal collection of roles in committees. The key to student participation *in* the curriculum is engagement with the experience *of* the curriculum, and as Schutz remarked, 'those experiences are meaningful which are grasped reflectively' (Schutz 1976, p. 69). The participatory school is not only active, it is also reflective, providing occasions when all its members can address its concerns as their own.

Summary

Responsibility and authority in the school curriculum are shared unevenly, between administrators and senior staff, class teachers, parents, students and outside bodies. Changes in the educational system have increased the complexity of roles and relationships in curriculum decision making, and attention has been largely focused on enhanced professional roles. Fresh efforts are now needed, to redefine parental and student roles. Participation in the curriculum is necessary for learning, but this participation has often been treated as a form of reception: parents and students receive curriculum decisions made by professionals. There is room for improvement, in the structuring and communicating of professionally made curriculum decisions. A still greater need is the articulation of new forms of student participation. Some educational systems have made progress in the matter of student participation in curriculum decisions and provide practical examples.

Three forms of curriculum participation are relevant to students. Child-centred education has provided a momentum in relating curricula to interests and needs. There are problems here, in the potential conflict between 'child', 'curriculum' and 'society', but they can be resolved and this is something to address in the process of curriculum planning. Procedures and techniques are available for teachers to use in identifying students' interests and needs, some of them already in widespread use.

A second form of student participation revolves around the activity curriculum. The principle of active student engagement with the curriculum is no more than a slogan unless it leads to specific roles and responsibilities for students where they have definite freedom of choice and opportunity for decision making. It is not sufficient to restrict the principle to a minority of students. There are ways of seeking to involve all students but these are likely to require substantial changes in the content and organization of the curriculum and of school life.

The third form of participation entails sharing certain planning and design responsibilities with students. The participation of the learner in the definition of the learning situation, in the determination of what is to be studied and in assessment and evaluation can be achieved in many different ways, which must be related to the experience, maturity and capabilities of the students. There are obstacles or difficulties: some structural, like external examinations and the existing methods of taking decisions; others attitudinal, in the minds of teachers themselves and in the community. The arguments for participation ultimately rest on ideas about human freedom and action. These need to be set against the objections, and connections must be established between fundamental educational values and goals and the steps taken in schools to bring them to fruition. Student participation in the curriculum is a justifiable aim, whose realization will bring about changes in the curriculum itself, in decision-making processes and in the organization of the school.

CHAPTER 10

CURRICULUM ACTION

'Resolutions of the will which relate to the future are merely deliberations of the reason about what we shall will at a particular time, not real acts of will. Only the carrying out of the resolve stamps it as will.' (Schopenhauer, *The World as Will and Idea*)

The movement of this book is towards what Schopenhauer identifies as real acts of the will. The deliberations of reason do not always lead us towards practical action but in the case of curriculum development that is their purpose and justification. Action and deliberation in the curriculum are different in feeling, style and format even when the content is similar; yet there is always a continuity, however veiled it may be, between them.

Actions on the curriculum will not arise spontaneously or evolve naturally out of the deliberations, nor are the deliberations necessarily and obviously focused through the actions. Often, in educational settings, it seems that they belong together only in a loosely assembled collection, lacking integration and coherence. This is nowhere more evident than in the different languages used in schools and about schools. The educational constructs, beliefs and values come from the same pool, but their expression and communication often divides rather than unites the educational profession. We do have a common language for the curriculum but its discourse is still rather limited and far from universal. The language difficulties point in two directions – to conceptual problems and to that ragged empiricism which characterizes a great deal of educational research. If, as is often alleged, the theory of curriculum and curriculum development is inadequately structured, or has been insufficiently grounded in educational action, it is not difficult to understand why those conceptual difficulties persist and the research retains its piecemeal and uneven character. However, curriculum theory may suffer no more in these respects than other kinds of theory that relate to human action. As theory, its problems lie in the partly charted regions between the domains of speculative, analytical and critical-empirical thought and the trans-actions and relations between teachers and learners in the social world. These regions are not only poorly charted, they are always in a state of flux. The problems of curriculum theory are not merely those of explaining and interpreting that social world (what *is* the case) or of applying psychological, sociological and other kinds of knowledge to 'practice'. They require us to project forward preferred actions, desirable values, intentions and aims for the future (what *ought, could* or *might be* the case). Decisions about what is to be done are not, therefore, simply a matter of practical choice or of technique. A much wider frame of action is required.

Our final set of questions addresses this wider frame of action, since to have a strategy for school-based curriculum development, and capability to carry it through, we must be able to interrelate the thinking, theories, global and strategic considerations, the national arena and all those other ways of contextualizing curriculum planning and development, and the organic and dynamic life of the school. Checklists *and* guidelines have their place but they, too, have to be contextualized and related to a theory of school action. To treat them as free-standing and self-justifying is to reduce the school to a functioning subsystem, whose action parameters are not of its own making. That is not the position that has been taken in this book. However, just as we have to approach curriculum development as a process of changing present reality into some desirable future state, so we have to find a continuity between the school and its actions and the wider society.

I have rejected the separation, as if into two distinct and opposing positions, of autonomous action on the curriculum in the school, and those larger transformations of society and culture whereby a national curric-ulum framework has emerged as a significant phenomenon of our educational system. The problem we face is to find in each of these tendencies whatever is valuable and dynamic and can contribute to the progress of education, through the development of schooling, learning and the curriculum. Their distinctiveness and differences will not disappear, nor can the opposition between them be dissolved, but there are possi-bilities for uniting them, maintaining a dynamic tension. School-based curriculum development, viewed in this way, is not a separate, marked-off enterprise, a kind of alternative to the big project or to national research and development; it is, rather, a way of planning and organizing the school for an effective fulfilment of its roles in systemwide curriculum development. Ways of doing this have been suggested and discussed. They require some very specific changes, to improve communications and effect closer working relationships and interchange, but also to establish new structures nationally as well as in the school itself for partnership, collaboration and a sharing of experience. Diversity and a tradition of localism characterize British society and others of a similarly democratic and open character, but need not prevent us from striving for unified policies and comprehensive programmes of action in which all schools play their part. The development of the curriculum thus requires action on many fronts. Within the school, that action is most often carried out within departments, or year groups, or in particular parts of the curriculum. My argument has been that this is not enough. Energies must go increasingly into review, evaluation and development of the whole curriculum, involving the whole school. It is in this direction that national policies for the curriculum are pointing, but it is only the school that can bring them to a practical realization.

Building a knowledge base

We are left, therefore, with the question of what is to be done. Our first answer is that we need to improve our knowledge and understanding of curriculum action in the school setting. School-based curriculum development already exists in British education on a wide scale, and is expanding in many countries with strong centralist traditions (OECD/ CERI 1979, 1982). Thus we can turn to the schools themselves for the necessary knowledge of practical issues. However, this is less easy than it sounds. The paucity of research on the topics of school-based, school-focused and school-initiated curriculum development is attested in several reviews and commentaries on the published literature (Connelly and Ben-Peretz 1980; Hargreaves, A. 1982; Kelly 1981; Knight 1983; OECD/CERI 1979; Taylor 1982). On the other hand, published case-studies of school reviews, institutional self-evaluation and local development are becoming available. These include personal and subjective reports which have a different contribution from surveys and scientifically designed experiments, but are often no less valuable (Cambridge Institute of Education 1977 onwards; DES 1983b; Eggleston 1980; Hammersley and Hargreaves 1983; Henderson and Perry 1981; Holt 1983b; Nixon 1981). Given this recent expansion of writing, we ought not to exaggerate our ignorance of curriculum innovations in schools. Thus, knowledge and understanding are accumulating from sources over and above what is reported in articles in research journals. This does not lessen the need for a further look at our information sources, our research base and our means of handling data.

The knowledge problem is threefold: (1) an inadequate framework for building knowledge and understanding and reaching judgements – a problem which has been addressed in this book; (2) a limited and rather weak capacity for gathering, storing, analysing and using the present miscellany of data sources including reports by schools on their own development work; (3) new ways to prepare and undertake research programmes – not simply isolated projects – in major issues and trends in school-based curriculum development. The second and third problems are illustrated by Stenhouse's concern to improve the documentation, comparison and systematic analysis of case-study material, much of it unpublished and inadequately reported (Skilbeck 1983a, pp. 15–17). Building up a knowledge base of school curriculum development is impracticable unless attention is given to the professional development and training programmes that will be required for school and LEA personnel. If school-based development is to emerge as a major thrust of curriculum policy, and if its scope and requirements are as I have discussed them in this book, it is necessary for us to treat the school as a place not only of curriculum development but also of research, documentation, and professional training and development, as Glen Evans argues in the *Readings*. For the moment, our attention is on just one aspect of this problem: knowing what is happening as schools undertake curriculum development, and identifying the issues and problems in practice itself.

It must become an object of policy to address the issues of research and documentation, just as it has been to lay out a framework of aims, content and assessment. Modern methods of data analysis could be used to handle the array of miscellaneous, unpublished documents. Experiments with national information centres, in the Schools Council and the Australian Curriculum Development Centre suggest that there may be little value – and great difficulty and expense – in simply collecting, collating, perhaps summarizing and storing material of this sort. On the other hand, we need to be in a better position than we are now to draw empirical generalizations from well-analysed evidence. Until we are, field initiatives in school-based curriculum development, support for these and policy positions will all be rather precarious: as much a matter of enthusiasm, pressure and hope as of carefully evaluated experience, well-reasoned theory and rational allocation of resources.

Local and regional centres for teachers were, some years ago, expected to be places to devise and operate curriculum documentation services. But for different reasons, including budget cuts, this has not been realized, except in isolated instances. However, there are other sources of information about school-based curriculum development in different parts of the country, one of them diploma and higher degree curriculum research reports. While they do not give us a complete or general picture, they are a useful and easily overlooked source. Conferences, reported observations by HMI and local advisers, the journal literature all provide additional, if often unsystematic, kinds of information. Putting all this together, we are forced to the conclusion that experience of school-based curriculum development is still not well understood, because it is unevenly and insufficiently reported, documented, analysed and evaluated. Thus we cannot feel confident that, in any educational system, we know what is happening in school development, and therefore we can make only provisional judgements about it. This serves both as a reminder that we do not know nearly enough about school-based curriculum development and as an argument that no national curriculum policy which presupposes major development roles for the school ought to proceed unless it includes provision for building up our knowledge base, and that includes large-scale surveys and evaluations as well as individual case-studies.

School-based curriculum development requires its own research agenda. Meanwhile, there are topics of obvious importance for us to be working on, in building up a knowledge base. The ten topics that follow are not meant to be exhaustive but to indicate research areas which are related to themes that have been explored in earlier chapters:

1. the scope and scale of typical within-school curriculum review, evaluation and development projects and programmes;
2. principal themes, topics, problems and issues addressed in school curriculum development, in sample schools;
3. typical ways of planning, organizing managing and resourcing development programmes in and between schools;
4. relationships between schools, local authorities and local or regional

support agencies and DES in respect of control, support and communications issues (not just policy implementation or accountability
studies);

5. examples of school developments which are participatory and collaborative (students, parents, community);
6. examples of whole-school or cross-departmental school development
programmes;
7. styles and procedures of planning, designing and evaluating the
curriculum in the school that have been successful and might have
wider applications;
8. values, perceptions and interests of participants and how these are
expressed in the course of school development projects;
9. sample studies of common core curricula, including collaborative
projects between schools;
10. characteristic problems encountered in school-based curriculum
development, together with ways of addressing them.

Such a research agenda, provisional as it is, sets targets for future action
and combines descriptive, interpretative, evaluative and action studies, all
of which are needed. The agenda envisages small as well as large-scale
projects, individual as well as collective research. There are relations
between the topics suggested to explore, and appropriate or possible
sources of research support to be identified. The agenda is suggestive, and
needs further work to serve as a programme for action. It is part of the
response that is needed in order to meet the criticism that school-based
curriculum development is being insufficiently researched.

It may be objected that, because of its intense practicality, what is
required for school-based development is not research but commitment,
action 'on the ground'. We do indeed need that action but the research
agenda is designed to assist in discovering what action there is, what
meanings and values it has, ways of communicating to other practitioners
the nature of the experience and the criteria of success, and of relating
school-based curriculum development to other forms of change and
development in education. If not exactly an action research programme
– whether defined as large-scale programmes of action undertaken both in
pursuit of policy goals and to test hypotheses or as small-scale self-
monitoring and self-evaluation by teachers of their own or colleagues'
teaching (Halsey, A.H. 1972, chapter 13; Kemmis 1981) – the rationale for
the proposed agenda includes improved practice and wider understanding
of problems of practice.

Action in the school

The kinds of activities that individuals, groups and institutions are engaged in when they are developing the curriculum may be viewed in many different ways, as earlier chapters show. They can be classified into two distinctive stances towards action: *what our conception of development suggests are appropriate normative tasks and opportunities,* and *what, from experience, we seem able to do and to plan for in schools as they are.* Although these are distinctive stances, they may be treated as two aspects of a single developmental process, since for every practical step taken there are norms or ideal reference points with which it can and ought to be contrasted. By this method, we do not only judge the actual by the ideal, but also lay open our conception of the ideal to the judgement of experience.

There are three clusters of activity which I shall discuss briefly:
1. the self-reflective, self-monitoring, self-evaluative teacher, or small group of teachers;
2. the problem-solving school;
3. the development network.

1. Self-reflection

No changes in institutional structures, resources, roles and relationships or other dimensions of social life are needed for self-reflection to occur, but moves to bring about such changes may well follow upon the critical questioning that is entailed by reflective inquiry. When discussing the processes of review, evaluation and development throughout this book, we have frequently alluded to reflection, self-evaluation and personal monitoring, but usually in reference to whole school planning. We need to see them also as individualized, personal experiences; for example, of teachers reviewing their practice, students evaluating their experience of the curriculum, or parents asking themselves about the criteria and standards they apply to the curriculum. These events may occur in personal reverie, the study circle, the small action research group, in course planning and so on.

The attractions of self-reflection as a principle in school-based curriculum development are its concern for inquiry, appraisal and deliberation on the immediate situation, its apparent simplicity and economy and its focus on personal values, individual perceptions and the self-determining individual or small group. Self-reflection can start anywhere and requires only a readiness to reflect on one's own actions and values as student, parent, teacher, and so on, to evaluate one's actions and beliefs, and to experiment with new practices. It sounds straightforward but is not. There is no need to spell out the complexities and demands of this activity, once it goes beyond the merely superficial and occasional overview. Just because self-reflection is so personal and idiosyncratic, the thought of extending and organizing it throughout a school seems strange, self-conscious and intrusive. Yet to leave it as a purely individual and voluntary activity is to ensure that it will not play a major role in the curriculum development process. Perhaps the school's main responsibility here is in providing conditions for self-reflection, quietly fostering and arranging informal study circles, rather than anything more explicit.

There are difficulties about self-reflection as a basis for curriculum action. The isolation of the teacher can be reinforced instead of being reduced; doubts and uncertainties and a paralysis of the will may occur as often in teachers or students as positive self-appraisal and renewal of commitment; if parents are involved in small-scale critical study circles, their judgement can be challenging, and self-reflection gives no guidance as to action except what the individual's own resources provide. This might be partially overcome through small, mixed-group, reflective discussions, although these need to be conducted in a manner that is open to others' experiences and influences.

As part of a repertory of processes in school-based curriculum development, self-reflection and small-group sessions on issues and ideas nevertheless can play an important role. Their introversion and subjectivity can be a valuable means of mitigating excessive zeal for administrative and organizational structures; they can be highly motivating and stimulating and thereby help to identify the individual with the processes that are under review; and they provide a vital link between the schematizations and generalizations of action plans and programmes, and the personal life-worlds of participants.

2. The problem-solving school

With the accumulating evidence of the 1970s that large-scale curriculum development projects did not seem to be having the success expected (or hoped) of them, increasing interest has been taken by innovation theorists in the so-called problem-solving school (OECD 1982, 1983). Can – or should – the school take charge of the process of curriculum renewal? We have seen already how the notion of teacher-based curriculum development was enlarged to incorporate roles for other important groups in or associated with the school, and we have examined many of the ways in which schools have successfully addressed problems in the curriculum: definition of the curriculum needs, preparation of curriculum plans and designs, selection of aims, determination of the needs of particular groups of students, deciding ways of assessing and evaluating, and defining and sometimes managing further professional development and staff training. It might seem, therefore, that in the final analysis curriculum development can be left in the hands of the problem-solving school. Such a school aims to be developmental in respect of the curriculum, and, in addition, to meet two other developmental needs of the school as an organization: staff or professional development including in-service education of teachers, and organizational development including procedures for improving school management and adjusting school organizational structures to accommodate students and their curricula. Thus three related strands of educational development can be brought together. The idea of the problem-solving school has the attraction of a responsible, well-equipped organization showing initiative and resourcefulness in identifying its own problems and finding practical ways of meeting them. This could have a particular appeal on the one hand to advocates of school autonomy and, on the other, to economy-conscious administrators. Further advantages are pointed up in Ray Bolam's overview of strategies, prepared for the OECD International School Improvement Project (OECD/CERI 1982).

The argument for identifying school-based curriculum development with the problem-solving school are persuasive yet there are certain difficulties, and only some of these are raised by Bolam in his review of issues. For example, the school has quite different classes of problems to address: those it 'finds' or which arise in its environment, those which its own actions generate, and those which are presented to it formally as requirements of the educational system. Do we assume that the school not only *solves* but also *defines* or helps define the problems? If so, as has been argued throughout this book, there is the difficulty that school autonomy becomes meaningful only when we pursue the relations of the school to the wider society and the educational system. Consequently, we have to extend the idea of the problem-solving school to include problem-receiving and problem-initiating. Doubtless the model can be extended in this way but once we begin to do so, the formulation of the problem-solving school loses some of its power and coherence.

The school is not only or perhaps not even primarily a problem-solving agency. It is an organic part of an environment to which it is adaptive and responsive; it has its own dynamic and patterns of relationships; it is evolving and changing in different ways; its typical activities are not so much problem solving as interactive, relational and developmental: problems in numerous external as well as internal contexts. Problem solving is a powerful image of the school which suggests corporate, self-directed, purposeful and forward-looking action. Problem solving requires us to seek out difficulties in practice, and to clarify them and elaborate their meaning – conceptualizing them as problems; it also requires that we formulate, implement and evaluate possible solutions to these problems. In doing all this, the school can be acting corporately and cooperatively through departmental and whole-school working parties and planning groups, it can be using instruments for observation and evaluation, and in other ways following the well-known institutional procedures for organizing for change.

All of these activities, we have seen, are highly relevant to school-based curriculum development. However, the other considerations mentioned above are also important. While it is appropriate that action on the curriculum take the form of the school identifying problems and taking practical steps to solve them, this is still not taking us far enough towards an understanding of those actions that need to be undertaken in order for school-based curriculum development to become a central and not a marginal feature of education.

3. The development network

We turn finally to what, for want of something more precise, I have termed *a development network*. This, or something like it, is the sort of phrase that captures the actions that are necessitated by our approach to school-based curriculum development. To recapitulate points made in earlier chapters:

1. The school is an organic community whose different categories of members all have rights and responsibilities in the curriculum.
2. Curriculum development is a planned, purposeful set of activities.
3. In addition to partial and piecemeal development activities, whole school curriculum development must be undertaken.
4. The school is not autonomous; its success as an educational agency depends on its relationships with other bodies.
5. Developments in educational policy, locally and nationally, envisage

new roles and relationships for schools: schools are being enlisted in a wider educational enterprise.

6. For teachers, students and parents to engage successfully with curriculum issues they need to feel involved, and to gain satisfaction and experience achievement.

These points are a reminder that the school not only has problems to solve, it has tasks to accomplish – not all of them of its own making or choosing – it needs to exercise its freedom to develop and to identify with and relate to a wider world, and it is an organism with its own inner patterns of development. This draws our attention towards issues like ways of improving the quality of experiences for all who live and work in the school, the way the school handles communications and relationships questions and the expectations it holds of itself and that others hold of it.

Action to effect curriculum development in the school cannot be taken independently of action elsewhere in the education system – this theme has been reiterated throughout this book. The school must work through its relations, discovering how these make its own development possible. For example, schools cannot proceed far in curriculum development unless they provide time and opportunity for teachers in key positions to improve their professional competence. Not all of this can be done in or by the school itself. If the right opportunities do not exist or are not taken, the school's development role suffers. The whole basis of the argument advanced in this book is that schools need a wider frame of reference than the school itself, and resources other than those they themselves control. The actions that schools take towards developing the curriculum are therefore but a part, albeit a key part, of what we mean by curriculum development. In taking those actions, it is less the independence and self-reliance of the school that need to be fostered than its readiness and ability, as an organization and a community, to think and act relationally. This means that the school will move towards a more organic and collaborative mode in curriculum development and that it will see itself as an agency for education whose visions and purposes will be realized through its creative responses to the culture and society of which it is part.

BIBLIOGRAPHY

Adams, J. (1899) *The Herbartian Psychology Applied to Education*, Boston, D.C., Heath and Company.

Aiken, W.M. (1942) *The Story of the Eight-Year Study: with Conclusions and Recommendations*, New York, Harper and Bros.

Alberty, H. (1953) Designing programs to meet the common needs of youth, in Nelson, H. (editor) *Adapting the Secondary School Program to the Needs of Youth*, Fifty Second Yearbook of the National Society for the Study of Education, Part 1, Chicago, University of Chicago Press.

Anyon, J. (1980) School curriculum: political and economic structure, and social change, *School Practice*, Spring, pp. 96–108.

Apple, M.W. (1979) *Ideology and Curriculum*, London, Routledge and Kegan Paul.

Apple, M.W. (1982a) *Education and Power*, London, Routledge and Kegan Paul.

Apple, M.W. (1982b) Common curriculum and state control, *Discourse*, 2.2, pp. 1–9.

Arnold, M. (1960) *Culture and Anarchy* (1869), edited by J. Dover Wilson, Cambridge, Cambridge University Press.

Ashenden, D., Blackburn, J., Hannan, B. and White, D. (1984) Manifesto for a democratic curriculum, *The Australian Teacher*, 7 February, pp. 13–21.

Ashton, P., Kneen, P., Davies, F. and Holley, B.J. (1975a) *The Aims of Primary Education: a Study of Teachers' Opinions*, Schools Council Research Studies, London, Macmillan Education.

Ashton, P., Kneen, P. and Davies, F. (1975b) *Aims into Practice in the Primary School*, London, University of London Press.

Assessment of Performance Unit (APU) (1984a) *Science Assessment Framework Age 13 and 15*, London, D.E.S.

Assessment of Performance Unit (APU) (1984b) *Science at Age 11*, London, H.M.S.O.

Assessment of Performance Unit (APU) (1984c) *Science at Age 13*, London, H.M.S.O.

Australian Ethnic Affairs Council (1977) *Australia as a Multicultural Society*, Canberra, Australian Government Publishing Service.

Australian National University National Clearinghouse on Transition from School (1981 – present) *Abstracts* and *Newsletters*, Canberra, Australian National University.

Ausubel, D. (1963) *The Psychology of Meaningful Verbal Learning*, New York, Grune and Stratton.

Ausubel, D. (1978) In defence of advance organizers: a reply to the critics, *Review of Educational Research*, 48, pp. 251–259.

Ayer, A.J. (1968) *The Origins of Pragmatism*, London, Macmillan.

Balogh, J. (1982) *Profile Reports for School Leavers*, London, Longman for Schools Council.

Banks, J.A. (1981) *Multiethnic Education Theory and Practice*, Boston, Allyn and Bacon.

Banks, J.A. (1984) Multicultural education and its critics: Britain and the United States, *The New Era* 65, 3, pp. 58–6.

Becher, T. (1984) The political and organizational context of curriculum evaluation, in Skilbeck, M. (editor) *Evaluating the Curriculum in the Eighties*, London, Hodder and Stoughton.

Becher, T. and Maclure, J.S. (1978) *The Politics of Curriculum Change*, London, Hutchinson.

Beeby, C.E. (1966) *The Quality of Education in Developing Countries*, Cambridge (Mass), Harvard University Press.

Bell, R. and Prescott, W. (editors) (1975) *The Schools Council: A Second Look*, London, Ward Lock.

Bennett, N. (1976) *Teaching Styles and Pupil Progress*, London, Open Books.

Bennis, W.G., Benne, K.D. and Chin, R. (editors) (1976) *The Planning of Change*, 3rd edition, New York, Holt Rinehart and Winston.

Berg, L. (1963) *Risinghill: Death of a Comprehensive School.* Harmondsworth, Penguin.

Bernstein, B. (1977) *Class, Codes and Control*, London, Routledge and Kegan Paul.

Bidney, D. (1967) *Theoretical Anthropology*, 2nd edition, New York, Schocken Books.

Biggs, J.B. and Collis, K.F. (1982) *Evaluating the Quality of Learning The Solo Taxonomy (Structure of the Observed Learning Outcome)*, New York, Academic Press.

Black, P., Harlen, W. and Orgee, T. (1984) *Standards of Performance – Expectations and Reality. A study of the problems of interpreting the APU Science Surveys*, London, D.E.S.

Black Papers (1969–1977) London:

1. Cox, C.B. and Dyson, A.E. (1969) *Fight for Education*, The Critical Quarterly Society.

2. Cox, C.B. and Dyson, A.E. (1969) *The Crisis in Education*, The Critical Quarterly Society.

3. Cox, C.B. and Dyson, A.E. (1970) *Goodbye Mr. Short*, The Critical Quarterly Society.

4. Cox, C.B. and Boyson, R. (1975) *Black Paper 1975*. London, Dent.

5. Cox, C.B. and Boyson, R. (1977) *Black Paper 5*, London, Temple Smith.

Blenkin, G.M. and Kelly, A.V. (1981) *The Primary Curriculum*, London, Harper and Row.

Blenkin, G.M. and Kelly, A.V. (editors) (1983) *The Primary Curriculum in Action*, London, Harper and Row.

Bloom, B.S. (1971) Mastery Learning and its implications for curriculum development, in Eisner, E.W. (editor) *Confronting Curriculum Reform*, Boston, Little Brown.

Bloom, B.S. et al. (1956) *Taxonomy of Educational Objectives: the Classification of Educational Goals, Handbook 1 – Cognitive Domain*, New York, David McKay.

Bloom, B.S., Hastings, J.T. and Madaus, G.F. (editors) (1971) *Handbook of Formative and Summative Evaluation of Student Learning*, New York, McGraw Hill.

Board of Education (1931) *Report of the Consultative Committee on the Primary School*, London, H.M.S.O. (Hadow Report).

Board of Education (1943) *Curriculum and Examinations in Secondary Schools*, Report of the Committee of the Secondary School Examinations Council (Norwood Report), London, H.M.S.O.

Boas, G. (1966) *The Cult of Childhood*, London, University of London Warburg Institute.

Bobbitt, F. (1913) *The Supervision of City Schools*, National Society for the Study of Education, Twelfth Yearbook, Chicago, University of Chicago Press.

Bobbitt, F. (1918) *The Curriculum*, Boston, Houghton Mifflin.

Bobbitt, F. (1924) *How to Make a Curriculum*, Boston, Houghton Mifflin.

Bolam, R., Smith, G. and Cantor, H. (1978) *LEA Advisers and the Mechanisms of Innovation*, Slough, National Foundation for Educational Research.

Boomer, G. (1978) Negotiating the Curriculum, *English in Australia*, 44, June, pp. 16–29.

Bradley, J., Chesson, R. and Silverleaf, J. (1981) *Inside Staff Development*, Windsor Berks, National Foundation for Educational Research.

Brinsley, J. (1917) *Ludus Literarius or the Grammar Schoole* (1627), edited by E.T. Campagnac, Liverpool, Liverpool University Press.

British Columbia (1976a) Ministerial Policy Statement (on Core Curriculum), *Education Today*, 3, 3, p. 4.

British Columbia Ministry of Education (1976b) *What should our children be learning? Goals of the Core Curriculum*, Victoria, British Columbia.

Broadfoot, P. (1979) *Assessment, Schools and Society*, London, Methuen.

Broudy, H.S., Smith, B.O. and Burnett, J.R. (1964) *Democracy and Excellence in American Secondary Education*, Chicago, Rand McNally and Company.

Brubacher, J.S. (1947) *A History of the Problems of Education*, New York, McGraw-Hill Book Company.

Bruner, J.S. (1966) *Toward a Theory of Instruction*, Cambridge, Mass., Harvard University Press.

Bruner, J.S. (1972) *The Relevance of Education*, London, Allen and Unwin.

Bruner, J.S. (1977) *The Process of Education*, New York, Random House, (published 1960).

Burgess, T. and Adams, E. (editors) (1980) *Outcomes of Education*, London, Macmillan Education.

Bush, R.N. (1976) Educational Research and Development: the next decade, Occasional Paper 11, Stanford Center for Research and Development in Teaching.

Butts, R.F. (1955) *A Cultural History of Western Education*, New York, McGraw-Hill Book Company.

Buxton, M. (1983) Autonomy and essential learnings: a critique of the Australian Curriculum Development Centre's view of core curriculum, *Curriculum Perspectives*, 3.2, pp. 29–32.

Callaghan, J. (1976) Towards a national debate, *Education*, 22, pp. 232–233.

Callahan, R.E. (1962) *Education and the Cult of Efficiency*, Chicago, Chicago University Press.

Cambridge Institute of Education (1977 onwards) *Classroom Action Research Network Bulletins*, Cambridge, Cambridge Institute of Education.

Case, R. (1978) Implications of developmental psychology for the design of effective instruction, in Glaser, R., Pellegrino, J. and Lesgold, A. (editors) *Cognitive Psychology and Instruction*, Hillsdale, New Jersey, Lawrence Erlbaum.

Cassirer, E. (1944) *Essay on Man: An Introduction to a Philosophy of Human Culture*, New Haven, Connecticut, Yale University Press.

Caston, G. (1971) The Schools Council in context, *Journal of Curriculum Studies*, 3.1, pp. 50–64.

Caswell, H. (1935) *Curriculum Development*, New York, American Book Company.

Caswell, H. (editor) (1937) *Readings in Curriculum Development*, New York, American Book Company.

Central Advisory Council for Education – England (1959) *15 to 18*, Vol. 1 (Report), (The Crowther Report), London, H.M.S.O.

Central Advisory Council for Education – England (1963) *Half Our Future*, (The Newsom Report), London, H.M.S.O.

Central Advisory Council for Education – England (1967) *Children and Their Primary Schools*, London, H.M.S.O. (The Plowden Report).

Centre for Contemporary Cultural Studies Education Group (1981) *Unpopular Education, Schooling and Social Democracy in England since 1944*, London, Hutchinson/Centre for Contemporary Cultural Studies, Birmingham.

Charters, W.W. (1923) *Curriculum Construction*, New York, The Macmillan Co.

Clark, D.L. (1967) Educational research and development: the next decade, in Morphet, E.L. and Ryan, C.O. *Implications for Education of Prospective Changes in Society*, Reports on Designing Education for the Future: an Eight State Project, Denver, Colorado, Eight State Project.

Cohen, D. and Harrison, M. (1977) *Perceptions of Decision Making in School Based Curriculum Development*, Curriculum Action Project, Report No. 1, Sydney, Macquarie University.

Cohen, D. and Harrison, M. (1978) *Curriculum Decision Making in Australian Secondary Schools*, Curriculum Action Project, Report No. 4, Sydney, Macquarie University.

Cohen, D. and Harrison, M. (1979) Curriculum decision making in Australian education: what decisions are made within schools? *Journal of Curriculum Studies*, 11, 3, pp. 257–267.

Connell, W.F. (1980) *A History of Education in the Twentieth Century World*, Canberra, Curriculum Development Centre; London, Harper and Row.

Connelly, M. and Ben-Peretz, M. (1980) Teachers' roles in the using and doing of research and curriculum development, *Journal of Curriculum Studies*, 12, 2, pp. 95–108.

Consultative Committee on the Curriculum (1977) *The Structure of the Curriculum in the 3rd and 4th Years of Scottish Secondary Schools*, (Munn Report), Edinburgh, Scottish Education Department/H.M.S.O.

Corey, S.M. (1953) *Action Research to Improve School Practice*, New York, Columbia University.

Craft, M. (1982) *Education for Diversity: the Challenge of Cultural Pluralism*, Nottingham, University of Nottingham.

Cremin, L.A. (1961) *The Transformation of the School*, New York, Alfred A. Knopf.

Cremin, L.A. (1971) Curriculum making in the United States, *Teachers' College Record*, 72, 2, pp. 207–220.

Crittenden, B. (1982) *Cultural Pluralism and Common Curriculum*, Melbourne, Melbourne University Press.

Crone, R. and Malone, J. (1983) *The Human Curriculum*, Belfast, The Far-Set Co-operative Press.

Croydon Education Committee, London Borough of Croydon (1984) *A Statement of Policy by the Education Authority on the Curriculum followed in the County Schools in Croydon*.

Curriculum Development Centre *School Based Curriculum Development Series* (1981), (Series Editor Malcolm Skilbeck), Canberra C.D.C.: Curriculum Development Centre *Core Curriculum for Australian Schools*; Fifield, J. et. al. *Core Curriculum: Descriptions of Practice in Nineteen Australian Schools*; Toomey, R. and Chipley, D.R. *Values and the Core Curriculum in Secondary Schools*; Davies, E. *Leadership Roles and Responsibilities*; Rawlinson, R. and Spring, G. *Support Services for Teachers and Schools*; Nettle, E.B. *Survey of Teachers' Perceptions*; Solimon, I. et. al. *A Model for School-Based Curriculum Planning*; Centre for the Study of Innovation in Education, La Trobe University *Core Curriculum and Values Education: a Literature Review*; Rawlinson, R. and Donnan, N. *Curriculum Development Styles and Structures for Australian Needs*; Walton, J., Hunt, J. and Maxwell, T. *Processes and the Involvement of Tertiary Institutions*; Curriculum Development Centre *Twenty Questions on Core Curriculum* (Video).

Davies, I.K. (1976) *Objectives in Curriculum Design*, London, McGraw Hill.

Dawson, J. (1984) The work of the A.P.U., in Skilbeck, M. (editor) *Evaluating the Curriculum in the Eighties*, London, Hodder and Stoughton.

Defoe, D. (1979) *A Tour Through the Whole Island of Great Britain* (1724–26), Harmondsworth, Penguin.

de Garmo, C. (1895) *Herbart and the Herbartians*, London, William Heinemann.

Department of Education and Science (1975) *A Language for Life*, (The Bullock Report), London, H.M.S.O.

Department of Education and Science (1976) Yellow Book (official use only), London, D.E.S.

Department of Education and Science (1977a) *Ten Good Schools*, Matters for Discussion, No. 1, London, H.M.S.O.

Department of Education and Science (1977b) Circular 14/77, London, H.M.S.O.

Department of Education and Science (1977c) *Education in schools a consultative document*, Green Paper, London, H.M.S.O.

Department of Education and Science (1977d) *Curriculum 11–16*, London, H.M.S.O.

Department of Education and Science (1977e) *A New Partnership for our Schools*, (Taylor Report), London, H.M.S.O.

Department of Education and Science (1977f) *Educating our Children: Four Subjects for Debate*, London, H.M.S.O.

Department of Education and Science (1978a) *Special Educational Needs*, Report of the Committee of Enquiry into the Education of Handicapped Children and Young People, (The Warnock Report), London, H.M.S.O.

Department of Education and Science (1978b) *Primary Education in England*, London, H.M.S.O.

Department of Education and Science (1979a) *Local Authority Arrangements for the School Curriculum, Report on the 14/77 Circular Review*, London, H.M.S.O.

Department of Education and Science (1979b) *Aspects of Secondary Education in England: a Survey by H.M. Inspectors of Schools*, London, H.M.S.O.

Department of Education and Science (1979c) *A View of the Curriculum*, (H.M.I. Matters for Discussion Series), London, H.M.S.O.

Department of Education and Science (1980a) *A Framework for the School Curriculum*, Proposals for consultation by the Secretaries of State for Education for England and for Wales, London, H.M.S.O.

Department of Education and Science (1980b) *A View of the Curriculum*, London, H.M.S.O.

Department of Education and Science (1980c) *Examinations 16 to 18: a Consultative Paper*, London, H.M.S.O.

Department of Education and Science (1980d) *A.P.U.: What it is, how it works*, London, D.E.S.

Department of Education and Science (1981a) *The School Curriculum*, London, H.M.S.O.

Department of Education and Science (1981b) Circular 6/81, London, D.E.S.

Department of Education and Science (1981c) *The Secondary Curriculum 11–16: A Report on Progress*, London, H.M.S.O.

Department of Education and Science (1981d) *Review of the Schools Council*, (Trenaman Report), London, D.E.S.

Department of Education and Science (1982a) *Examinations at 16 Plus: A Statement of Policy*, London, H.M.S.O.

Department of Education and Science (1982b) *The New Teacher in School*, Report by H.M.I., London, H.M.S.O.

Department of Education and Science (1982c) *Mathematics Counts*, (The Cockcroft Report), London, H.M.S.O.

Department of Education and Science (1983a) Circular 8/83, London, H.M.S.O.

Department of Education and Science (1983b) *Curriculum 11–16: Towards a Statement of Entitlement*, London, H.M.S.O.

Dewey, J. (1902a) *The Child and the Curriculum*, Chicago, University of Chicago Press.

Dewey, J. (1902b) *The School and Society*, Chicago, University of Chicago Press.

Dewey, J. (1910) *How We Think* (revised edition 1933), Boston, D.C. Heath and Company.

Dewey, J. (1916) *Democracy and Education*, New York, The Macmillan Company.

Dewey, J. (1920) *Reconstruction in Philosophy*, New York, Henry Holt and Company (revised edition, Boston, Beacon Press, 1948).

Dewey, J. (1929) *Experience and Nature*, New York, W.E. Norton and Company.

Dewey, J. (1938) *Experience and Education*, New York, Macmillan Company.

Dines, P. (1984) Examinations and evaluation, in Skilbeck, M. (editor) *Evaluating the Curriculum in the Eighties*, London, Hodder and Stoughton.

Dow, G. (editor) (1982) *Teacher Learning*, London, Routledge and Kegan Paul.

Dunning, J. (Chairman) (1977) *Assessment for All. Report of the Committee to Review Assessment in the Third and Fourth Years of Secondary Education in Scotland.* Edinburgh, H.M.S.O.

Education Department of Victoria Australia (1980a) *Green Paper on Strategies and Structures for Education in Victoria*, Melbourne, Department of Education.

Education Department of Victoria, Australia (1980b) *White Paper on Strategies and Structures for Education in Victorian Government Schools*, Melbourne, Government Printer.

Eggleston, J. (1980) *School-based Curriculum Development in Britain. A Collection of Case Studies*, London, Routledge and Kegan Paul.

Eisner, E.W. (1969) Instructional and expressive educational objectives: their formulation and use in curriculum, in *Instructional Objectives* A.E.R.A. Monograph Series on Curriculum Evaluation, Chicago, Rand McNally and Company.

Eisner, E.W. and Valance, E. (editors) (1974) *Conflicting Conceptions of Curriculum*, Berkeley, California, McCutchan Publishing Company.

Elliott, J. (1982) Facilitating action-research in schools; some dilemmas, Cambridge, Cambridge Institute of Education, Mimeo.

Engels, F. (1969) Ludwig Feuerbach and the end of classical German philosophy, in Feuer, L.S. (editor) *Marx and Engels Basic Writings on Politics and Philosophy*, London, Collins.

Entwhistle, H. (1970) *Child Centred Education*, London, Methuen and Company.

Erasmus (1957) *Ten Colloquies* (The Godly Feast), New York, Liberal Arts Press.

Eraut, M. (1984) Institution-based curriculum evaluation, in Skilbeck, M. (editor) *Evaluating the Curriculum in The Eighties*, London, Hodder and Stoughton.

Expenditure Committee of the House of Commons (1976) *Policy Making in the D.E.S. Department of Education and Science*, Sessions 1975–76, Cmd. 6678, London, H.M.S.O.

Fifield, J. (1981) Core Curriculum: *Descriptions of Practice in 19 Australian Schools*, Canberra, Curriculum Development Centre.

Foshay, A.W. and Beilin, L.A. (1969) Curriculum, in *Encyclopaedia of Educational Research*, New York, Macmillan, pp. 275–279.

Foucault, M. (1970) *The Order of Things. An Archaeology of the Human Sciences.* London, Tavistock Publications.

Foucault, M. (1977) *Language, Counter-Memory, Practice. Selected Essays and Interviews*, edited by D.F. Bouchard, Oxford, Basil Blackwell.

Fowler, G. (1975) Department of Education and Science, ministers and the curriculum, in Bell, R. and Prescott, W. *The Schools Council: a Second Look*, London, Ward Lock Educational.

Freeman, K.F. (1907) *Schools of Hellas*, London, Macmillan (Concluding essay: The Schools of Hellas).

Fullan, M. (1983) Evaluating program implementation: what can be learned from Follow Through, *Curriculum Inquiry*, 13, 2, pp. 215–227.

Further Education Curriculum Review and Development Unit (1981) *ABC in Action* Report on the piloting of A Basis for Choice, London, Further Education Unit.

Gagné, R.M. and Briggs, L.J. (1974) *Principles of Instructional Design*, New York, Holt Rinehart and Winston.

Galton, M., Simon, B. and Croll, P. (1980) *Inside the Primary Classroom*, London, Routledge and Kegan Paul.

Galton, M. and Willcocks, J. (eds.) (1983) *Moving from the Primary Classroom*. London, Routledge and Kegan Paul.

Gammage, P. (1982) *Children and Schooling*, London, Unwin Education Books.

Ginsburg, H. and Opper, S. (1979) *Piaget's Theory of Intellectual Development*, Englewood Cliffs, New Jersey, Prentice Hall.

Gipps, C. and Goldstein, H. (1983) *Monitoring Children: an Evaluation of the Assessment of Performance Unit*, London, Heinemann Educational Books.

Giroux, H. (editor) (1980) *Journal of Education*, 162.1 (Special issue on educational ideology and the hidden curriculum).

Glatter, R. (editor) (1977) *Control of the Curriculum Issues and Trends in Britain and Europe*, Proceedings of the fifth annual conference of the British Educational Administration Society, London, University of London Institute of Education.

Goacher, B. (1983) *Recording Achievement at Sixteen Plus*, London, Longman for Schools Council.

Golding, W. (1980) *Rites of Passage*, London, Faber and Faber.

Good, H.G. (1956) *A History of American Education*, New York, The Macmillan Company.

Goodlad, J.L. (1964) *School Curriculum Reform in the United States*, New York, Fund for the Advancement of Education.

Goodlad, J.L. (1983) *A Study of Schooling*, New York, McGraw Hill.

Goodlad, J.L. with Stoephasius, R.V. and Klein, M.F. (1966) *The Changing School Curriculum*, New York, The Fund for the Advancement of Education.

Gordon, D. (1982) The concept of the hidden curriculum, *Journal of Philosophy of Education*, 16, 2, pp. 187–198.

Gordon, P. and Lawton, D. (1978) *Curriculum Change in the Nineteenth and Twentieth Centuries*, London, Unibooks.

Graham, P.A. (1967) *Progressive Education: From Arcady to Academe*, New York, Teachers' College Press.

Gray, K.R. (1974) What can teachers contribute to curriculum development? *Journal of Curriculum Studies*, 6, 2, November, pp. 120–132.

Halpin, D. (1982) School-based curriculum review: what vocabulary should prevail? *Curriculum*, 3, 1, pp. 17–33.

Halsey, A.H. (editor) (1972) *Educational Priority*, Vol. 1, London, H.M.S.O.

Halsey, P.H. (1969) Curriculum innovation: national efforts, in Bar R.M. (editor) *Curriculum Innovation in Practice in Relation to Colleges of Education*, Ormskirk, Lancashire, Edge Hill College of Education.

Hamlyn, D.W. (1967) The logical and psychological aspects of learning, in Peters, R.S. (editor) *The Concept of Education*, London, Routledge and Kegan Paul.

Hammersley, M. and Hargreaves, A. (editors) (1983) *Curriculum Practice Some Sociological Case Studies*, London, The Falmer Press.

Hargreaves, A. (1982) The rhetoric of school centred innovations, *Journal of Curriculum Studies*, 14, 3, pp. 251–266.

Hargreaves, D.H. (1982) *The Challenge for the Comprehensive School*, London, Routledge and Kegan Paul.

Harlen, W. (editor) (1978) *Evaluation and the Teacher's Role*, Schools Council Research Series, London, Macmillan Educational.

Harman, G. and Smart, D. (editors) (1982) *Federal Intervention in Australian Education Past Present and Future*, Melbourne, Georgian House.

Harris, A. (1977) The impossibility of a core curriculum, *Oxford Review of Education*, 3, 2.

Harrison, A.W. (1982) *Review of Graded Tests*, Schools Council Examinations Bulletin 41, London, Methuen Educational.

Hayward, M. (1983) The Russian Empire, in his *Writings in Russia 1917–1978*, edited and with an Introduction by Patricia Blake, London, Harvill Press.

Heath, R.W. (editor) (1964) *New Curricula*, New York, Harper and Row.

Henderson, E. and Perry, G. (editors) (1981) *Change and Development in Schools*, London, McGraw Hill.

Her Majesty's Inspectorate (1984) *Report by Her Majesty's Inspectors on the Effects of Local Authority Expenditure Policies on the Educational Services in England*, London, H.M.S.O.

Herrick, V.E. and Tyler, R.W. (eds.) (1950) *Towards Improved Curriculum Theory*, Supplementary Educational Monograph No. 71, Chicago, University of Chicago Press.

Hersom, N. (1978) The British Columbia core curriculum: a case study in recentralisation, Prepared for the Fourth International Intervisitation Program in Educational Administration, Vancouver, University of British Columbia, Mimeo.

Hirst, P.H. (1965) Liberal education and the nature of knowledge, in Archambault, R.D. (editor) *Philosophical Analysis and Education*, London, Routledge and Kegan Paul.

Hirst, P.H. (1974a) *Knowledge and the Curriculum*, London, Routledge and Kegan Paul.

Hirst, P.H. (1974b) The logical and psychological aspects of teaching a subject, in *Knowledge and the Curriculum*, London, Routledge and Kegan Paul.

Holmes, E. (1911) *What Is and What Might Be – A Study of Education in General and Elementary Education in Particular*, London, Constable and Co.

Holt, M. (1983a) Vocationalism: the new threat to universal education, *Forum*, 25, 3.

Holt, M. (1983b) *Curriculum Workshop – An Introduction to Whole Curriculum Planning*, London, Routledge and Kegan Paul.

Hunt, A.J. and Lacy, N. (1979) *Aims and Objectives of Education in Victoria*, Ministerial Statement, Melbourne, Parliament of Victoria.

Illich, I.D. (1971) *Celebration of Awareness*, London, Calder and Boyars.

Imperial Chemical Industries (1983) *Steam*, No. 1.

Inner London Education Authority (1983) *Race, Sex and Class*, London, I.L.E.A.

Jackson, P.W. (1968) *Life in Classrooms*, New York, Holt Rinehart and Winston.

Johnson, M. (1967) Definitions and models in curriculum theory, *Educational Theory*, 17, 2, April.

Joseph, Sir Keith (1984a) Speech to the North of England Education Conference, Sheffield, 6 January, London, D.E.S.

Joseph, Sir Keith (1984b) Public letter to Chairman of Schools Curriculum Development Committee, London, D.E.S.

Judge, H. (1976) The great curriculum row, *New Society*, 21 October, pp. 119–121.

Kaufmann, W. (1971) Introductory Essay, in Schacht, R. *Alienation*, London, George Allen and Unwin.

Kearney, N.C. and Cook, W. (1960) Curriculum, in Harris, C.W. (editor) *Encyclopaedia of Educational Research*, 3rd edition, New York, Macmillan, pp. 358–365.

Keeves, J.P. (1983) A reply to Malcolm Skilbeck, *The Australian Journal of Education*, 27, 2 August, pp. 111–120.

Kelly, A.V. (1981) Research and the primary curriculum, *Journal of Curriculum Studies*, 13, 3, pp. 214–225.

Kelly, A.V. (1982) *The Curriculum: Theory and Practice*, 2nd edition, London, Harper and Row.

Kemmis, S. (1981) Research approaches and methods: action research, in Anderson, D. and Blakers, S. (editors) *Transition from School: An Exploration of Research and Policy*, Canberra, Australian National University Press.

Kemmis, S., Cole, P. and Suggett, D. (1983) *Orientations to Curriculum and Transition: Towards the Socially Critical School*, Melbourne, Victorian Institute of Secondary Education.

Kilpatrick, W.H. (1929) *The Foundations of Method*, New York, Macmillan.

Kilpatrick, W.H. (1951) *Philosophy of Education*, New York, Macmillan.

King, A.R. and Brownell, J.A. (1966) *The Curriculum and the Disciplines of Knowledge*, New York, Wiley, (Reprinted New York, Krieger, 1976).

Kirby, N. (1981) *Personal Values in Primary Education*, London, Harper and Row.

Klein, M.F. (1976) Tyler and Goodlad speak on American Education, *Educational Leadership*, May.

Kliebard, H.M. (1969–70) The Tyler Rationale: a reappraisal, *School Review*, pp. 259–272.

Kliebard, H.M. (1979) The drive for curriculum change in the United States, 1890–1958, 1. The ideological roots of curriculum as a field of specialisation, *Journal of Curriculum Studies*, 11, 3, pp. 191–202.

Kliebard, H.M. (1979) The drive for curriculum change in the United States, 1890–1958, 2. From local reform to a national preoccupation, *Journal of Curriculum Studies*, 11, 4, pp. 273–281.

Knight, P. (1983) *English School-Based Curriculum Development*, Unpublished MA Thesis, University of Lancaster.

Kogan, M. (1978) *The Politics of Educational Change*, London, Fontana.

Krathwohl, D.R., Bloom, B.S. and Masia, B.B. (1964) *Taxonomy of Educational Objectives: the Classification of Educational Goals, Handbook 2, The Affective Domain*, New York, David McKay Company.

Lacey, C. (1984) The Schools Council: an evaluation of a major curriculum agency, in Skilbeck, M. (editor) *Evaluating the Curriculum in the Eighties*, London, Hodder and Stoughton.

Lawton, D. (1980) *The Politics of the School Curriculum*, London, Routledge and Kegan Paul.

Lawton, D. (1983) *Curriculum Studies and Educational Planning*, London, Hodder and Stoughton.

Lindblad, S. (1984) The practice of school-centred innovation: A Swedish case, *Journal of Curriculum Studies*, 16, 2, pp. 165–172.

Linton, R. (1936) *The Study of Man*, New York, D. Appleton-Century Company.

Locke, M. and Bloomfield, J. (1982) *Mapping and Reviewing the Pattern of 16–19 Education*, London, Schools Council.

Lounsbury, J.H. and Vars, G.F. (1978) *A Curriculum for the Middle School Years*, New York, Harper and Row.

Lundgren, U. (1983) Social production and reproduction as a context for curriculum theorising, *Journal of Curriculum Studies*, 15, 2, pp. 143–154.

Mager, R.F. (1962) *Preparing Objectives for Programmed Instruction*, Palo Alto, California, Fearon.

Mannheim, K. (1943) *Diagnosis of our Time*, London, Routledge and Kegan Paul.

Mannheim, K. (1951) *Freedom, Power and Democratic Planning*, London, Routledge and Kegan Paul.

Marland, M. (1981) Drawing up a scheme of work, in Marland M. and Hill, S. (editors) *Departmental Management*, London, Heinemann Educational Books.

Marrou, H.I. (1956) *A History of Education in Antiquity*, London, Sheed and Ward.

Marx, K. (1904) *A Contribution to the Critique of Political Economy*, translated from the second German edition by N.T. Stone, Chicago, Charles W. Kerr and Company.

Ministry of Education (1964) *Report of the Working Party on the Schools' Curriculum and Examinations*, (Lockwood Report), London, H.M.S.O.

Mitchell, P. (1984) Institutional evaluation: the process within a school, in Skilbeck, M. (editor) *Evaluating the Curriculum in the Eighties*, London, Hodder and Stoughton.

Moore, T. and Lawton, D. (1982) Authority and participation, in Lee, V. and Zeldin, D. (editors) *Planning in the Curriculum*, London, Hodder and Stoughton in association with the Open University, pp. 35–40.

Morrell, D. (1963) Curriculum study: the freedom of the teacher, *Educational Research*, V, Feb.

Morris, B. (1972) *Objectives and Perspectives in Education*, London, Routledge and Kegan Paul.

Mortimore, J. and Mortimore, P. (1984) *Secondary School Examinations*, London, University of London Institute of Education.

MacDonald, B. and Walker, R. (1976) *Changing the Curriculum*, London, Open Books.

MacDonald-Ross, M. (1973) Behavioural objectives – a critical review, *Instructional Science*, 2, pp. 1–51.

Maclure, S. (1968) *Curriculum Innovation in Practice*, Report of the Third International Curriculum Conference, London, H.M.S.O.

McClure, R.M. (1971) The reforms of the fifties and sixties: an historical look at the near past, in National Society for the Study of Education, Seventieth Yearbook: *The Curriculum: Retrospect and Prospect*, Chicago, N.S.S.E., pp. 45–73.

McTaggart, R. et. al. (1982) *The Action Research Planner*, Waurn Ponds, Victoria, Deakin University Press.

National Inquiry into Teacher Education (1980) *Report*, Canberra, Australian Government Publishing Service.

National Union of Teachers (1981) *Curriculum and Examinations*, (Memorandum of evidence submitted by the National Union of Teachers to the Education, Science and Arts Committee on curriculum and examinations for the 14–16 age group), London, National Union of Teachers.

Neill, A.S. (1960) *Summerhill*, New York, Hart Publishing Company.

Nisbet, J. (1976) Contrasting structures for curriculum development: Scotland and England, *Journal of Curriculum Studies*, 8.2, pp. 167–170.

Nisbet, J. (1979) An international perspective, in Ramsay, P. (editor) *Issues in Curriculum Development*, Auckland, New Zealand Institute of Education.

Nixon, J. (editor) (1981) *A Teachers' Guide to Action Research*, London, Grant McIntyre.

The Open University (1976) *E203 Case Study 2, The West Riding: Changes in Primary Education*, Milton Keynes, Bucks, The Open University.

O.E.C.D. (1975) *Educational Development Strategy in England and Wales*, Paris, O.E.C.D.

O.E.C.D. (1983) *Compulsory Schooling in a Changing World*, Paris, O.E.C.D.

O.E.C.D./C.E.R.I. (1973) *Case Studies of Educational Innovation: IV Strategies for Innovation in Education*, Paris, O.E.C.D.

O.E.C.D./C.E.R.I. (1975a) *Handbook of Curriculum Development*, Paris, O.E.C.D.

O.E.C.D./C.E.R.I. (1975b) *Educational Development Strategy in England and Wales*, Paris, O.E.C.D.

O.E.C.D./C.E.R.I. (1978) *Creativity of the School*, Paris, O.E.C.D.

O.E.C.D./C.E.R.I. (1979) *School-based Curriculum Development*, Paris, O.E.C.D.

O.E.C.D./C.E.R.I. (1982) International School Improvement Project: strategies for school improvement, Paris, O.E.C.D., Mimeo.

O.E.C.D./C.E.R.I. (1983) International School Improvement Project: contributions to the discussion on strategies of change in a centralized educational system, the case of France, Paris, O.E.C.D., Mimeo.

Parsons, C., Steadman, S.D. and Salter, B.G. (1983) Communication and the curriculum, the Schools Council's national projects, *Curriculum*, 4.2, pp. 25–30.

Passmore, J.A. (1970) *The Perfectibility of Man*, London, Duckworth.

Peters, R.S. (1959) Must an educator have an aim? *Authority Responsibility and Education*, London, George Allen and Unwin Limited.

Peters, R.S. (1964) Education as initiation, London, University of London Press and Evans Brothers.

Peters, R.S. (1972a) Education and the educated man, in Dearden, R.F., Hirst, P.H. and Peters, R.S. (editors) *A Critique of Current Educational Aims*, London, Routledge and Kegan Paul, pp. 1–16.

Peters, R.S. (1972b) Education and human development, in Dearden, R.F., Hirst, P.H. and Peters, R.S. (editors) *Education and Reason*, London, Routledge and Kegan Paul.

Popham, W.J. (1969a) Objectives and instruction, in Popham, W.J. et. al., *Instructional Objectives*, American Educational Research Association Monograph

Series on Curriculum Evaluation, Chicago, Rand McNally, pp. 32–64.

Popham, W.J. (1969b) Probing the validity of arguments against behavioural goals, in Anderson, R.C. et. al. (editors) *Current Research on Instruction*, Englewood Cliffs, New Jersey, Prentice Hall, pp. 66–72.

Popham, W.J. (1975) *Educational Evaluation*, Englewood Cliffs, New Jersey, Prentice Hall.

Popper, K. (1962) *The Open Society and its Enemies*, Vols. 1 and 2, London, Routledge and Kegan Paul.

Raven, J. (1980) *Parents, Teachers and Children*, London, Hodder and Stoughton.

Raven, J. (1982) *Competence in Modern Society*, London, W.K. Lewis.

Reid, M.I. (1978–79) The common core curriculum: reflections on the current debate, *Educational Researcher*, 21.2, pp. 47–102.

Reid, W.A. (1978) *Thinking about the Curriculum: the nature and treatment of curriculum problems*, London, Routledge and Kegan Paul.

Reid, W.A. (1981) The deliberative approach to the study of the curriculum and its relation to critical pluralism, in Lawn, M. and Barton, L. (editors), *Rethinking Curriculum Studies*, London, Croom Helm, pp. 160–187.

Reynolds, J. and Skilbeck, M. (1976) *Culture and the Classroom*, London, Open Books.

Rooper, T.G. (1907) Handiwork in education, in Tatton, R.G. (editor), *Selected Writings of Thomas Godolphin Rooper H.M.I.*, London, Blackie and Son.

Rosenbloom, P. (editor) (1964) *Modern Viewpoints in the Curriculum*, New York, McGraw Hill.

Ross, J.A. (1980) The influence of the principal on the curriculum decisions of teachers, *Journal of Curriculum Studies*, 12.3, pp. 219–230.

Rousseau, J.J. (1911) *Emile* (1762) translated by B. Foxley, London, Dent.

Rowntree, D. (1977) *Assessing Students: How Shall We Know Them?* London, Harper and Row.

Rowntree, D. (1982) *Educational Technology in Curriculum Development*, 2nd edition, London, Harper and Row.

Salis, J. (1979) Beyond the market place: a parent's view, in Lello, J. (editor) *Accountability in Education*, London, Ward Lock Educational, pp. 110–116.

Salter, B. and Tapper, T. (1981) *Education, Politics and the State*, London, Grant McIntyre.

Schaff, A. (1970) The Marxist theory of social development, in Eisenstadt, S.N. (editor), *Readings in Social Evolution and Development*, Oxford, Pergamon Press.

Schilpp, P.A. (editor) (1939) *The Philosophy of John Dewey*, Evanston, Illinois, Northwestern University Press.

Schon, D. (1971) *Beyond the Stable State: Public and Private Learning in a Changing Society*, Harmondsworth, Middlesex, Penguin Books.

Schools Commission (1978) *School Based Decision Making Parts 1 and 2*, Reports of a National Conference, Canberra, Schools Commission.

Schools Commission (1981) *Report for the Triennium 1982–84*, Canberra, Schools Commision.

Schools Council (1967a) *The New Curriculum: a presentation of ideas, experiments and practical developments, selected from Schools Council Publications 1964–67*, London, H.M.S.O.

Schools Council (1967b) *The First Three Years, 1964–67*, London, H.M.S.O.

Schools Council (1969) *With Objectives in Mind*, London, Macdonald and Company.

Schools Council (1973) *Pattern and Variation in Curriculum Development Projects*, Schools Council Research Studies, London, Macmillan for the Schools Council.

Schools Council (1975) *The Whole Curriculum 13–16*, Working Paper 53, London, Evans/Methuen Educational.

Schools Council (1978) *Constitution of the Schools Council for Curriculum and Examinations as from 1 September 1978*, London, Schools Council.

Schools Council (1979) *Principles and Programmes*, London, Schools Council.

Schools Council (1981) *The Practical Curriculum*, Working Paper 70, London, Methuen Educational.

Schools Council (1982) *Issues and Achievements*, London, Schools Council.

Schools Council (1983a) *Planning One-Year 16–17 Courses*, Schools Council Pamphlet 21, London, Schools Council.

Schools Council (1983b) *Primary Practice*, Working Paper 75, London, Methuen Educational.

Schools Council (1984) *The Final Years 1982–84*, London, Schools Council.

Schopenhauer, A. (1907) *The World as Will and Idea*, translated by R.B. Haldane and J. Kemp, London, Kegan Paul, Trench, Trubner and Co.

Schubert, W.H. (1980) *Curriculum Books: The First Eighty Years*, Lanham Md., The University of America.

Schutz, A. (1976) *The Phenomenology of the Social World*, translated by G. Walsh and A. Lehnert, London, Heinemann Educational Books.

Schwab, J.J. (1969) The practical: a language for curriculum, *School Review*, November.

Schwab, J.J. (1971) The practical: arts of eclectic, *School Review*, August.

Schwab, J.J. (1983) The practical 4: something for curriculum professors to do, *Curriculum Inquiry*, 13.3, Fall, pp. 239–265.

Secretary of State for Education and Science (1982) *The Secondary School Curriculum and Examinations – Initial Government Observations on the Second Report from the Education, Science and Arts Committee, Session 1981–82*, London, H.M.S.O.

Seddon, T. (1981) Intention and reality of school-based curriculum development, *Curriculum Perspectives*, 2, 1, pp. 9–16.

Seeley, W.C. (1867) Liberal education in universities, in Farrar, F.W. (editor) *Essays on a Liberal Education*, London, Macmillan.

Seguel, M.L. (1966) *The Curriculum Field – Its Formative Years*, New York, Columbia University Teachers College Press.

Selleck, R.J.W. (1969) *The New Education*, Melbourne, Pitman.

Skilbeck, M. (1974) School based curriculum development and teacher education policy, Paris, OECD Mimeo.

Skilbeck, M. (1975) The school and cultural development, in Golby, M. et al, *Curriculum Design*, London, Croom Helm and The Open University Press, pp. 27–35.

Skilbeck, M. (1981) The framework takes shape, *The Times Educational Supplement*, 4 December, p. 4

Skilbeck, M. (1982a) *A Core Curriculum for the Common School*, London, University of London Institute of Education.

Skilbeck, M. (1982b) Three educational ideologies, in Horten, T. and Raggatt, P. (editors) *Challenge and Change in the Curriculum*, London, Hodder and Stoughton and The Open University, pp. 7–18.

Skilbeck, M. (1983a) Lawrence Stenhouse: research methodology, *British Educational Research Journal*, 9, 1, pp. 11–20.

Skilbeck, M. (1983b) Education and change in South Australia, *The Australian Journal of Education*, 27, 2, pp. 99–110.

Skilbeck, M. (editor) (1984a) *Readings in School Based Curriculum Development*, London, Harper and Row.

Skilbeck, M. (editor) (1984b) *Evaluating the Curriculum in the Eighties*, London, Hodder and Stoughton.

Skilbeck, M. (1984c) Curriculum development: from R-D-D to Review, Evaluate, Develop (R-E-D), in Nisbet, M. (editor) *World Yearbook of Education 1984/85*, London, Kogan Page.

Smart, D. (1978) *Federal Aid to Australian Schools*, Brisbane, University of Queensland Press.

Smith, B.O., Stanley, W.O. and Shores, J.H. (1957) *Fundamentals of Curriculum Development*, revised edition, New York, Harcourt, Brace and World.

Smolicz, J.J. (1979) *Culture and Education in a Plural Society*, Canberra, Curriculum Development Centre.

Sockett, H. (1976) *Designing the Curriculum*, London, Open Books.

Steadman, S.D. et al. (1978–81) *Reports in the Impact and Take-Up Project*, London, Schools Council.

Stenhouse, L. (1971) Pupils into students, *Dialogue*, Schools Council Newsletter 5, pp. 10–12.

Stenhouse, L. (1975) *An Introduction to Curriculum Research and Development*, London, Heinemann.

Stenhouse, L. (editor) (1980) *Curriculum Research and Development in Action*, London, Heinemann.

Stent, M.D., Hazard, W.R. and Rivlin, H.N. (editors) (1973) *Cultural Pluralism in Education*, New York, Appleton Century Crofts.

Taba, H. (1962) *Curriculum Development: Theory and Practice*, New York, Harcourt Brace and World.

Tasmania Department of Education (1978) *Report of the TEND Committee* (Tasmanian Education: Next Decade), Chairman, W.F. Connell, Tasmania, Department of Education.

Tawney, D. (editor) (1973) *Evaluation in Curriculum Development: Twelve Case Studies*, Schools Council Research Series, London, Macmillan.

Tawney, D. (editor) (1976) *Curriculum Evaluation Today*, Schools Council Research Series, London, Macmillan.

Taylor, P.H. (1982) Curriculum research: retrospect and prospect, *Journal of Curriculum Studies*, 14, 1, pp. 53–59.

Tetroe, J. and Woodruff, E. (1980–81) The education of an educator – Jerome Bruner interviewed, *Interchange*, 11, 2, pp. 30–38.

Thomas, N. (1979) Primary education in England, *Primary Education Review*, Spring, 6, pp. 4–6.

Travers, R.M. (1966) Towards taking the fun out of building a theory of instruction, *Teachers College Record*, 68, 1, pp. 49–60.

Travers, R.M. (1977) *Essentials of Learning*, 4th edition, New York, Macmillan.

Tripp, D. (1981) The overcrowded core: a cause for concern, *Curriculum Perspectives*, 1, 2, pp. 51–56.

Tripp, D.H. and Watt, A.J. (1984) Core curriculum: what it is and why we don't need one, *Journal of Curriculum Studies*, 16, 2, pp. 131–141.

Turner, M. (1981) Contemporary moves for core curriculum, in Centre for the Study of Innovation in Educaton, School of Education, La Trobe University, *Core Curriculum and Values Education: A Literature Review*, Canberra, Curriculum Development Centre, pp. 85–106.

Tyler, R.W. (1949) *Basic Principles of Curriculum and Instruction*, Chicago, University of Chicago Press. (also 1969).

Tyler, R.W. (1964) Some persistent questions on the defining of objectives, in Lindvall, C.M. (editor) *Defining Educational Objectives*, Pittsburgh, University of Pittsburgh Press, pp. 77–83.

UNESCO (1978) *Fifth Regional Consultation Meeting on the Asian Programme of Educational Innovation for Development, Final Report*, Bangkok, UNESCO.

Victorian Institute of Secondary Education (1981) Discussion Paper on Guidelines for Descriptive Assessments, Melbourne, VISE.

Waterhouse, P. (1983) *Managing the Learning Process*, London, McGraw Hill.

Weinstock, A. (1976) I blame the teachers, *The Times Educational Supplement*, 23 January.

Westbury, I. and Wilkof, N.J. (editors) (1978) *Science, Curriculum and Liberal Education*, Chicago, University of Chicago Press.

Weston, P. (1979) *Negotiating the Curriculum. A Study in Secondary Schooling*, Windsor, Berks, NFER Publishing Company.

White, J. (1975) The end of compulsory education, in *The Curriculum: The Doris Lee Lectures*, London, University of London Institute of Education.

White, J. et al. (1981) *No Minister: a critique of the Department of Education and Science paper – The School Curriculum*, London, University of London Institute of Education.

Whitehead, A.N. (1932) The organisation of thought, in *The Aims of Education and Other Essays*, London, Ernest Benn.

Williams, R. (1968) *Communications*, Harmondsworth, Middx, Penguin.

Williams, R. (1981) *Culture*, London, Fontana.

Willis, P. (1979) *Learning to Labour, How Working Class Kids get Working Class Jobs*, London, Saxon House.

Wright, D. (1983) Why not ask the pupils, *Multicultural Teaching*, Annex 4, Autumn, pp. 31–32.

Wrigley, J. (1970) The Schools Council, in Butcher, H.J. and Pont, H.B. (editors) *Educational Research in Britain 2*, London, University of London Institute of Education, pp. 21–24.

Wrigley, J. (1978) APU team leading way to common core, Report of an interview, *The Times Educational Supplement*, 8 September.

Wrigley, J. (1980) Is a common form of curriculum feasible and desirable in a changing society?, *Curriculum*, 1, 2, Autumn.

Wrigley, J. (1981) Confessions of a curriculum man, Leicester, University of Leicester School of Education, Mimeo (Published in revised form in *Curriculum*, 4, 2, 1983)

INDEX OF NAMES

INDEX OF SUBJECTS